SEEING THROUGH CLOSED EYELIDS

Can a work of art help us know our world differently? In this first scholarly study of Giuseppe Penone, art historian Elizabeth Mangini argues that the Italian artist's engagement of the body's multiple senses constitutes a new theory of sculpture as a means to connect with and know the phenomenal world. Through close readings of signal works across Penone's five-decade career – from his emergence in the context of 1960s Arte povera to his position as a pre-eminent contemporary artist today – Mangini demonstrates how Penone refuses modernist opticality, recasts artistic labour, and emphasizes a non-anthropocentric concept of time. Penone's approach challenges viewers to broaden their sensory and temporal perceptions, creating structurally significant new ways to understand human experience.

Giuseppe Penone is best known for his engagement with trees, which he employs as raw material, imagery, and an active force in the creative process. *Seeing Through Closed Eyelids* suggests that such works materialize the perceptible tensions between any organism and its environment. By locating Penone's art in its social context and connecting it to broader discourses about art's status, theories of phenomenology, and the anthropocene, this book offers an original reading of Penone's work, as well as a wider view of the artistic generation for whom sculpture was a means to probe the nature of experience itself at the dawn of postmodernism.

(Toronto Italian Studies)

ELIZABETH MANGINI is an associate professor at California College of the Arts, San Francisco.

Seeing Through Closed Eyelids

Giuseppe Penone and the Nature of Sculpture

ELIZABETH MANGINI

UNIVERSITY OF TORONTO PRESS
Toronto Buffalo London

Toronto Buffalo London
utorontopress.com

Reprinted in paperback 2023

ISBN 978-1-4875-0058-0 (cloth)
ISBN 978-1-4875-5696-9 (paper)
ISBN 978-1-4875-3693-0 (EPUB)
ISBN 978-1-4875-1134-0 (PDF)

Toronto Italian Studies

Publication cataloguing information is available from Library and Archives Canada.

Cover design: Louise OFarrell
Cover image: Giuseppe Penone, *Alpi Marittime – Continuerà a crescere tranne che in quel punto* (*Maritime Alps – It Will Continue to Grow except at That Point*), 1968/2003. Tree, bronze; arm, 15 ¾ × 4 × 5 ⅛ inches. Installation view, Maritime Alps, near San Raffaele Cimena, Italy, 2008. © Archivio Penone.
Photograph © Archivio Penone.

We wish to acknowledge the land on which the University of Toronto Press operates. This land is the traditional territory of the Wendat, the Anishnaabeg, the Haudenosaunee, the Métis, and the Mississaugas of the Credit First Nation.

This book has been published, in part, with the assistance of grants from California College of the Arts, San Francisco, and the Italian Art Society, as well as the generosity of artists who gave permission to illustrate their works.

University of Toronto Press acknowledges the financial support of the Government of Canada, the Canada Council for the Arts, and the Ontario Arts Council, an agency of the Government of Ontario, for its publishing activities.

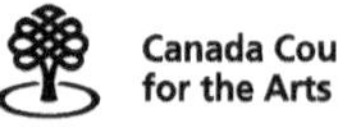

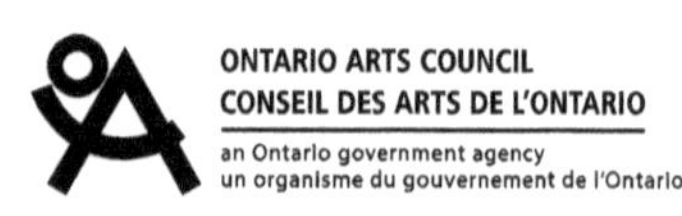

Funded by the Government of Canada
Financé par le gouvernement du Canada

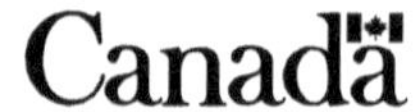

Contents

Illustrations

Acknowledgments

In the research and writing of this book, I have benefited from the wisdom and support of many individuals and institutions. I foremost wish to thank the artist Giuseppe Penone, through whose work I have found new ways to engage in ideas and issues pertinent to art, aesthetics, ecology, botany, and Italian history. I am also grateful to Dina Carrara, Ruggero Penone, and everyone at Archivio Penone, who, together with the artist, generously opened their doors to me numerous times, starting with my first visit to Turin in 2006, and who continue to respond with patience and candour to my many queries. Others in and around Turin who through friendship, conversation, and a myriad of small kindnesses helped with my research include Gilberto Zorio; Grazia Toderi; Gian Enzo Sperone; Simona Crovetto, the Lentini family; Norma Mangione; Filippo and Jennifer Fossati; Matteo and Lidia Castella; Stefano Musso and his staff at the Biblioteca d'Arte dei Musei Civici di Torino; and Marcella Beccaria, Carolyn Christov-Bakargiev, and Maria Massina at Castello di Rivoli.

Several artists and photographers, including Giuseppe Penone, have given permission for the reproduction of their works and images in service of the book's arguments, and I am especially grateful to Joan Jonas, Yayoi Kusama, Paolo Mussat Sartor, and Nanda Lanfranco. I further appreciate those who helped facilitate or gave permission for the use of the images to which they hold or administer rights, including Sebastiano Pellion di Persano, Sylvie Rondeau, Agnese Boschini at Fondazione Piero Manzoni, Lori Zajkowski at ARS NY, and Joyce Faust at Art Resource. Polity Press graciously granted permission for the use of quotations from Roberto Esposito, and MAMBo provided permission for the reproduction of excerpts from their published translations of Penone's writings.

Friends and colleagues in and around the field of Italian art have supported this work at various stages through conversations, collaborations, invitations, and reading of drafts, as well as through their own excellent research, writing, and exhibitions. I thank Christopher Bennett, Tenley Bick, Germano Celant, Maddalena Disch, Adrian Duran, Richard Flood, Jacopo Galimberti, Giorgia Gastaldon, Sharon Hecker, Daniela Lancioni, Christine Mehring, Ara Merjian, Graziella Parati, Valentina Pero, Lucia Re, Antonella Soldaini, Marin Sullivan, Denis Viva, and Anthony White, who each in the their own way improved this project. This work has been enhanced from access and advice provided by professionals in the field, including Marian Goodman and Barbara Gladstone; Charlie Spalding and Jennifer Knox White at Gagosian Gallery; Gavin Brown's Enterprise; Nora Severson at the Glenstone Museum; Peter Blank and Roy Viado at the Bowes Art & Architecture Library at Stanford University; Virginia Mokslavesk at the Getty Research Library; Bart Brouns at the Stedelijk Bibliotek; the librarians and archivists at the Walker Art Center; and the staff at the Nasher Sculpture Center.

My editors, Mark Thompson and Robin Studniberg, at University of Toronto Press displayed incredible confidence in this project from the start. Their patience and counsel, along with initial project support from Siobhan McMenemy, made this book a reality. I am also grateful to Tim Griffin, Michelle Kuo, David Velasco, and the many excellent editors at *Artforum* who have supported and published my writing on Giuseppe Penone and Arte povera for many years.

The publication of this book, its associated research, and especially its illustrations were made possible by faculty development and travel grants from the California College of the Arts (CCA), and a publications grant from the Italian Art Society. The writing and revision of the manuscript, in particular, would not have been possible without a sabbatical from teaching at CCA in 2018–19, for which I am especially grateful to Provost Tammy Rae Carland and President Steven Beal. The warm community of CCA colleagues enriched me by providing opportunities, guidance, and intellectual stimulation. I especially thank my program chairs, co-instructors, writing group members, and the college librarians including Mitchell Schwarzer, Maria Makela, Tirza Latimer, Juvenal Acosta, Tina Takemoto, Ted Purves, Karen Fiss, Jackie Francis, Jeanette Roan, Max Leung, Linda Geary, Patricia Lange, Donald Smith, Nancy Chan, Teri Dowling, and Paul Navarette. I am fortunate to have learned from and alongside many colleagues and students in the History of Art and Visual Culture, Visual and Critical Studies, Curatorial Practice, and Graduate Fine Arts programs at CCA over the past decade.

From formal mentorship and reading of drafts to invitations to present my research, and from talking through ideas over windy walks on the Great Highway to engaging in intellectual arguments at shared meals, this book was enhanced by the generosity and good cheer of several friends. I am grateful to Gwen Allen, Juana Berrio, Scott Cataffa, Vincent Fecteau, Gary Garrels, Philip Glahn, Mark Haxthausen, Richard Hoblock, Anthony Huberman, Geoff Kaplan, Pam Lee, Anna Mecugni, Marina Pugliese, Alexandra Quinn, Dean Rader, and Apsara di Quinzio.

It is to my entire family that I owe the largest debt for their unflagging support on the long road to this book's publication. Each in their own way, they have nourished me when I needed it most. They have followed me from coast to coast, and sometimes across the Atlantic, as my engagement with the discipline and the material deepened. They have been conscripted to undertake more museum visits (and personalized art history lectures) than perhaps they would otherwise choose. I can only be in awe of your love, humour, and fortitude. Most especially this is true of Jordan Kantor, who has seen me and this project from the first flickers of ideas through to the last image permissions, never refusing to lend his shoulder for support or his sharp mind for countless drafts and details. This book is for O. and N.

SEEING THROUGH CLOSED EYELIDS

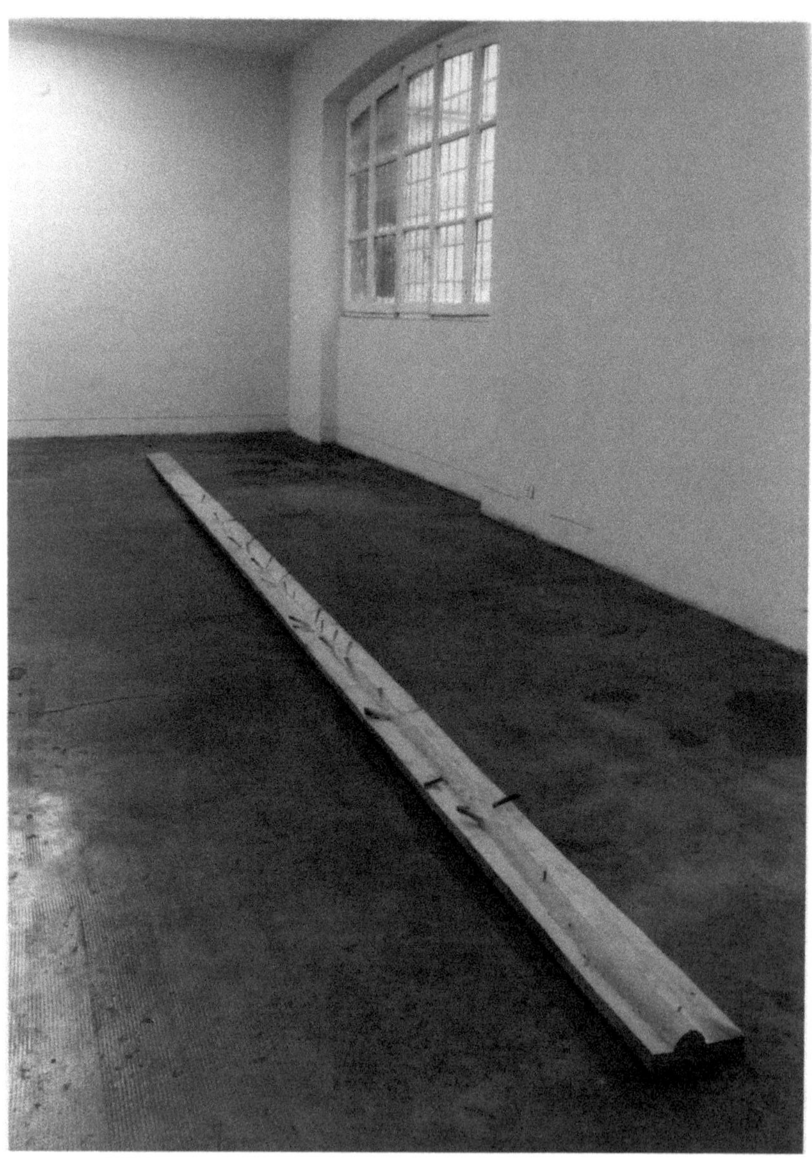

0.1 Giuseppe Penone, *Il suo essere nel ventiduesimo anno di vita in un'ora fantastica* (*His/Its Being in the Twenty-Second Year of Life at a Fantastic Hour*), 1969. Wood, 800 x 20 x 12 cm (destroyed).

Photograph: Paolo Mussat Sartor, © Paolo Mussat Sartor

Introduction
His Being in the Twenty-Second Year of Life at a Fantastic Hour

My work began in the latter half of the sixties, a moment of strong reaction to the political and social system, which didn't allow indifference. Strong social criticism accompanied a desire to reset values, in order to be able to rebuild on the basis of a rediscovered identity. / The choice to work with natural elements is the logical consequence of an idea that excluded the product of society and that sought relationships of affinity with matter. / The desire for an equal relationship between my person and things is the origin of my work. / Man is not a spectator or actor but simply nature.

– Giuseppe Penone, *Writings*

A grainy black-and-white photograph shows a long, thin object laid horizontally on a concrete floor (figure 0.1). The photograph is an installation view of Giuseppe Penone's sculpture *Il suo essere nel ventiduesimo anno di vita in un'ora fantastica* (*His/Its Being in the Twenty-Second Year of Life at a Fantastic Hour*, 1969), temporarily on view at Gian Enzo Sperone Gallery in Turin, Italy. The artist had carved around the knots in a wooden board to reveal what the tree from which the board had been milled would have looked like when it was twenty-two years old, identical to the artist's age at the time of its making. The sculpture is in relief, allowing a simultaneous reading of tree and lumber and connoting the ways in which wood can be seen as a product of both nature and society. Its display was one of the first times Penone exhibited at the cosmopolitan gallery, marking his entry into the city's vibrant artistic scene, in which he soon became a central and lasting figure.

Penone was still a teenager when, three years before showing the tree sculpture at Sperone, he moved from the semi-rural town of Garessio to Turin, the urban capital of Piedmont. The immediate post-war years had been a period of rapid growth for this Baroque city nestled at the base of the Alpine foothills: between 1951 and 1967 the population of the urban centre almost doubled, and it increased by nearly 80 per cent in the neighbouring suburbs.[1] Manufacturing and engineering jobs in the Italian automobile industry, which was booming in the 1950s and early 1960s, drew most of the new arrivals to Piedmont. Some came for Turin's renowned university, which had educated the likes of Marxist philosopher Antonio Gramsci, anti-Fascist author and activist Natalia Ginzburg, the novelist Italo Calvino, and the second president of the Italian Republic, Luigi Einaudi. Still others were drawn by the convergence of intellectual life and politics in Turin's storied cafés, where the 1861 unification of Italy (the Risorgimento) had been plotted, and which continue to be central to refined Torinese culture today. Penone moved to Turin for its art school, the Accademia Albertina di belle arte di Torino.

Despite, or perhaps due to, its central role in Italian industrialization, the once-royal city designed by Filippo Juvarra had plenty that catered to its discerning inhabitants in the late 1960s, including theatres, commercial art galleries, and non-profit exhibition spaces. It also had a museum of modern art, newly reopened in 1959 with an exhibition of blue-chip works from local private collections.[2] Giulio Einaudi, son of the aforementioned Luigi, was among the best publishers of Italian fiction and non-fiction, and his eponymous publishing house on Turin's Via Achivescovado was known for translating a diverse catalogue of international books for the Italian audience. Many of the artworks Penone made in his first decade of living in Turin attest to the rich diversity of its cultural milieu. During this period the young artist began to develop a theory of sculpture through material experimentation, intellectual exchange, and thoughtful reflection. Over the next decades the implications of these ideas came to fruition through the works themselves.

To say that Turin was an international artistic crossroad in the 1960s sounds like a cliché, but indeed it *was* one of a few places in Italy, if not Europe, where so many artists of different generations, nationalities, and aesthetic tendencies could be seen cheek by jowl. For instance, Japanese Guta'i artists showed there, alongside European exponents of Art Informel and members of Situationist International. It was possible to see the works of American Pop and Neo-Dada artists exhibited with those of the (mostly French) New Realists. This diversity created a unique critical context in which ideas hatched in one corner of the world resonated with conversations arising from artistic circles that were continents away. Itinerant critics and curators like Germano Celant, Daniella Palazzoli, and Michel Tapié helped marshal a wide range of international artists into Turin's contemporary art spaces. This richness spurred the Genoa-born Celant to reminisce about these years: "For me, Turin was the center of the world."[3]

Another vector for such exciting discourses crossed through Turin's wide range of commercial art galleries, including, most notably, Notizie, Gian Enzo Sperone, and Christian Stein.[4] They nurtured regional dialogues via collaborative exhibitions and broadened local perspectives by exchanging artists with international galleries.[5] In April 1967, for example, a group exhibition at Sperone's gallery included Turin-based artists Giovanni Anselmo, Michelangelo Pistoletto, and Gilberto Zorio, alongside such Americans as Andy Warhol, Dan Flavin, and James Rosenquist.[6] Turin's culture was further enriched by the presence of a lively performing arts scene, with spaces that accommodated music, theatre, and experimental performance practices like the Living Theater and, later, Pistoletto's *Zoo*. In 1968, art critic Lea Vergine surveyed the scene, boasting: "Turin, over the course of the last two years, has been able to insert itself among the liveliest centres of Europe."[7] For her, as for many creative people, the city's arcade-lined piazzas were the back-drop to an exchange of ideas that had the potential to impact culture beyond the local art world.

Turin was a hotbed as much for radical politics in the late 1960s as for emerging art and culture. Indeed, the University of Turin was the site of major student protests in 1967.[8] These protests initially aimed to remediate stale teaching methods, outdated facilities, and overcrowded conditions at the university, but they soon telescoped to address larger social and ideological issues like industrialization, consumerism, and class divisions. The students' uprising, as historian Paul Ginsborg has remarked, "was an ethical revolt, a notable attempt to turn the tide against the predominant values of the time."[9] Organized students and factory workers then recognized their shared interests, and by 1969 had joined in solidarity with one another to agitate for widespread social change. In the late sixties and throughout the early seventies the high percentage of skilled labour and university students in Turin, combined with its stratified social structures, made this period one of the flashpoints in a decade of political and social unrest known retrospectively as the *Anni di piombo* (Years of lead).

This leaden decade, marked on the one hand by the theorization of an equitable society through the liberation of the worker, and on the other hand by extremist domestic terrorism, is part of the socio-political context in which Penone's artistic practice emerged. He has often maintained that his work is not overtly political and, indeed, that the poetic language of art is incompatible with the directness required to effect political change. Yet, his work may be read as reflecting aspects of these conditions, which permeate his approach to materials, forms, and artistic labour.[10] The theoretical connection between labour and identity is, for instance, evident in seemingly apolitical sculptures like the carved tree he showed at Sperone, because of the way its very form is linked to the body of the artist. Reading the larger relevance of such works is justified by the way social politics saturated the fabric of everyday life in Turin, from the housing built for factory workers, to stores supplying materials to the city's industry, to the philosophy being discussed in the university's lecture halls. That is, Penone is of the same generation as that of the students who had occupied the piazzas and made alliances with workers. He had moved to Turin as a student to attend the art academy where his elder brother Giovanni was already studying.

Penone was eager to connect with like-minded artists at the urban art school, although the foundational courses in which he was enrolled ultimately served to teach him what he did *not* want to do as an artist. While he respected his professors, Penone bristled against the pedantic exercises of nineteenth-century pedagogy still in practice there – copying the works and styles of acclaimed "masters" – and he quickly recognized that this academic program was ill suited to the concerns of young artists like him, who had been born after the Second World War. The whole world had changed, so how did it make sense to keep imitating the works of modernist artists like Giacometti, let alone those of the Italian Renaissance?[11] Penone could easily do the traditional tasks being assigned to him in art school – indeed, others recognized his skill early on – but like any teenage art student, he was wary of the many limitations laid upon artistic making at school.

Penone did not overtly rebel against his teachers or rebuff historical art; rather, he considered introspectively each instance of discomfort. It was an approach that would nurture the conceptual aspects of his budding practice. When he was assigned by a professor to draw a leaf, for example, Penone realized how many conventions were already dictating the way he viewed the tasked representation: the choice of materials, the disciplinary constructions of drawing, and the linguistic concept of the leaf itself.[12] Together these were influencing the outcome of this simple exercise before he had even begun. A desire to get outside of these dogmatic principles initially spurred him towards sculpture, particularly the avenues it presented for subverting representation and formal convention. Moreover, many of his early works could be considered actions as much as sculptures. Despite the academy's generally ill fit, Penone stayed in school during this period, augmenting his studies by frequenting contemporary galleries and connecting with other like-minded artists in Turin.[13] The city, it seems, offered him more of the education he desired than the academy could provide. This is how he came to be included among the many artists whom curator Germano Celant would champion as pursuing Arte povera.

Arte povera is a label today referring to ten to fifteen artists who showed together in a series of exhibitions organized by Celant or who were written about in essays he published between 1967 and 1972. Arte povera was never a movement, in the sense that the artists never signed a manifesto proclaiming their ideas or identifying itself with a common cause. Only later did museums and galleries consistently apply the term to shows of these Italian artists.[14] Originally Arte povera was a powerful idea in which Celant captured several aspects born of the Torinese art scene. Among these factors was the prevalence of sculptures that eschewed predetermined meaning in favour of the phenomenological experience of objects and situations, not a "poverty" of materials but of preloaded signification. According to Celant, this approach allowed more latitude for the viewer to become a co-conspirator in the production of meaning, which in turn revealed the critical-conceptualist bent of many of the artists towards their own roles. His earliest uses of the term also denote the proximity of these artistic practices to the larger socio-political struggles of the time. This is nowhere better indicated than in the provocative title Celant used to introduce his concept to the international art scene on the pages of *Flash Art* in its November/December 1967 issue: "Arte povera: Appunti per una guerriglia" (Arte povera: Notes for a guerilla war).[15]

The young Penone was not mentioned in that early text, and although today he is considered among the central Arte povera artists, his work did not appear in any of Celant's exhibitions until late 1969. Even in 1976, Italian critic and art historian Lea Vergine left Penone out of the artists listed in the "Arte povera" section of her important book *Dall'Informazione alla Body Art dieci voci dell'arte contemporanea: 1960/70* and instead included him in the "Body Art" section.[16] The point here is not to argue about whether or not Penone is an Arte povera artist but simply to demonstrate that such terms were far more fluid and expansive in their initial theorization than they turned out to be later when used as commercial labels. The present study will therefore examine Penone's development of a distinct voice within his artistic milieu, rather than homogenize it with the diverse practices of a dozen artists in service of a single curatorial concept like Arte povera.

None of this is to suggest that the profound cultural changes happening in Italian post-war society were absent from the art and art criticism of the era, or that connections and affinities among artists

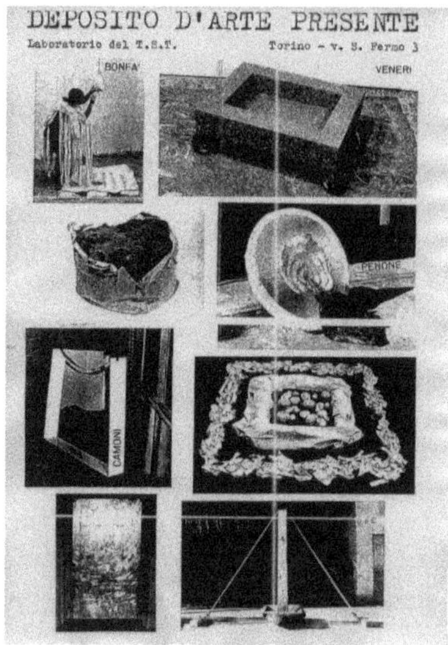

0.2 Broadsheet announcing exhibition including work by Penone at Deposito d'Arte Presente, Turin, June 1968.

Photograph: © Archivio Penone

did not exist. Indeed, Penone had already met artist Gilberto Zorio at art school, and they were united in their rejection of its musty means of working. Zorio introduced him to Sperone, who displayed several of Penone's early works at the Deposito D'Arte Presente (Warehouse of Contemporary Art) (figure 0.2). It was then through Sperone that the younger artist met Anselmo, Paolini, Pistoletto, and the other artists around whom Celant had already begun to construct his critical frame.[17] In a 1972 interview Zorio recounted his first introduction to his fellow student at the Accademia Albertina di belle arte di Torino: "It was an extraordinary meeting; by the end of the first days [Penone] demonstrated an exceptional modeling ability (his maternal grandfather was a sculptor). In the turn of a year he had exceeded the praxis of modelling and had completely changed his type of work."[18] Zorio describes here that Penone was not content simply to make forms correctly, and that his work had taken a strong conceptual dimension from the very start. This is what Penone shared with Zorio and several other artists of his generation: a desire to get to the root of the experience of encountering objects, to communicate directly, without the tropes of representation, and to welcome experimentation in all its material forms. A community of like-minded artists was indeed incubating in Turin.[19]

The conversation among Penone's peers was developing its own language and terms. They sought a way of understanding art-making and art objects that was fundamentally in opposition to the predominance of style among the earlier generation of painters and sculptors. Instead of continuing the development of abstraction as a language that could transcend the everyday, these younger artists pursued the concept of the artwork as an invested part of a nexus of exchange among artist, viewer, material, and phenomenological context. While not aiming to overturn the working conditions of Turin's factories, many of the artists showing at Sperone were making works that addressed the spectator in ways that foregrounded shared agency and solidarity rather than separation and hierarchy.[20] Penone shared this desire to rewrite the codes of communication through art, a fact that was recognized by his peers. "[Penone] had seen things," Zorio remarked, "that served him for the liberation of language that he sought, and he entered into it with incredible fluency."[21] Penone's material experiments, which were aimed at a new way of understanding art as simultaneously sign and object, constituted a distinct voice within the rich cultural scene from which they emerged, as well as a potent force in international discourses about art.

Penone's early concerns were born of the post-war aesthetic discourse, in that his works elaborate a new theory of sculpture as a discipline, but they also model new ways of engaging the complex, fragmentary, and mediated means of communication inherent to sculpture. When his artworks invite viewers to perceive aspects of form, object, and material beyond the limitations of human vision and the strictures of language, they preview some of the central ideas of postmodern theory. This book investigates both the means by which Penone's artistic project accomplishes this and the resonances that his approach has with major intellectual discourses of the period, specific to art conversations and beyond. Each chapter investigates focused aspects of his work and relies upon a different theoretical model. Further, each is tethered, by varying degrees, to the social and cultural history of the era. The analysis of a half century of artworks unfolds over four central chapters, and the critical approach of the present study – without aspiring to be a complete survey or catalogue raisonné – is maintained throughout in order to reveal the broader cultural value of Penone's sustained artistic pursuit. Phenomenology, and its emphasis on the embodied nature of experience, is employed as a historical reference and a methodological tool.

Exhibition catalogues dominate the current field of books on Giuseppe Penone, which necessarily focus on limited strands of the artist's work according to the exhibition rationale and checklist. These catalogues most often comprise one or two short essays by the curators, an interview with the artist, the reproduction of some of his writings, and copious illustrations of the works surveyed. Important examples include Jean-Christophe Amman's *Giuseppe Penone: Bäume, Augen, Haare, Wände, Tongefäss* (1977), which documented the artist's solo exhibition at the Kunstmuseum Luzern; Ida Gianelli's *Giuseppe Penone: Scultura di Linfa* (2007), in conjunction with the artist's installation at the Venice Biennale; and Matthew Teitelbaum's *Giuseppe Penone: The Hidden Life Within* (2013), produced for the artist's show at the Art Gallery of Ontario. Such books provide valuable documentation of distinct parts of Penone's project, as well as historical context for the reception and analysis of individual bodies of work.

More general retrospectives of the artist's project follow a similar structural pattern: short essays by different authors, selections of the artist's writings, and illustrations of works. Germano Celant edited the first major exhibition monograph in 1989, using his own theory of Arte povera to drive his interpretation of Penone's work in the main essay, "Intertwining Metamorphoses."[22] In this text Celant relies heavily on biography, painting a picture of the artist and the first twenty years of his project as rooted almost entirely in his rural upbringing. Two years later the Castello di Rivoli produced a catalogue for its retrospective exhibition, including a wider range of voices on the artist and his project.[23] In 2013 curator Laurent Busine edited a book that functions like a visual survey, including an interview between Penone and art historian Benjamin Buchloh, one short text each by Busine and art historian Didier Semin, and a handful of brief (single-page) thematic catalogue entries by Italian curator Daniela Lancioni to accompany its generous illustrations.[24]

Outliers among books on the artist (excluding those few conceived by the artist) include a book of his writings that accompanied a 2009 retrospective in Bologna.[25] Available in English and Italian, this volume consists of primary texts, making it an essential resource for the poetic writings that constitute a significant part of Penone's practice. In 2008 French philosopher and art historian Georges Didi-Huberman published a short monograph on Penone, which was translated into English in 2016.[26] Through analyses of select works, Didi-Huberman argues that the artist's work centres on the relationship between touch and thought. Comparisons between artistic precedents and aspects of Penone's project support its relevance to considerations of the nature of artistic work, but Didi-Huberman does not read Penone's work in its full cultural contexts. The present study makes use of many of the sources listed here for documentation of important installations and evidence of the works' historical reception through their essays and interviews. This is, however, the first sustained scholarly monograph on the Italian artist that places Penone's work in its local, international, and intellectual contexts in order to recognize his contribution to each.

The first chapter of this book analyses the artist's earliest series of works against the prevailing artistic discourses of the early to mid-1960s. These first works contain the kernels of concerns that Penone would follow over the ensuing decades, including his questioning of the primacy of the visual aspects of art, a correlation of artistic identity with the body, a repositioning of the act of making as a negotiation of forces, and a cultivation of expanded temporal frames for his works. Each of these topics is emergent in such early works as the *Alpi Marittime* (Maritime Alps, 1967–8), a series of photographically documented actions that highlight touch, process, and duration. When read in the context of mid-century artistic discourses focused on gesture, the *Maritime Alps* works illuminate the transnational quality of his concerns and the distinctiveness of his response.

Chapter 2 studies Penone's early identification of the centrality of touch as a resistance to and complication of what Martin Jay has called the "ocularcentrism" of modernism.[27] Many of Penone's works of the early to mid-1970s engage sight, only to refuse it, delay it, or otherwise undermine its primacy among the five senses. Through such an approach the artist gives plastic, palpable form to some of the twentieth century's most complex philosophies of perception. Many of Penone's works from this period take the body as the starting point for sculptural exploration, manifesting the argument of French phenomenologist Maurice Merleau-Ponty that the senses are so entwined with the body that the body itself forms a theory of perception.

The third chapter reads Penone's early body-perceptual experiments as demonstrations of the radically reciprocal relationship between the artist's body and materials. It is a relationship he came to view as ontological to sculpture. Many works from this period foreground the relative passivity of the artist and, conversely, the action of the material. In one series begun during the early 1970s, breath emerges as a symbolic, fluid material that transgresses the body's border through both active and passive respiration. By the end of the decade the artist had begun to conceive of his body's labour as being equivalent to the movements of a stream or to the force of a storm. These works connote aspects of the social context of late 1970s Italy, in which bodily presence figured predominantly in debates about labour and political power. Read through thing theory and biopolitics, his works' persistent visual reliance on the human body is reframed as primarily anti-anthropocentric due to the works' ultimate demonstration of material entanglement.

Chapter 4 weaves together many strands of Penone's practice through a transhistorical investigation of his works with trees over five decades. This break from the chronological progression of the previous chapters is intentional, for as much as socio-historical context is crucial to reading the works at some stages, this chapter aims to counterbalance the temporal strictures that historians are apt to place on artistic practices. In Penone's oeuvre, trees are more than simply iconographic forms or instrumentalized symbols of nature. Rather, he uses trees to explore vastly expanded perspectives on time. From the earliest recovered trees, like *His/Its Being in the Twenty-Second Year of Life at a Fantastic Hour* (1969), to large-scale bronze trees installed in public parks, the temporal aspect of such works underscores sculpture's address to the phenomenology of human experience, its entreaties to the body and all the senses, and its potential material durability. The tree sculptures, specifically, emerge from a politically charged historical moment, and looking at them diachronically here reveals how they, more than any single political slogan or social ideal, expand one's perception of time. This has a radical, profound, and lasting impact.

Penone likely already had a notion of what it meant to be an artist when he arrived in Turin, and, at the time, it was one of the most interesting places for a young artist to be. The ideas and artworks produced there were a force that a young artist could work with and against in the search for a definition of art that could be both intensely personal and widely impactful. Reading five decades of Penone's art in the context of its intellectual, cultural, and social environment, one discovers the main tenets of his own theory of sculpture embedded in the works themselves. Through material exploration, phenomenological awareness, and correlation with the body, he demonstrates what it means to be an artist and ultimately proposes what it might mean to be human.

Recalibrating human perception of and relationship with the phenomenal world has ethical and political implications that permit Penone's works to extend beyond the confines of twentieth-century art.

Indeed, recognizing the human impact on the material world is central to current and ongoing debates about the survival of present-day economies, political structures, and even the human species. I argue throughout the book that Penone's work addresses the concerns of his generation, which was directly facing the rapidly changing realities of post-war Italy, through a distinct anti-anthropocentrism. Today this approach resonates with contemporary debates about the human role in the larger structures of the physical world, with the threat of human-induced climate change haunting geopolitical alliances and scientific debates alike. In its constant search for ways of being in the changing social and material world of the post-war era, Penone's art reflects the time in which it was made and predicts some of the central issues of the twenty-first century. Giuseppe Penone had arrived in Turin in his nineteenth year, at a fantastic hour.

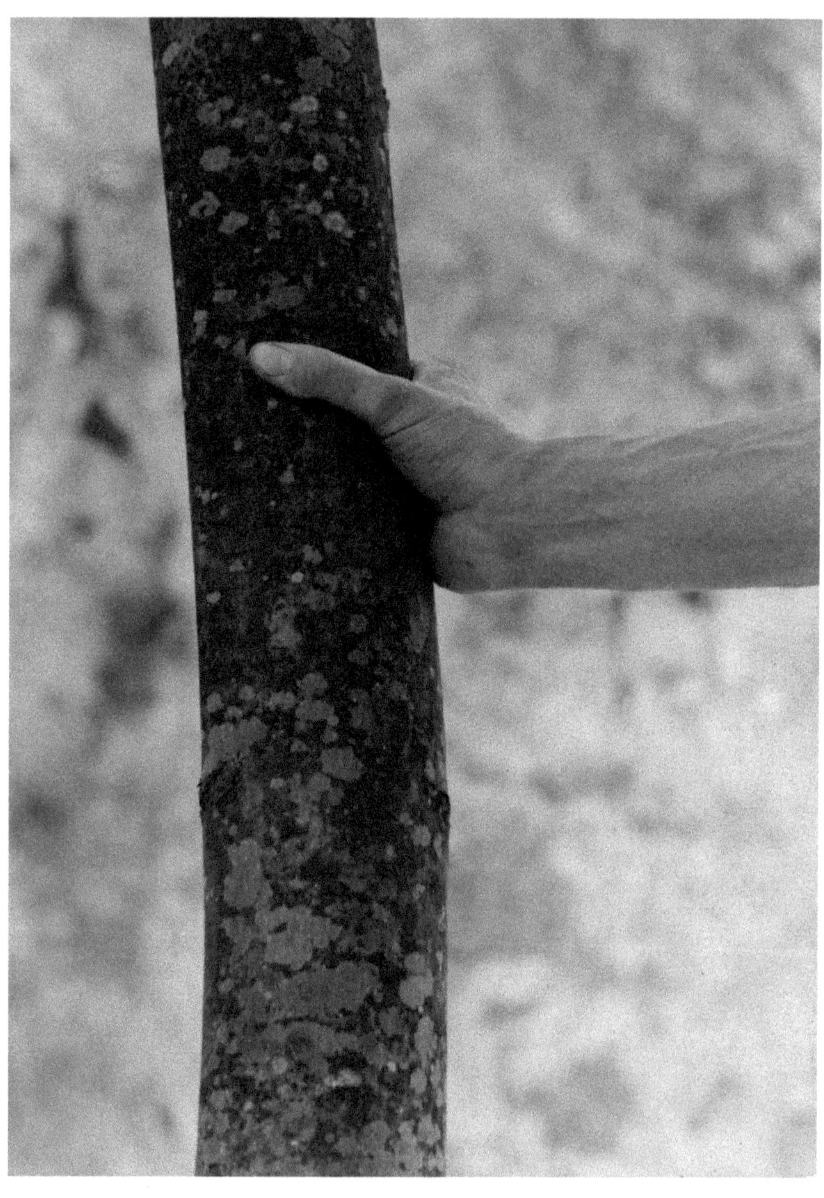

1.1 Photographic documentation of Giuseppe Penone making *Continuerà a crescere tranne che in quel punto* (*It Will Continue to Grow except at That Point*), from *Alpi Marittime* (Maritime Alps), 1968.

Photograph: Claudio Basso, ©Archivio Penone

1
Presentness and Trace

The hand that grasps and holds is one of the distinguishing features of the human species.

– Roberto Esposito, *Persons and Things*

Penone's critical considerations of the material production of sculpture began to blossom during an interval in his formal studies at the academy. When he was back home in Garessio in the winter of 1968, a respite from the growing tensions of Turin's student and labour movements, he began to formulate new ways of demonstrating the work of the artist.[1] On land that had been tended by his family for generations, the artist's sentimental valuation of his family home aligned with a new, less abstract concept of soil as a material employed in the production of a sculptural form. That is, he recognized that the land, which seemed "natural" by comparison with Turin's Baroque urban plan, had in fact been similarly shaped by a sum of man-hours – 14,520 hours of work between 1881 and 1969, by Penone's later calculations.[2] He began to see agricultural labour as sculptural – the intentional investment of contact between humans and materials, resulting in a form that could not be achieved independently by either: a landscape.

Penone's upbringing in this area had also taught him that, for example, the wood used by a sculptor was not just a passive recipient of the artist's touch but a living thing to be cultivated, with careful attention directing its growth and development. His recent exposure to new art practices in Turin, as well as his studies of materials and traditional modelling techniques at the academy, allowed him to view nature with fresh eyes. Penone saw his materials as more than inert matter; they were "forces" against which he could juxtapose other forces, such as his own, to provoke a reaction.[3] Is carving a milled piece of wood fundamentally different from training, grafting, or trimming a tree's branches? What if tactics borne of planting, plowing, harvesting, or tending could be brought back to the studio, or, inversely, what if the studio could be brought outside to the forest? What kind of sculpture would result from this non-hierarchical way of approaching the relationship between the artist and the material? Concurrent with a generational interrogation of the old ways of understanding authority, process, and labour, Penone began to orient his artistic practice to the aesthetic potentialities of similar questions, using his personal experiences to develop a unique voice.[4]

Walking through the woodland area near his childhood home that winter, Penone began to act on this new consideration of sculpture as a confrontation between the presence of the human artist and the latent energy of the material. He first applied his own force to the organic processes of the area known as the Maritime Alps, a mountain range that connects the alpine region of Piedmont and the coastal region of Liguria. In the most literal example of exerting his artistic will on this forest, Penone grasped the slender trunk of a tree with his right hand (figure 1.1). Having marked the spot, he attached an iron sculpture of his hand to the tree at the same location.[5] Photographs were made to document the initial action as well as the sculptural intervention. The artist scrawled on the photographic print of the latter: "L'albero continuerà a crescere tranne che in quel punto" (The tree will continue to grow except at that point) (figure 1.2).

Could making sculpture be as fundamental as placing one's hand on another material or object? It seems simple, yet the work has at least five distinct parts: the concept/plan, the corporeal action, a material incursion, photographic documentation, and the captioning of the resulting image. Together these steps comprise key aspects of a nascent theory of sculpture: sculpture is the result of a physical (tactile) encounter; the artist and the material both exert a certain amount of force to arrive at a form; the formal outcome of the encounter does not have to be predetermined (and may continue to change over time); and the reception of the work is inextricable from its production. This formulation, of course, is diametrically opposed to the concept of modernist sculpture as instantaneously and wholly manifest, which was being defended by Michael Fried, contemporaneously, in the pages of *Artforum*.[6] Instead, Penone's experiments in the forest were essentially a means to test hypotheses about the nature of sculpture, and they provided evidence of the possibilities still latent in the discipline.

Speaking about what first drew him to sculpture, the artist argued that sculpture was relatively less encumbered from the conventions and

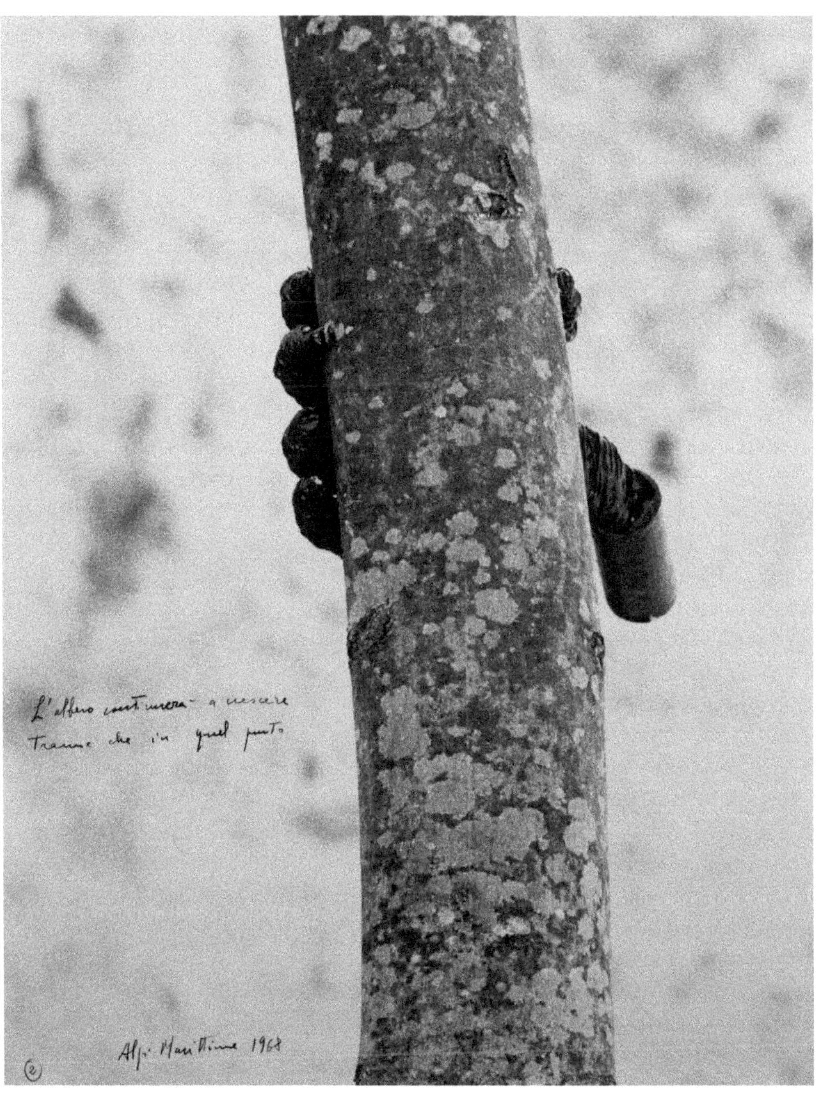

1.2 Giuseppe Penone, *Continuerà a crescere tranne che in quel punto* (*It Will Continue to Grow except at That Point*), from *Alpi Marittime* (Maritime Alps), 1968. Black-and-white photograph, 64 x 49 cm.

Collection of the artist, Turin. Photograph: Claudio Basso, ©Archivio Penone

semantics of art-making. He notes, using an example of an everyday object, that when you make a table, it is a table first and then maybe a sculpture. If you draw a table, however, it is always a drawing; it is always locked into the codes and conventions of visual representation.[7] For Penone then, sculpture's alignment with the body in phenomenological space and time seemed to offer the clearest path to presenting an object, rather than merely representing it. The potential correspondence between the sculptural object and its material make-up, the way it replaced artistic intuition with process, was as important for Penone as it was for others of his generation.[8]

In grasping the tree with his hand and marking where it would *not* continue to grow, the artist identified sculpture's double identity – material and object – in this case, wood and tree. In 1955 Giulio Carlo Argan, one of Italy's premier post-war art historians, had cited the inability to solve a similar material paradox as the central problem of Italian sculpture at mid-century.[9] In his "Difficoltà della scultura," Argan identified a "Catholic" desire to preserve the visibility of the material within a representation as the primary limiting factor to Italian sculpture flourishing in the same way as sculpture was flourishing in Northern Europe and the United States during the early post-war period. In his view, contemporary Italian sculptors were too cautious, and they still struggled against the opacity of the material. Penone's simple act of grasping a tree trunk demonstrates the opposite impulse: the wood only represents itself and its encounter with the artist. Argan's critique forms part of the theoretical framework for post-war sculpture, a national conversation that may have reached Penone through his coursework at art school or in conversations with other artists.

As if answering Argan's call, Penone used this intervention – part of a body of work known collectively by its site as the *Alpi Marittime* (Maritime Alps, 1967–8) – to investigate the nature of sculpture with neither foreseen outcomes nor representational, iconographic aspirations. Penone would return to and photograph this tree over ensuing decades, regularly documenting the plant's adjustment to the "presence" of his hand. From the very beginning, the surrogate hand was projected to remain in place indefinitely to mark the location and therefore the future potential of the artist's touch. The larger series includes such interventions as the artist plaiting the trunks of three saplings so that they would grow together; constructing a cage around a tree's crown that would be lifted as the tree grew against this obstacle; and periodically adding weights to a tree to counter its upward growth. Each action was documented with photographs at its initiation, and most were recorded regularly for years to come. Like many of Penone's works from this early period, they are known primarily through these photographs, yet they are not fundamentally photographic works. Instead they contain essential kernels of the lines of inquiry about sculpture that he would pursue for decades to come.

The circulation of the *Maritime Alps* photographs at the time underscores their importance to his oeuvre and to the larger conversations about sculptural making. It was precisely these black-and-white photographs that provided his material connection to other young sculptors working in Turin and his informal entry into the arena of Arte povera. After showing the images to Gian Enzo Sperone, Penone exhibited them in a May 1969 group show at the gallery that included works by many of the newly christened Arte povera protagonists. By the end of that same year, Penone had had his first solo show at the gallery, and Germano Celant had reproduced the images in the first defining publication of the nomenclature: *Arte povera* (Milan: Mazzotta, 1969).[10] Charting a path through the *Maritime Alps* to Penone's November 1969 solo show at Sperone, one can see the artist's emergent theory of sculpture in its various contexts.

Read in terms of international aesthetic discourses, the *Maritime Alps* actions and their documentation constitute the artist's opening riposte to the late modernist obsession with gesture. *It Will Continue to Grow except at That Point* provides a clear example of the artist's early wrestling with action and gesture. Indeed, by exhibiting a photograph of a cast of his hand on the tree, Penone already begins to challenge the auratic presence of the artist's body through the double absence implied by the coincidence of an indexical surrogate and its photographic record. The status of such works as both actions and documentary photographs locates Penone's initial approach to art-making beyond the stale binary of abstraction and representation. Finally, their non-hierarchic approach to material and their potential for extended duration constitute the artist's first enunciation of a complex investigation of the temporal and multisensory aspects of process, production, and reception.

Sculpture and/against Gesture

Like so many experimental works of the late 1960s and early 1970s, *Maritime Alps* interventions like *It Will Continue to Grow except at That Point* highlight an action, specifically that by which an artwork may be manifest. The concept of a dematerialized gesture, disentangled from the presence of an object, was most notably chronicled at the time by Lucy Lippard, who maintained that a move towards highly conceptual art emerged from the dual notions of art as idea and art as action.[11]

In her book, which counted writings by Celant among those catalogued as evidence, Lippard maintained that this was a decentralized, international trend. She argued that it aligned artists with prevailing distribution theories as well as the political struggles of youth movements across the globe, such as those affecting Turin's university and factories.

The value placed on nimble tactics and improvisational materials was already evident in late 1960s Italy, both in art and in politics. In Tommaso Trini's review of the fall 1967 exhibition *Arte povera e IM Spazio* at Genoa's Galleria La Bertesca, the first exhibition to use the term in its title, and one that did not yet include the young Penone among its artists, the critic argued that a coincidence of action and concept was central to the way in which curator Germano Celant proposed to view the artworks gathered under this new term. Using Alighiero Boetti's assemblages as examples, Trini wrote, "The action, and the event to which it gives rise, becomes as important as the object." He further marvelled at the effect of this attitude: "these works are to be looked at with indifference: the more indifferent, the better perceived their beauty."[12] His words affirm that however physical the process, the result is fundamentally conceptual and poetic, unaffected by the traditional rules of formal aesthetics. Could such manifest indifference to the formalities of the object be a way out of the difficulty facing Italian sculpture, which so concerned mid-century critics like Argan?

While they may not appear to prioritize traditional measures of craft and facture, most of the Arte povera artists, in Turin especially, do approach materials with great sensitivity. The material is integral to the meaning of the work, for what it can do within the context of the work or for how its own properties meet the demands of the artist. Lippard, too, maintained a nuanced position in relation to the materiality of the object, stating that what mattered most was not "how much materiality a work has, but what the artist is doing with it."[13] In the United States, for example, much of the discourse around process and material during the 1950s and 1960s was grappling with the legacy of the New York School, whose post-war abstractions were read alternately as visual records of artistic gesture or as an embrace of the irreducible limitations of each medium. In Italy the theoretical implications of this American abstract painting were only really felt in the 1960s, and even then the New York School model – upon which Clement Greenberg's and Harold Rosenberg's opposing theories had been based – was by no means the only example of gestural abstraction.[14]

A 1961 issue of the Milan-based journal *Il Verri* demonstrates how porous the discourse was from a European perspective: it contained not only Greenberg's 1948 review of a Jackson Pollock exhibition at the

Betty Parsons Gallery and an excerpt of Rosenberg's 1952 "American Action Painters" but also texts by Lucio Fontana and Michel Tapié.[15] Tellingly, the issue also includes both a passage written by Pollock in which he talks about being "in" the painting, and an essay in which Greenberg argues for painting becoming more attentive to "surface texture and tactile qualities"; neither artist nor critic is represented in these pages as championing opticality.[16] A distinctly international combination of voices in this issue – including the writings of Italian theorists and critics such as Argan, Umberto Eco, and Enzo Paci – clearly places the reception of the New York School in the European context of Art Informel, known in Italy as Informale. This, in turn, was rooted in the materialism of the broadly European avant-garde of the pre-war years. Further, Paci's essay in that issue, "Fenomenologia e Informale" is critical of the abstract and fetishistic aspects of informal art, which he argues is already radically alienated from lived experience. The Italian philosopher calls for reading this art as materially and sensorially connected to the *Leib* (Edmund Husserl's concept of the lived body), signalling that the discourses of gestural abstraction and modernist idealism in Italy were already tied to phenomenology and were moving beyond the American terms of the discourse.[17]

Italian artists of Penone's generation therefore had the vocabulary and conceptual framework to approach the antagonism between opticality and action painting from a transnational point of view. Indeed by 1968, on the evidence of exhibitions such as *Con temp l'azione* and *Spazio dell'immagine*, Italian critic Marisa Volpi warned against reading the influence of the New York School in European action-based art, a troubling tendency she assigned to the lack of international critical attention to the Italian artistic discourse in the post-war years. Instead, she argued that the differences between the historical and post-war conditions of the two countries gave rise to different possibilities for art as a form of communication. Italian artists, who did not have to compete with the kind of mass culture, the scale of social divisions, or the hot art market present in the United States in the late 1960s, were thus "already more 'far out' than the Americans, their terrain of action was more limited, and their force of penetration was more profound and more subtle."[18] Volpi claims that unlike the work of New York–based artists of the same generation, who were directly responding to the imposing figures of Abstract Expressionism and gaining the attention of art institutions and collectors, the work of European artists "refutes assertiveness and spectacle." Pistoletto rolling a giant ball of newspapers between Turin's art galleries, and Marisa Merz wearing a knitted-copper pair of shoes with her feet propped against the gallery wall, are distinct actions, yet they are neither auratic performances nor diaphanous happenings. Action and gesture in Italian art were not undertaken in the same heroic terms as they were in the United States, and it is in their deployment of an intentionally weak gesture and their occupation of a distinctly *poveristi* position that they were toeing the cusp of postmodernism.[19]

In the Italian context, Penone's attention to materials within his action-based works presents a unique response to international art discourses by probing the issues of artistic agency and material specificity in a distinctly anti-auratic, anti-authoritarian way. Instead of the body versus the material, the body is figured as the point at which the concept and the object converge, in terms of both making and reception. Penone's early work is particularly rich in this kind of repositioning of artistic authority and labour. Here the machismo often attributed to mid-century gestural abstraction, and noted by Volpi as having been carried forward in the work of American artists like Donald Judd, is supplanted by the non-hierarchical position of the artist's body in relation to the natural world. For instance, in the *Maritime Alps* episode subtitled *La mia altezza, la lunghezza delle mie braccia, il mio spessore in un ruscello* (*My Height, the Length of My Arms, My Breadth in a Brook*, 1968), the artist fashioned a concrete form that corresponded to the three-dimensional measure of his outstretched body. Impressions of his hands, feet, and his upturned face are visible on the interior of the frame (figure 1.3). This rectangular concrete form was then laid horizontally into a stream-bed, where it disrupted the current of water, which nevertheless continued to flow over and around this obstruction (figures 1.4 and 1.5). It is an object that allows the artist's corporeal form to continuously divert the stream by a material stand-in.

This open-ended proposition of the artist's body in nature is consonant with the anti-representational aspects of Arte povera's Torinese protagonists. It finds echoes in many contemporaneous dematerialized projects in its move outside of the spatial confines of traditional sculpture, and it also foreshadows Penone's career-long critique of artistic agency as a means to explore the fundamental nature of sculpture. To the last point, the action of lying by proxy in the stream-bed can be read to take aim at the nature of artistic authority that action-painting arguments attempted to reinforce. For instance, the well-circulated photographs of Jackson Pollock making drip paintings show the American artist standing over a canvas laid out on the floor (figure 1.6). These and similar images of the painter were widely published in international magazines, testifying to the popular, American notion that gestural abstraction preserves the motion, if not emotion, of the artist in a direct, super-linguistic form. In short, they aim to evidence the American artist's mastery over the elusive, liquid material.

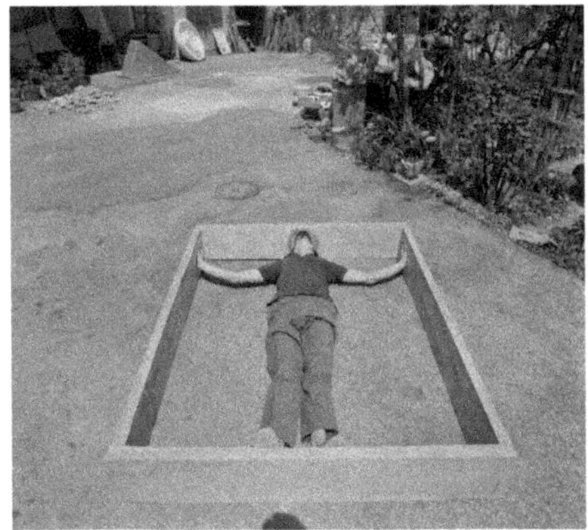

1.3 Photographic documentation of Giuseppe Penone making *La mia altezza, la lunghezza delle mie braccia, il mio spessore in un ruscello* (*My Height, the Length of My Arms, My Breadth in a Brook*), from *Alpi Marittime* (Maritime Alps), 1968.

Photograph: Claudio Basso, ©Archivio Penone

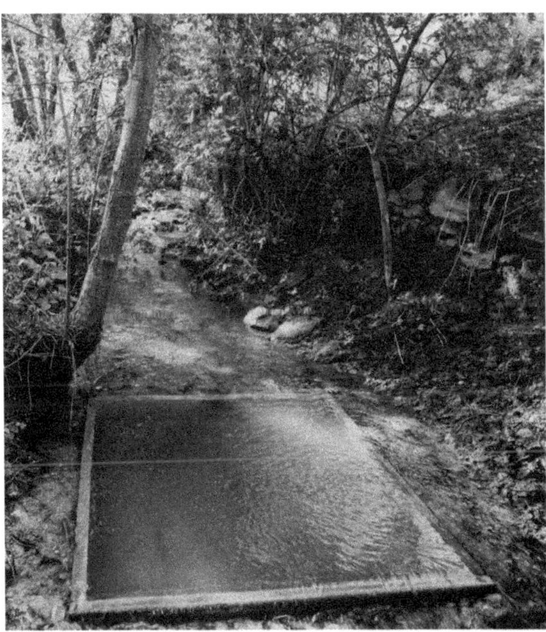

1.4 Giuseppe Penone, *La mia altezza, la lunghezza delle mie braccia, il mio spessore in un ruscello* (*My Height, the Length of My Arms, My Breadth in a Brook*), from *Alpi Marittime* (Maritime Alps), 1968. Black-and-white photograph, 64 x 49 cm.

Collection of the artist, Turin. Photograph: Claudio Basso, © Archivio Penone

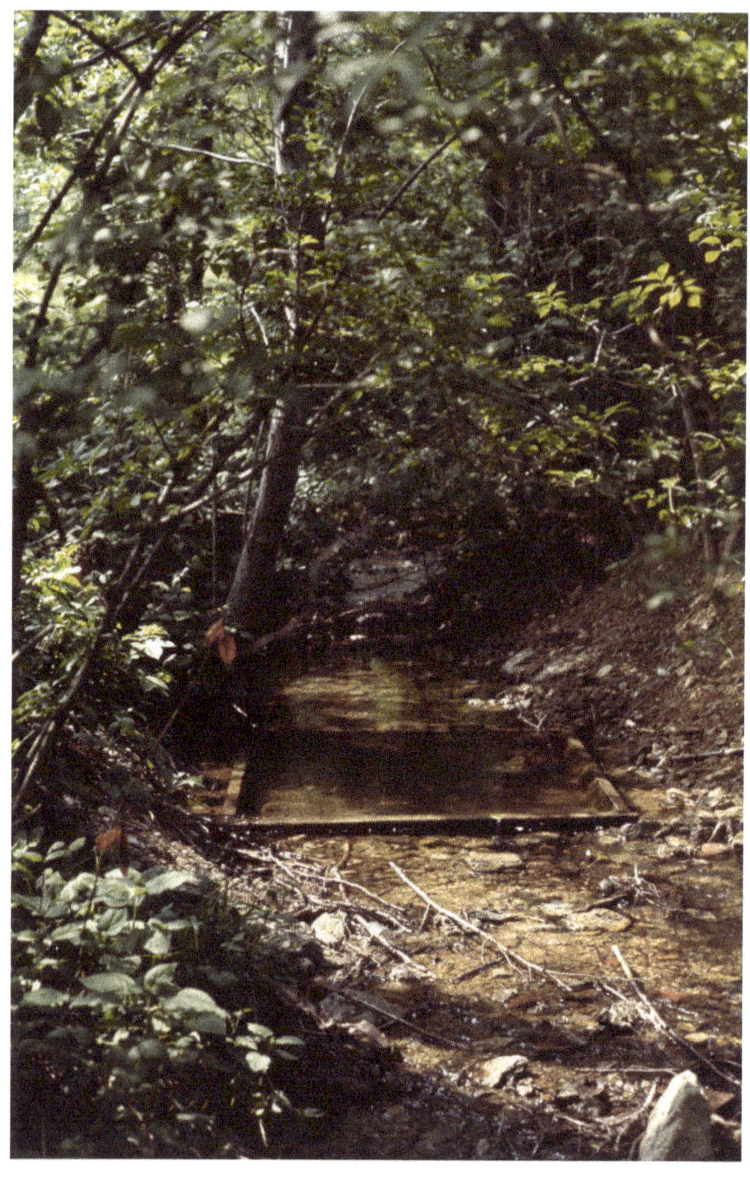

1.5 Giuseppe Penone, photographic documentation of *La mia altezza, la lunghezza delle mie braccia, il mio spessore in un ruscello* (*My Height, the Length of My Arms, My Breadth in a Brook*), from *Alpi Marittime* (Maritime Alps), 1968. Colour photograph, 64 x 49 cm.

Collection of the artist, Turin. Photograph: Claudio Basso,

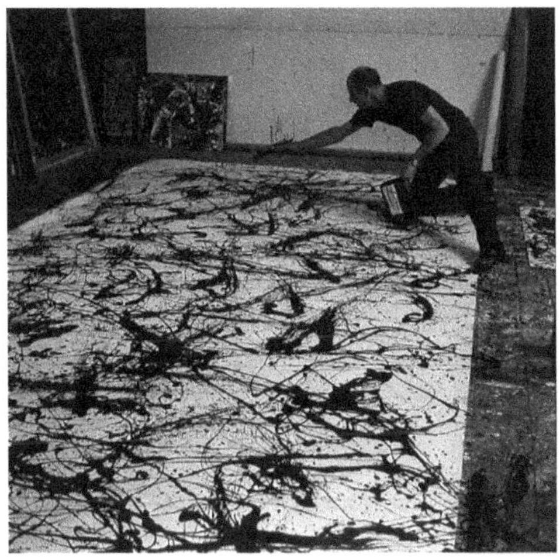

1.6 Rudy Burckhardt, *Jackson Pollock at Work*, 1950.

Image: Archives of American Art, Smithsonian Institution. Photograph: © 2021 Estate of Rudy Burckhardt / Artists Rights Society (ARS) New York. Pollock Art: © The Pollock Krasner Foundation / Artists Rights Society (ARS), New York.

Reading the documentary photographs of Penone's stream-bed action against Burkhardt's photograph of Pollock painting clarifies the radical departure of the younger artist's approach to his own identity vis-à-vis the material. Penone's body is positioned coincident with the horizontal plane of Pollock's substrate, problematizing both artistic authority over the material world and the presumed transparency of gestural abstraction.[20] Penone does not stand erect, looking out over the landscape, nor is he skilfully controlling the flow of liquid. Although the artist's body – via a surrogate – affects the movement of the stream, Penone's documentary image attests that it is no different from a stone or a fallen tree branch. His body here sculpts the stream as water passes over and through the concrete obstruction, but it neither dominates the stream-bed nor diverts the water for human ends. Rather, the artist here lowers himself to the same plane as the water, the earth, and the stones. That is, his body enters into the work but does not dictate the field or the form. The horizontal "surface," meanwhile, is not flat and submissive like Pollock's canvas, but deep and dynamic.

Penone's work thus proposes a different order of relationship between artist and material, as well as between artist and viewer. An action like this testifies to the fact that the mythologizing of abstraction, and gestural abstraction in particular, no longer held sway in the late 1960s. For Penone, like other artists of his generation, abstraction is still a language and therefore remains exclusionary in the sense that it still functions as a symbolic, one-way, hierarchical message from artist to viewer.[21] The artist inputs or codes a message, and the viewer must receive or decipher it. Penone's work, like that of many of his peers, was instead aimed at removing the barriers to direct experience by reducing representation to a minimum. Occupying a literal and conceptual horizontal plane was a key strategy to undermining metaphorically the entrenched hierarchies among and within artistic disciplines.

Art historian Rosalind Krauss charts the centrality of such deconstruction and reconsideration of art's disciplinary tendencies as part of a larger move towards postmodernism. In her 1979 essay "Sculpture in the Expanded Field" she identifies the historicization of challenges to the category of sculpture as obscuring what is truly radical about it: that it challenges the placelessness of modernist sculpture, which sought to free itself from the logic of the monument.[22] While Krauss does not deal with Italian Arte povera artists in period writings about sculpture, her analyses of American post-war artists provide a lens through which to read Penone's early work in relation to the larger concerns of artists and critics of his generation. For instance, in *The Optical Unconscious* (1993) Krauss provides an analysis through which *vertical* and *horizontal* can be considered to be key terms corresponding to the visual and tactile aspects of Penone's early practice. In her book, which is rooted in psychoanalysis and post-structuralist theory, Krauss outlines critical attempts to sublimate Pollock's fundamentally horizontal process to fit Greenberg's and, later, Michael Fried's formalist theories of modernism.[23] Despite the dominance of Greenberg's critical model among *critics*, Krauss argues that many *artists* saw the implications of Pollock's drip differently. She demonstrates how Cy Twombly, Andy Warhol, and Robert Morris each took up the non-optical aspects of the drip. While rooted in the North American context, Krauss's argument is relevant to the landscape of Penone's Turin since these three artists were showing at Sperone's gallery in the 1960s and 1970s.[24]

In building a context for the reception of Penone's *Maritime Alps*, Krauss's analysis of Robert Morris is most fitting since he was exhibiting at Sperone in 1969, just after he had begun to make soft, "anti-form" works. In fact, Morris's solo show at the gallery directly preceded the group show *Disegni progetti* (*Drawings, Plans*, May 1969), in which the

Maritime Alps photographs and attendant drawings were featured. In this period, Morris was exhibiting soft felt sculptures, which, according to Krauss, were a means to return horizontality to Pollock's liquid gesture.[25] Her argument follows a way of thinking about process that was defined by Morris in his own 1968 essay "Anti-form." There, the American artist argued that some process-driven art was a means to refute the idea that the end product of such encounters had to be an idealized form or a foreseen result.[26] Works made of soft materials, Morris claimed, were especially suited to a new way of thinking about making art because they implicitly yielded to the vagaries of gravity, time, and circumstances.

Ceding authority to the material and environmental context is a concept at the core of Penone's early works like the *Maritime Alps*. Further evidence of this tactic, arrived at on his own, if simultaneously with Morris, can be seen in the unassumingly titled *Pietra, corda, sole / Pietra, corda, pioggia* (*Stone, Rope, Sun / Stone, Rope, Rain*, 1968). In this work Penone photographically documents the ongoing interrelation of materials and natural processes: a stone, tied to a tree by a piece of rope, is "raised" by the tension created when the rope fibres absorb rainwater, and lowered when they dry out. The artist introduces the ingredients for an action or interaction, but he, like the viewer, is a witness to the "work," which unfolds over time, without actively managing it. The nuanced concept of gesture and artistic labour seen here echoes that of works like *It Will Continue to Grow except at That Point*. In both examples, Penone retreats from a theological "single moment of creation" to identify instead the complex unfolding of the work over time and among various constituents. Such works simultaneously mark and challenge the artist's agency.

When Penone invokes gesture in the *Maritime Alps*, he inevitably does so in subtle, anti-heroic terms: as a negotiated relationship between artist and matter, not as human dominance over the material world. For instance, in another of the actions in the series the artist wrapped his arms and legs around a tree trunk (figure 1.7). He then marked the outline of this embrace – the outline of his entire body – with a thin galvanized wire nailed into the tree. This intervention forecast that as the sapling grew, vestiges of the artist's silhouette would have an impact on the form of the tree. His artistic gesture therefore does have an effect on the material and its eventual form, but the action is brief and minor in comparison to the extended response of the tree.

In this work as in the others, the artist initiates contact, but the ultimate form is determined by the way the tree actively responds to this touch, a touch that is no longer steeped in the theology of artistic

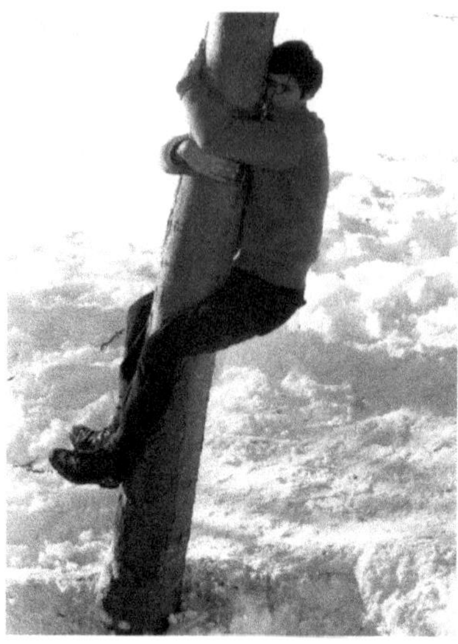

1.7 Photographic documentation of Giuseppe Penone making *L'albero crescendo ricorderà i punti del mio contatto* (*The Growing Tree Will Remember the Points of My Contact*), from *Alpi Marittime* (Maritime Alps), 1968.

Photograph: Claudio Basso, ©Archivio Penone

creation. The artist's touch is just one of many factors affecting the tree's growth, others of which include soil conditions, weather, water, fire, and disease, as well as encounters with other, non-human animals. A tree like an acacia, for instance, often grows more, larger thorns in areas where it has been trimmed, been damaged by the elements, or had its leaves eaten by an animal. Such a tree is emphatically more than a raw material; it is a force of nature. This negotiated relationship between the forces of man and matter is a recurrent theme that connects Penone's work to larger philosophical discourses, ranging from phenomenology to biopolitics, and which will be tracked in future chapters.

Sculpture and/as the Scent of Bread

The material encounters that Penone staged in the *Maritime Alps* may initially recall modernist antecedents and their focus on artistic gesture as the foundation of form, but the muted tenor of his reprisal of these codes can be read in his deployment of surrogates, photographs, and textual supplements. In international post-war discourses, such traces are often read as marks of absence as much as presence.[27] Direct Italian precedents for such thinking about trace include *décollagiste* Mimmo Rotella, whose ripped and reassembled fragments of advertising posters had challenged the creative act by linking it directly with destruction and appropriation. Similarly, Lucio Fontana's slashed and punctured monochromes literalized the violence of artistic gesture. The holes and tears that characterize many of his canvases are evidence of an already-past encounter between artist and material. Penone's clearest invocation of the trace is his use of surrogates in the *Maritime Alps*: models of his hand reformed in metal, the frame of his figure set into a stream, or silhouettes of the body marked by wire. Less obvious, at first glance, are the connotations inherent to the photographic documentation of these interventions and the written captions that accompany them.

Photography, in fact, provides a significant means for Penone to counter the subjective, auratic implications of action and gesture through mechanical "objectivity." Like many artists of this period working beyond the confines of the white cube, Penone turned to the camera for its documentary practicality as well as for its suggestion of transparent communication. In this period, objectivity was needed, and black-and-white photography provided a means to suggest basic testimony to what had been done.[28] In 1977 it was again Krauss who called into question the supposed pluralism of 1970s art by arguing that a consistent use of photography for its indexical qualities was a tactic that united many artists who aimed to free themselves from the articulated language of aesthetic convention.[29] Penone's use of photography in the 1968 *Maritime Alps* aligns with a generational use of the medium as an evidentiary, non-representational communication of presence and, as such, foreshadows the fundamentally postmodern attitude present in Penone's larger artistic project.

While it may seem paradoxical, the photograph became the ideal tool for Penone to work through some of the central concerns of sculpture because it allowed him to circumvent the twinned encumbrances of subjective representation and materialism still lingering in the discipline. That he considered photography to have an uncoded, indexical status is supported by the text or captions overwriting the mute, serial images. In his famous essay "The Work of Art in the Age of Mechanical Reproduction," Walter Benjamin describes a change in the functions of photographs when they are no longer primarily used as portraits, which in his words are the last vestiges of the cult value of images. Proposing Eugene Atget's pictures of the deserted streets and parks of Paris as evidence, he argues that photographs free of recognizable human figures become evidentiary, and they require a different kind of approach than "free-floating contemplation." This is an important example because here Benjamin also argues that captions, such as those appended to serial photographs in illustrated magazines, function in a means altogether different from titles. Instead, they direct the reading of a series of images to lead the viewer to a specific meaning because none is available in the single image alone.[30]

In Penone's *Maritime Alps*, handwritten notations on the photographs visually interrupt the transparency of the photographic document. The very presence of these "captions" and their linguistic strategies frustrate both photographic neutrality and artistic authority because the textual fragments refer to the artist's action and to the "action" of the living material. For instance, for the action in which he marked the embrace of his body with wire and nails, he inscribed one version of the photograph with a detailed description of his clinging to the tree and an arrow directing attention to the application of nails, as well as the phrase "L'albero crescendo conserverà la mia azione" (The growing tree will preserve my action) (figure 1.8). This focuses the viewer's attention on the action performed by the artist and positions the tree as a recipient of the action. Penone ultimately exhibited another version of the same image, captioned with a simple phrase "L'albero crescendo ricorderà i punti del mio contatto" (The growing tree will remember the points of my contact) (figure 1.9). Both inscriptions suggest some negotiation between the artist's intervention and the tree over time, but the latter phrase is especially interesting because his choice of words signals a specific understanding of the tree as a living, sentient organism. Instead of merely "preserving" a trace as a passive function of a material acted upon, Penone uses the Italian verb *ricordare* to imply that the tree, as a living organism, actively records or, more suggestively, "remembers" the encounter with his body, which merely leaves a trace.

Throughout the *Maritime Alps* series Penone mines the razor-thin space between an indexical photographic image and its caption through such short handwritten texts on the photographs. In the images, the hand and body of the artist is in a non-hierarchical relationship to the material (trees, stream, etc.), while *on* the images, a handwritten text reasserts an authorial voice, directing the reading of the image back to the artist who initiated the intervention. The clash of these opposing modes in the same visual document introduces an instability that is characteristic of the most critical postmodern art practices of the 1970s and 1980s.[31]

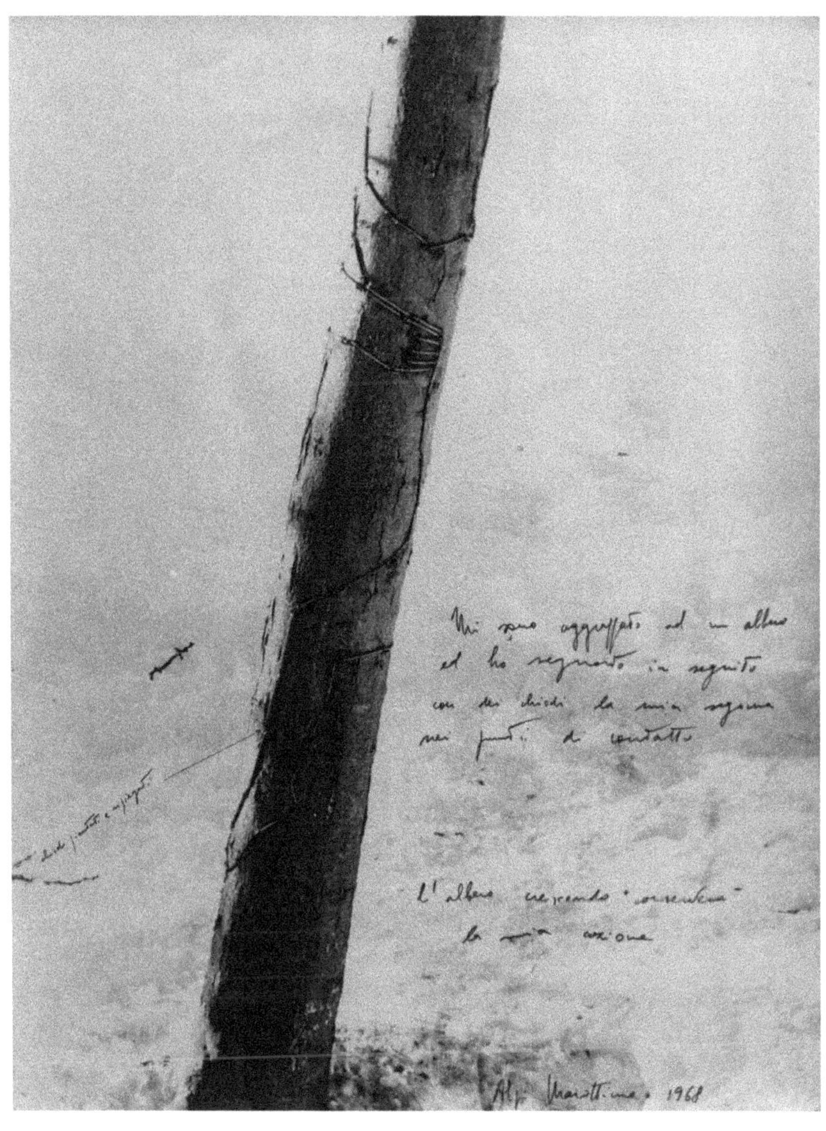

1.8 Giuseppe Penone, *Mi sono aggrappato ad un albero (I Clung to a Tree)*, from *Alpi Marittime* (Maritime Alps), 1968. Black-and-white photograph, 64 x 49 cm.

Collection of the artist, Turin. Photograph: Claudio Basso, ©Archivio Penone

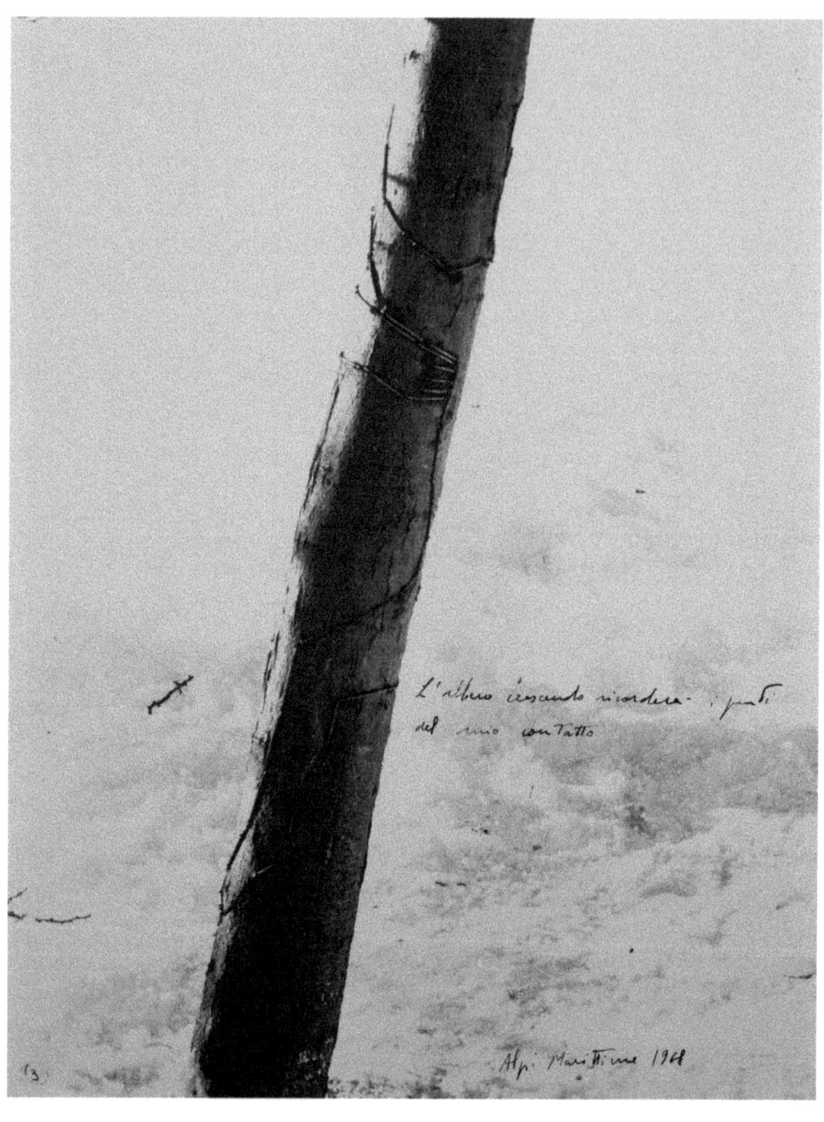

1.9 Giuseppe Penone, *L'albero crescendo ricorderà i punti del mio contatto* (*The Growing Tree Will Remember the Points of My Contact*), from *Alpi Marittime* (Maritime Alps), 1968. Black-and-white photograph, 64 x 49 cm.

Collection of the artist, Turin. Photograph: Paolo Mussat Sartor, ©Archivio Penone

Penone's own critique of the distinction between the cultural conventions of language and the putatively uncoded status of photographic images and natural objects reoccurs in a number of other works from this period. In particular, *Scrive, legge, ricorda* (*Write, Read, Remember*, 1969) and *Pane alfabeto* (*Alphabet Bread*, 1969) exemplify his engagement of semiotics and representation. In *Write, Read, Remember,* a photograph documents the artist driving a sharpened iron wedge into a tree trunk (figure 1.10). The metal bears the twenty-one letters of the Italian alphabet on one side and the ten Arabic numerals (integers) on the other. Because the letters and numbers appear in the reversal of a typesetter's characters, the action must be read as positing the tree as a factory for books, their flesh a potential future repository of human knowledge. The intervention poetically suggests the possibility of writing a book as the tree grows, rather than after it has been felled and made into paper.[32] Yet the quixotic absurdity of physically preloading the tree with such symbolic systems, combined with the demonstrable violence of the action, mocks the anthropocentrism of such an instrumentalized relationship between two organisms. *Write, Read, Remember* marks the indifference of the tree to human conventions and codes and, simultaneously, suggests that language is attained at the expense of other kinds of encounters.

The lesson about the limitations of an anthropocentric perspective is redoubled in *Pane alfabeto* (*Alphabet Bread*, 1969), in which a piece of stainless steel formed into the joined-up letters of the alphabet is baked into an oversized loaf of bread, which, to the delight of the local pigeons, is then left outside (figure 1.11). To the birds, the letters revealed by their nibbling are merely an obstruction to the crumbs that nourish their bodies. The transparency of their instinctual desire for food contrasts with the alphabet's opaque incomprehensibility. Reflecting on the attempt to harness such straightforwardness in his art, the artist mused: "Managing to make a work as effective as an odor that acts on the animal unconscious that governs us. A work like the scent of bread."[33] Can an artwork wash over us as effortlessly as a perfume? Might it affect us as forcefully and immediately? Language has some of this facility but not the immediacy. That is, once one knows how to read, alphabetic codes are deciphered with little effort or intention, but comprehension and meaning are often more elusive and often depend on the context of their reception.

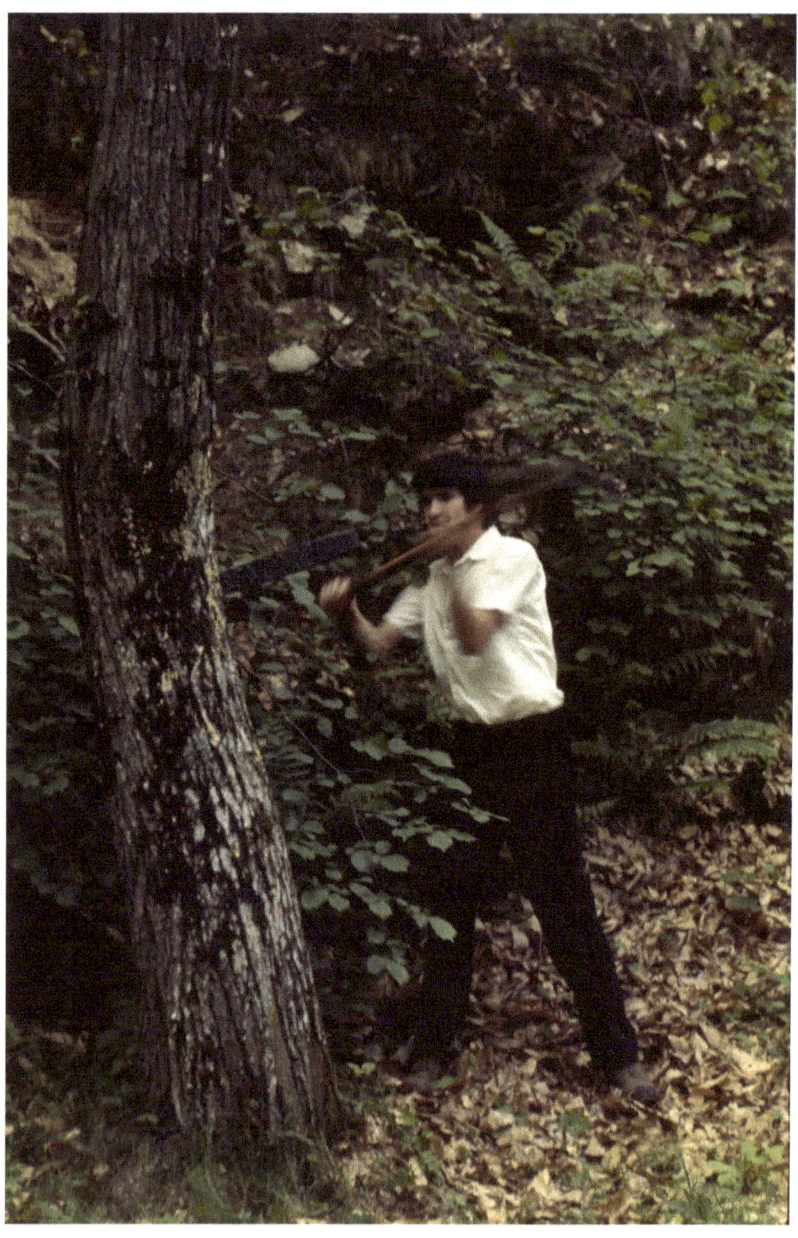

1.10 Giuseppe Penone, *Scrive, legge, ricorda* (*Write, Read, Remember*), 1969. Colour photograph. Galleria Multipli, Turin.

Photograph: Paolo Mussat Sartor, © Paolo Mussat Sartor

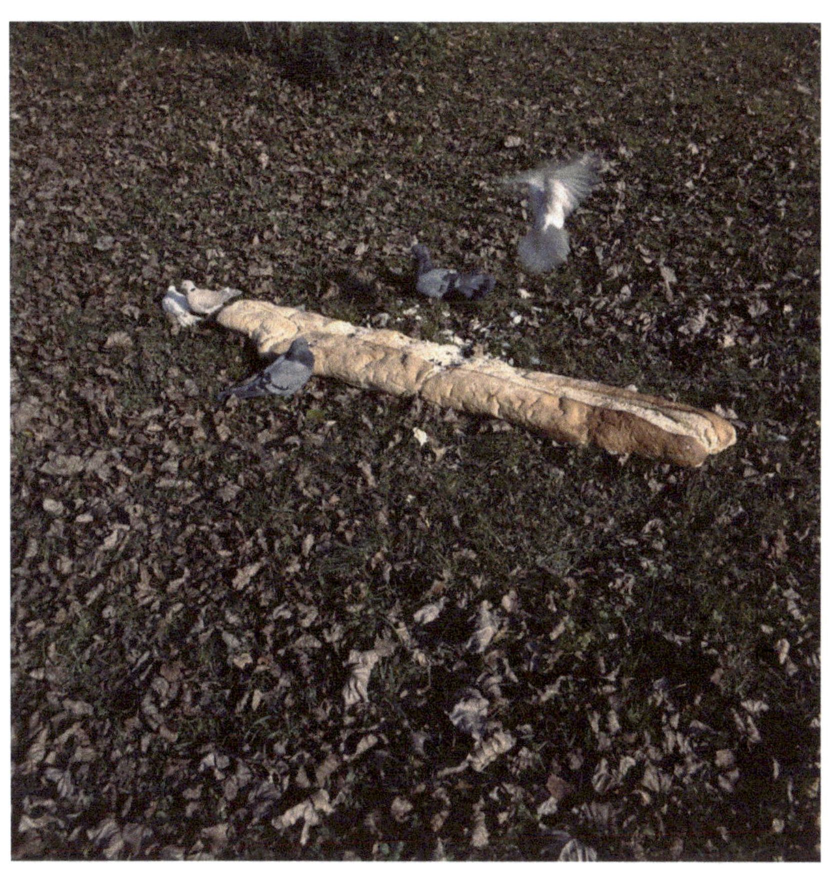

1.11 Giuseppe Penone, *Pane alfabeto* (*Bread Alphabet*), 1969.
Bread, steel letters, 200 x 50 x 20 cm.

Photograph: Paolo Pellion di Persano, © Archivio Penone

The varied action-intervention documentations of this period, from *Maritime Alps* to *Pane alfabeto*, function as a clearing out of many received concepts – material passivity, artistic agency, and the a-temporal transcendence of an artwork. Seen this way, art is a diagnostic tool through which Penone began to reconsider the nature of an artwork's messages and the means of its reception. Visual apprehension, whether of a photographic image or of written language, does not compare with the instinctual reaction to the aroma of food or the feeling of a material in hand. Sculpture, and its appeal to the non-visual senses, might be one means to achieve this immediacy.

Sculpture and/as Encounter

In early 1969 the *Maritime Alps* photographs were the primary vehicle through which Penone's practice gained an important context, one that would frame his work for decades to come. In addition to their inclusion in two group shows and one solo show at Sperone, the photographs were reproduced in Celant's *Arte Povera* book, published simultaneously in Italian, English, and German in late 1969.[34] Penone's contribution to the book was flanked by the works of Keith Sonnier and Franz Erhald Walther, thus formally inducting the artist into the local context of Arte povera as well as aligning his work with the international discourses of process, land art, and conceptualism. The *Maritime Alps* actions unfold over six pages, through a collection of drawn sketches and numerous documentary photographs of their making, as well as long-form, descriptive captions (figure 1.12). Not yet solidified into the suite of editioned art objects that they would eventually become, Penone's *Maritime Alps* here retained the freshness of an investigation in process.

The *Maritime Alps* works were still emergent projects when they were printed in the 1969 book, and their full temporal aspects were still unrealized, projecting into the future through their attendant captions. Statements like "The growing tree will raise the cage" would only appear valid after years or decades. Therefore, it is not surprising that Penone's explorations of artistic identity, process, and temporality also found form in some more immediate demonstrations. For instance, in *Gli anni dell un albero più uno* (*The Age of a Tree plus One*, 1969) Penone brought a small tree into Sperone's gallery during an interstice between shows. After laying it on the concrete floor, the artist covered the trunk of the felled sapling in wax, applied by hand (figure 1.13). The wax formed an additional layer on the tree's

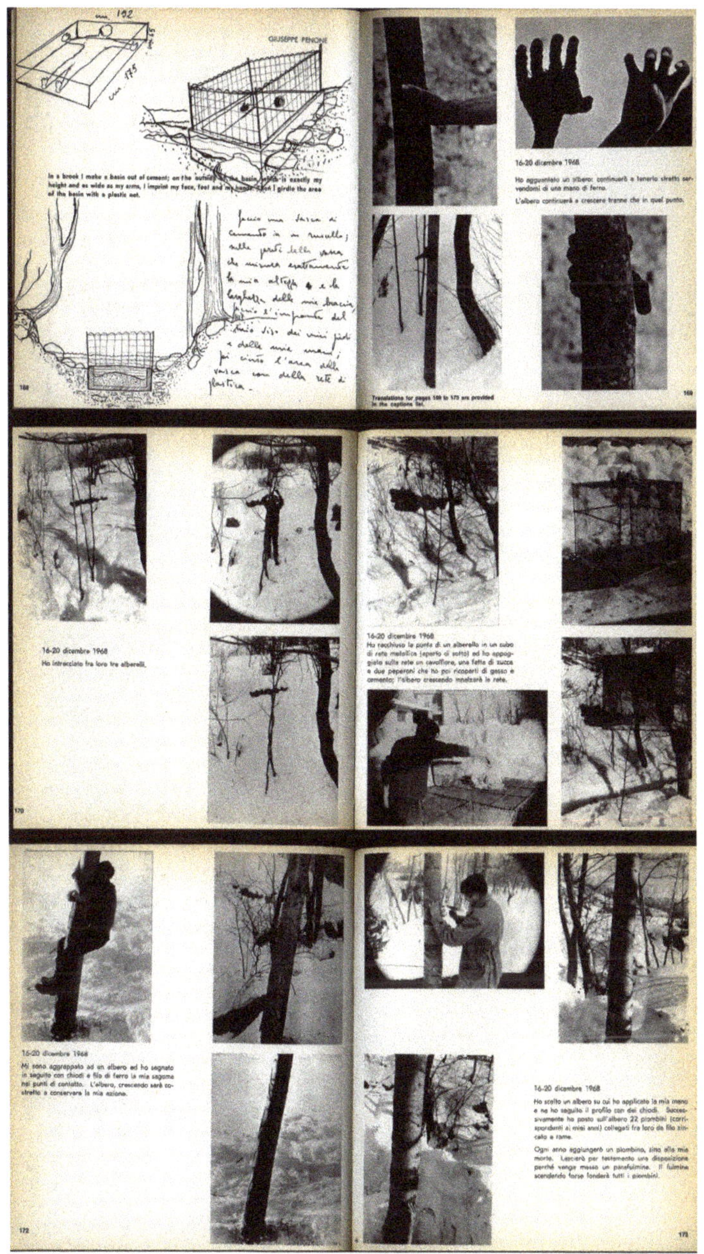

GIUSEPPE PENONE

In a brook I make a basin out of cement; on the outside of the basin, which is exactly my height and as wide as my arms, I imprint my face, feet and my hands. Then I girdle the area of the basin with a plastic net.

168

16-20 dicembre 1968

Ho agguantato un albero: continuerò a tenerlo stretto servendomi di una mano di ferro.

L'albero continuerà a crescere tranne che in quel punto.

Translations for pages 168 to 173 are provided in the captions list.

169

16-20 dicembre 1968

Ho intrecciato fra loro tre alberelli.

170

16-20 dicembre 1968

Ho racchiuso la punta di un alberello in un cubo di rete metallica (aperto di sotto) ed ho appoggiato sulla rete un cavolfiore, una fetta di zucca e due peperoni che ho poi ricoperti di gesso e cemento; l'albero crescendo innalzerà la rete.

16-20 dicembre 1968

Mi sono aggrappato ad un albero ed ho segnato in seguito con chiodi e filo di ferro la mia sagoma nei punti di contatto. L'albero, crescendo sarà costretto a conservare la mia azione.

172

16-20 dicembre 1968

Ho scelto un albero su cui ho applicato la mia mano e ne ho seguito il profilo con dei chiodi. Successivamente ho posto sull'albero 22 piombini (corrispondenti ai miei anni) collegati fra loro da filo zincato e rame.

Ogni anno aggiungerò un piombino, sino alla mia morte. Lascierò per testamento una disposizione perché venga messo un parafulmine. Il fulmine scendendo forse fonderà tutti i piombini.

173

1.12 Pages 168–73 in Germano Celant's *Arte Povera* (Milan: Mazzota, 1969).

Photographs: Elizabeth Mangini

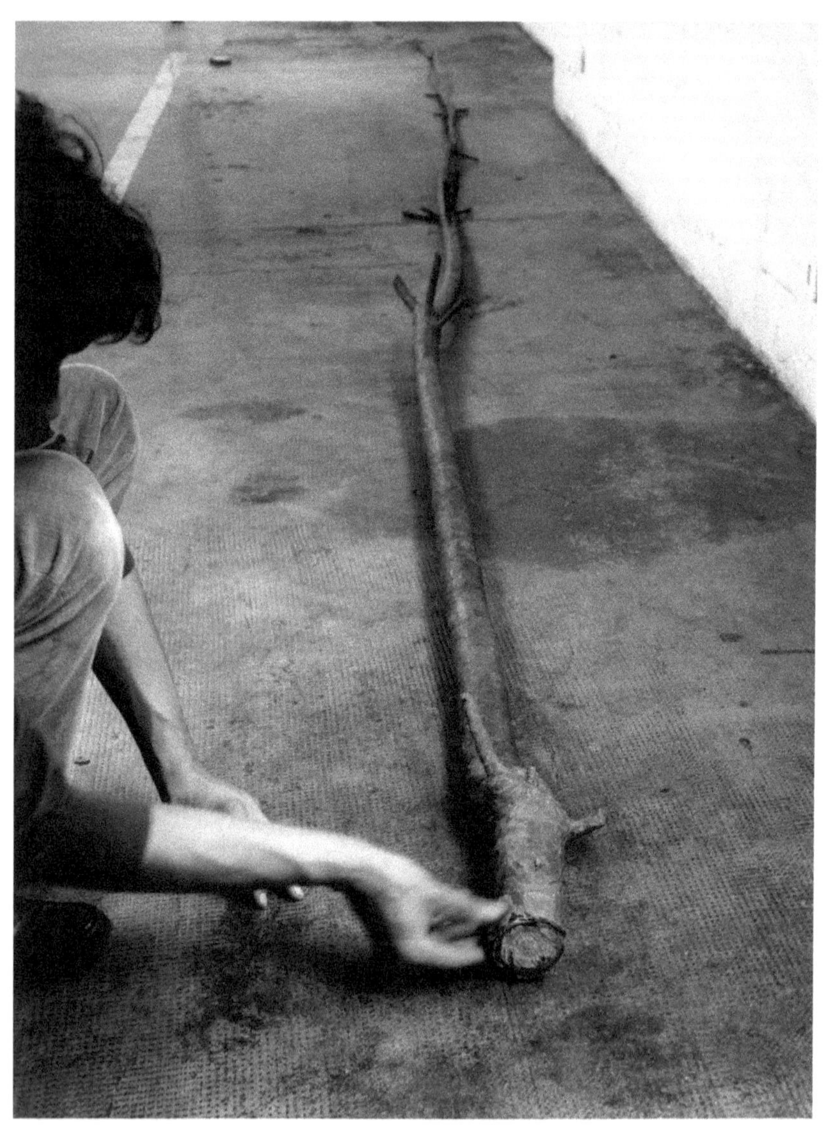

1.13 Giuseppe Penone, *Gli anni dell'albero più uno* (*The Age of a Tree plus One*), 1969.
Branch, wax, 800 cm x 6 cm diameter (destroyed).

Photograph: Paolo Mussat Sartor, © Paolo Mussat Sartor

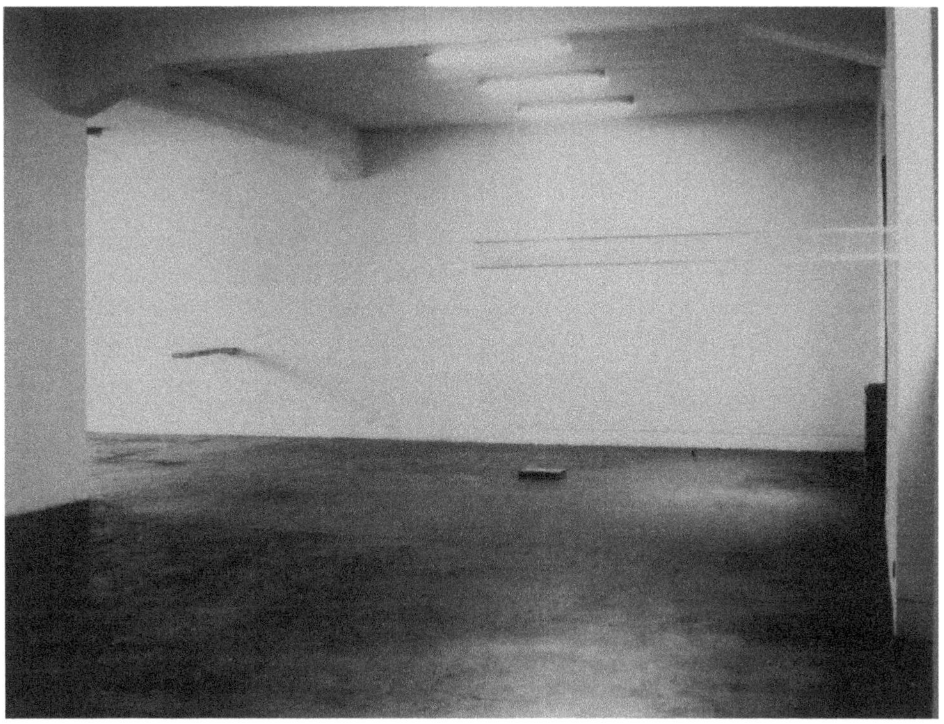

1.14 Installation view of *Giuseppe Penone: Indicazioni di uno spazio* at Galleria Gian Enzo Sperone, Turin, December 1969.

Photograph: Paolo Mussat Sartor, © Paolo Mussat Sartor

surface, a theoretical growth ring. In this way the artist artificially accelerated time through his manipulation of the material: he aged the tree one year in a matter of hours.

The Age of a Tree plus One demonstrates that Penone was beginning to think about ways in which the ideas generated by his interventions in nature could be received more directly by the viewer, rather than through photographic documentation.[35] The coda to this first, investigatory phase of the artist's project came in December 1969, with Penone's first solo exhibition at Sperone. Here the artist presented a critique of the stereotypical white cube of commercial galleries by reorienting viewers towards embodied experience: the multisensory, the material, and the temporal. Collectively titled *Indicazioni di uno spazio* (*Indications of a Space*), the show was spare: just three works inhabiting the gallery for a period of eleven days. The exhibition included *Indicazione del pavimento* (*Indication of the Ground*), *Indicazione del muro* (*Indication of the Wall*), and *Indicazione dell'aria (barra d'aria)* (*Indication of the Air (Bar of Air)*), all 1969 (figure 1.11). These were not objects as much as they were modifications to the room itself, further transferring the tactics he had developed in the *Maritime Alps* from the forest to the urban art gallery. Still seeking a minimum definition of sculpture, Penone's interventions in the gallery altered the presumed transparency of the conditions of viewing art by drawing attention to the physical space.

Indication of the Ground, for instance, posits sculpture at its most basic definition as something that sits on the ground. By setting a short row of bricks directly on the gallery floor, Penone effectively raised the floor by a single step. *Indication of the Wall* comprises a similar row of rectangular forms, cantilevered into the empty space of the room a metre above the ground. This piece demonstrates that sculpture takes up a position in space, whereas one typically looks at a painting hanging flat against a wall. For *Indication of the Air* Penone inserted a rectilinear glass tube into an opening in the gallery's window. It channelled icy winter winds directly into the gallery, constituting a literal bridge between the "real" world and the space of art, and lending temporary form, palpability, and sound to an otherwise invisible aspect of spatial experience: air. Each of these interventions functioned to focus the reception of art on the time-based, multisensory apperception of a space: the zero point of his own thinking about sculpture.

Between 1968 and 1969 Penone worked through some basic assumptions about sculpture. With the *Maritime Alps* he challenged received notions of representation and artistic authority by foregrounding the reciprocity inherent to material encounters, instead of covering it up. The tactics he developed in these works, including the use of casts and surrogates, allowed him to demonstrate process and to indicate artistic labour without eclipsing the materials or reducing them to visual signs. These interventions, as well as experiments like *Write, Read, Remember*, initiated a way of working that positioned the artist as both active agent and passive observer. In works like *Bread Alphabet*, *The Years of a Tree plus One*, and *Indications of a Space* the artist began to explore the ways in which a sculptor communicates to an audience through the body, and in which the meaning of sculptural encounters can transform over time. Embodied perception, material reciprocity, and temporal perspectivism are central themes that emerge in Penone's works of this early period and pervade his project – and, therefore, his theory of sculpture – for decades to come.

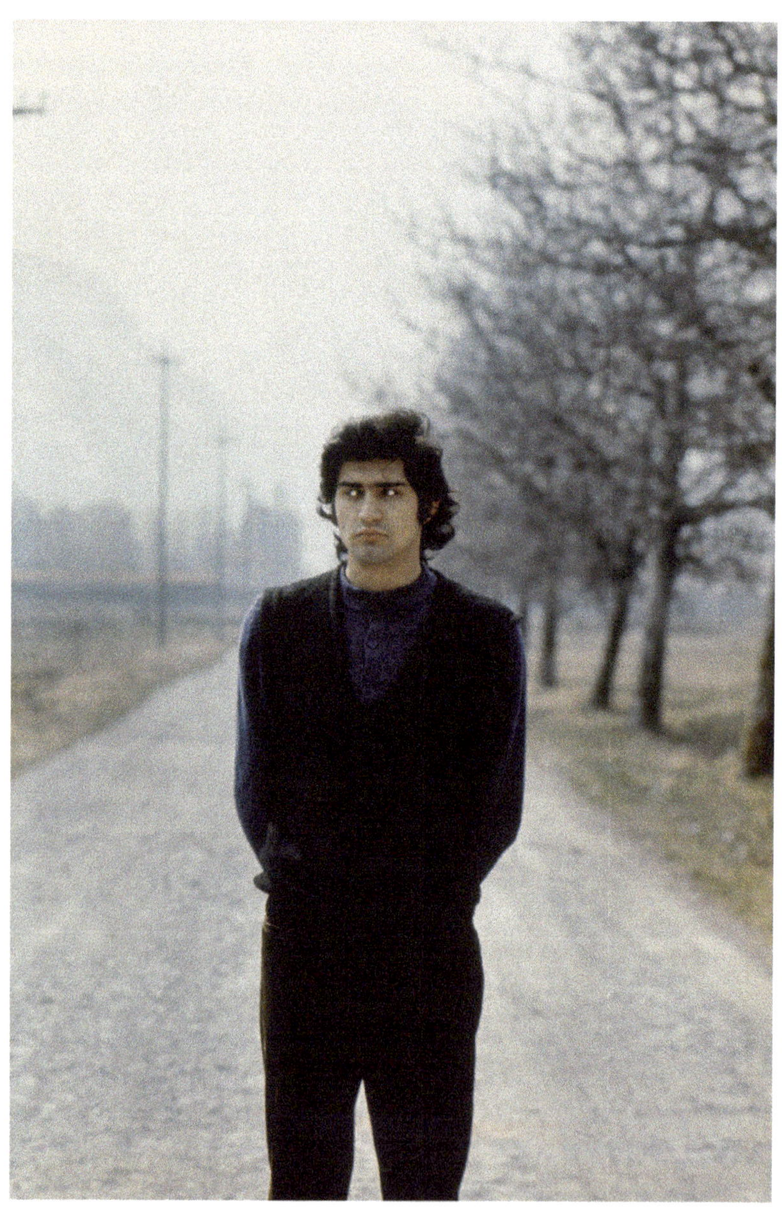

2.1 Giuseppe Penone, *Rovesciare i propri occhi* (*Reversing One's Eyes*), 1970. Slides and projector, documentation of 3 March 1971, Via Lepetit, Garessio (detail).

Photograph: © Archivio Penone

2
An Artist Turned Inside Out

At the root of becoming phenomenological operates this ethical choice: it is necessary to start over again, to reject observable reality as directly deterministic, since it is not only what is outside of us, but it educates and conditions us from within.

– Paolo Pompei, "Merleau-Ponty, Politica e morale"

A slide projector casts an image in which, at a distance, a lone figure stands still in the centre of a narrow country road (figure 2.1).[1] Trees and telephone poles line opposite sides of the path, recalling studies of single-point perspective. Slow, steady clicks of a slide projector bring the mysterious figure closer into view. Soon one discerns more details: it is a man, wearing a knitted sweater and sporting shaggy dark hair, wisps of which are being carried astray by a gentle wind. Eventually the landscape falls away, and the viewer is forced to look upon something that has remained opaque, even as the figure comes into full focus: his gaze (figure 2.2). The unsettling vacancy of the photographed visage attracts and repels with equal measure. The standing figure is Giuseppe Penone himself, and his blank stare is the result of his eyes being covered with mirrored contact lenses, which reflect the path ahead of him and render the artist temporarily blind. In collaboration with an array of photographers, amateur and professional alike, Penone repeated and documented this action numerous times around 1970.[2]

For most humans with sight, the eye is the most trusted witness to the existence of the self in the world, allowing one to understand oneself as distinct from other things.[3] In his 1637 discourse on light and optics, French mathematician and natural scientist René Descartes famously claimed sight to be the most noble of the senses, and this

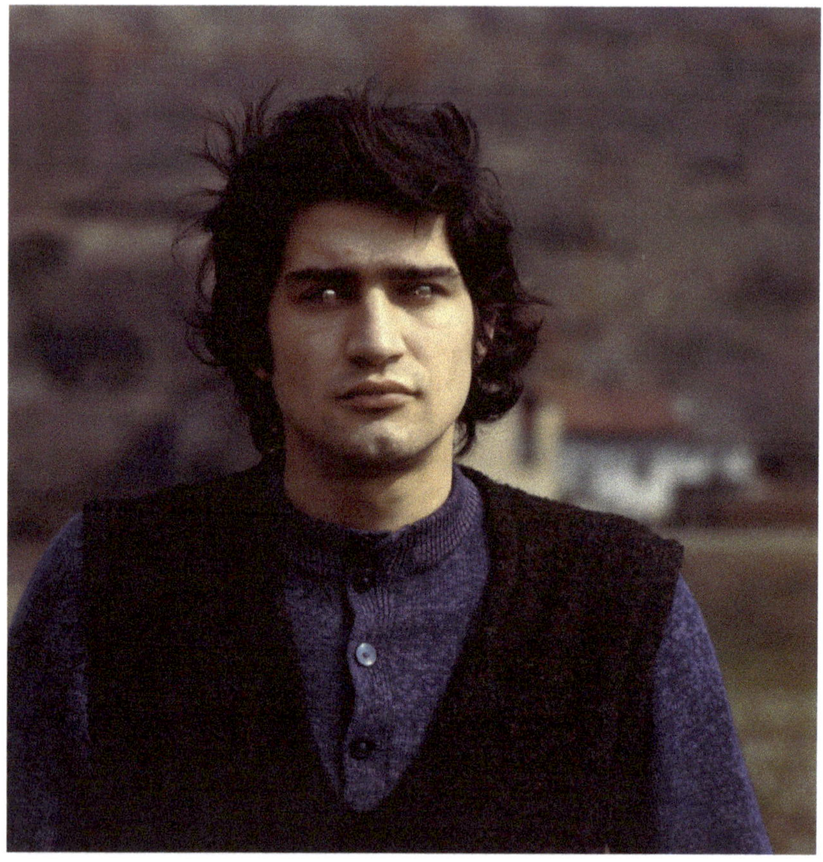

2.2 Giuseppe Penone, *Rovesciare i propri occhi* (*Reversing One's Eyes*), 1970. Slides and projector. Documentation of 3 March 1971, Cascine Ruffini, Garessio (detail).

Photograph: © Archivio Penone

eponymous Cartesian view persisted through the Enlightenment up through the modernist period.[4] Yet as far back as Plato's cave, vision alone – the eye set loose, without experience and grounding in the other senses – has also been understood to be unreliable. Not wanting to be fooled by shadows, Penone choreographed scenarios in which he had to experience the world with his flesh instead of his eyes and in which his eyes were no longer transparent windows but were subject

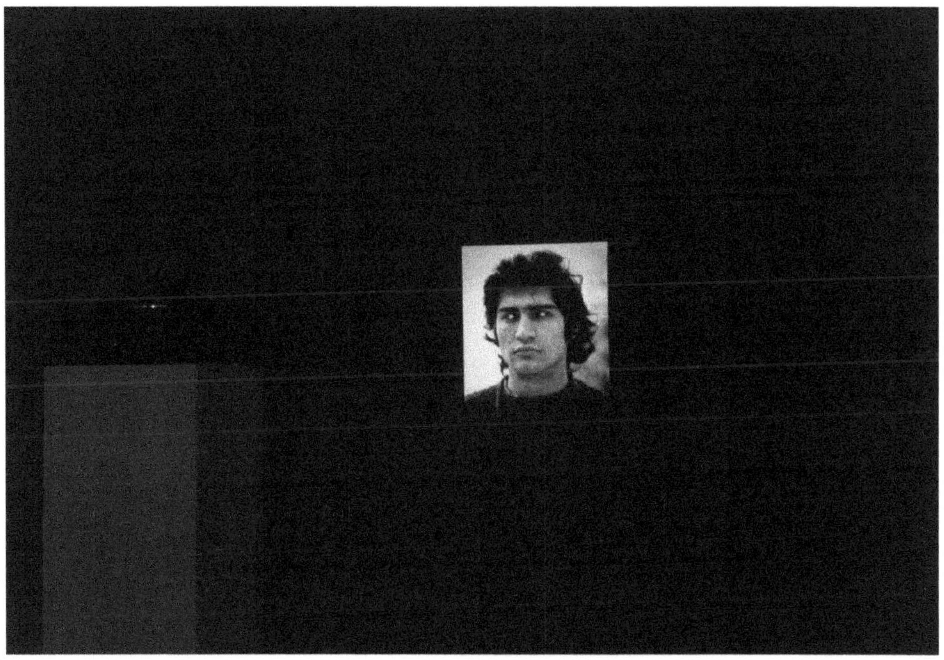

2.3 Giuseppe Penone, *Rovesciare i propri occhi* (*Reversing One's Eyes*), 1970. Six slides sequence. Installation view at Museo de la Ciudad, Quito, 2009.

Photograph: © Archivio Penone

to physical contact with objects.[5] The slide projection and related stills are known as *Rovesciare i propri occhi (To Turn One's Eyes Inside Out*, or *Reversing One's Eyes*, 1970–7) (figure 2.3). They are a collection of experiments as much as they are finished works, and they exemplify key aspects of Penone's investigation of artistic making and perceptual experience in his maturing practice. *Rovesciare* can also be translated into English as "to overthrow, topple, or overturn"; therefore, the reference to these works by a shortened version of the Italian title throughout this chapter maintains the revolutionary aspects of the Italian verb.[6] Holding onto these strong connotations is integral to the reading of these works as marking Penone's position vis-à-vis the Cartesian privileging of vision.

In *Indications of a Space* (Sperone, 1969) Penone had used palpable clues to help chart the phenomenal space of Sperone's gallery. The

Rovesciare works, however, engender a sense of perceptual uncertainty.[7] The fragile social dynamic of image-driven communication dissolves when the viewer is unable to connect with the figure in an imagined exchange of glances. Despite the young artist's squarely facing the camera in these images, the mirrors frustrate "eye contact."[8] Moreover, Penone's mirrored irises reflect the landscape's horizon line, which creates confusion between the vanishing point behind the figure and the one before him. The viewer of these images sees both what is in front of them and, theoretically, what is behind them (a street, a stream, a standing figure who, jarringly, is not really there). The misrecognition and doubling that occurs with the coincidence of the mirrored contact lenses and the mechanical registration of the camera's view produces a profound perceptual disturbance. Together, these social and perceptual cues destabilize the viewer's confidence in the stability of visual experience. That is, paradoxically, the short-circuiting of sight evokes its embodiment. Sight allows us to extend our sensorial limits to a far-off horizon and to "reach" perceptually beyond what is physically graspable. Images like these interrupt that projection, instead reminding us that vision is rooted in two socket-bound, fleshy orbs.

That vision is rooted in the body and that it has a tactile aspect is something we are habituated to ignore. Yet, trust in what one sees is not innate; rather, it is learned through experimentation and sensory experience. Children are less conditioned to trust what they see than adults are, and therefore touch is often the primary means through which humans first learn. Indeed, infants and toddlers instinctually reach out to grab whatever they see, pulling it close to the body and taking in its textures, heft, smells, and tastes with multiple sensory apparatuses. Penone claims that he wanted to put something of this fundamentally physical mode of discovery back into discussions about art, which to him seemed too focused on vision at the time.[9] The challenge was finding ways to do this within existing forms of artistic discourse without resorting to the arch-didacticism of happenings and other participatory works.

In *Rovesciare*, Penone captured automatic, instantly reflected images in the mirrored lenses before he saw them.[10] The resultant photographs, most of which were published in an artist's book, are therefore twofold: they document his refusal of vision, and they present the viewer with visual evidence of the same event. The gap between the artist's multisensory experience and its visual documentation is palpable. In these images the artist probes the traditional disparity between artist and viewer. He does so by locating their different orders of sensory experience and concurrently bringing them together (for the artist, like the viewer, does not visualize the event until later, when the lenses have been removed and the photographs developed).[11] This element of delay further destabilizes visual priority and questions the hierarchical separation between artist and viewer.

It might seem all too obvious to read Penone's image of the artist "blinded" as resisting the primacy of vision in art and its reception, but as they are photographs, some critics have understood *Rovesciare* in decidedly Cartesian terms. For instance, in a 2013 essay on the role of sight in Penone's work, curator Daniela Lancioni concludes that "Giuseppe Penone is showing simply this: we are what we look at."[12] Such assessments underscore the idea of vision's singularity, and its noble centrality to what it means to be human. Celant, however, suggests that Penone's rural upbringing is at the root of his emphasis on tactility, arguing that it reveals a "primitive" way of being in the world.[13] I read *Rovesciare* and other fundamentally visual, mostly photographic works from the early 1970s as neither an anthropocentric claim to visual primacy nor a regressive refusal of imagistic technology (indeed, we are talking about photographs). Rather, Penone's repudiation of sight in *Rovesciare* catalyses a sophisticated recognition of sight's embeddedness in the body and its implication in the intricate social and physical aspects of experience.

Penone oriented his early practice towards redefining one's perception of reality through the elaboration of a tactile approach to the visual, a concept for which there is a clear precedent in both art history and philosophy.[14] Curator Daniel Soutif has argued for using the term *haptic* to describe the artist's self-blinding actions, recalling art historian Alois Riegl's differentiation of the purely optic from the visual apprehension of space and volume.[15] Soutif submits that in *Rovesciare* the concept of vision is framed more like that understood by the Ancient Greeks, who used *haptikos* to describe the way in which they thought sight and touch were united, with light rays issuing from the eye and "touching" the regarded object. Penone's denial of pure opticality and his attention to the tactile aspects of the visual in *Rovesciare* can indeed be considered haptic, figuratively, because vision is here proposed as only one of multiple co-ordinated senses engaged in the creation and reception of the work.

Penone's own writings provide a key to understanding the philosophical relationship between opticality and his emerging sculptural practice. For instance, in 1970 the artist wrote: "The closed, sightless, body is defined in space. / And becomes sculpture."[16] His theory of sculpture, elaborated in words and works, thus integrates sight and vision in ways that are analogous to the body's ability to unify multiple sensory inputs. This attitude can be best understood as a re-reading of ocularcentrism in mid-twentieth-century European philosophy, which, as scholar Martin Jay has argued, maintains that the modern era has been dominated by the discourse of sight in a way that the premodern and postmodern have not.[17] In Jay's book *Downcast Eyes,* an investigation of what he terms *anti-ocularcentrism* in twentieth-century French philosophy, he argues that Jean-Paul Sartre and Maurice Merleau-Ponty were hinge figures in a theoretical resistance to the domination of sight, which later bore fruit in the philosophical and artistic elaboration of the postmodern.[18] Although Sartre's mistrust of images contributed to nihilistic nausea because it failed "to overcome the meaningless absurd thingness of the world," Merleau-Ponty was more temperate in his critique of the visual world.[19] The latter's work on perception critically engages with the Cartesian scopic regime and is therefore useful to reading Penone's photographic critique of the visual.[20]

The recourse to phenomenology is particularly apt because the University of Turin was one of the main conduits of such European philosophy in the post-war years. Following the death in 1953 of the Neopolitan Benedetto Croce, whose idealist philosophy dominated much of Italian thought in the early twentieth century, Turin-based scholars Norberto Bobbio and Luigi Pareyson were among the first to move in the direction of hermeneutics and phenomenology. Their students Gianni Vattimo and Umberto Eco subsequently carried these streams into aesthetics and popular culture. Eco served on the editorial board of the art-and-culture magazine *Marcatré* with Germano Celant, and, more importantly, his idea that an artwork could be structured to allow for its completion by the viewer, in "The Open Work," was reflected in Celant's theorization of Arte povera. Thus, while Penone may or may not have directly read any of Merleau-Ponty's texts, phenomenology's prevalence in the local intellectual context certainly permeated the art criticism of the day.[21] When Penone's mirrored-eye photographs isolate and disrupt the viewer's expectations of a scopic experience, one can read them as engendering a distrust of vision without rejecting it altogether, just as Merleau-Ponty critiqued the Cartesian disembodiment of vision without abandoning it. Indeed, since humans do have eyes, to ignore the visual altogether would be as problematic as over-privileging it. Instead, Penone's works draw attention to sight's limited role within the context of the body's perceptual system.[22] By using photography, Penone explores different orders of sensory perception and their imprinting on the body, which ultimately form the foundations of a larger claim for sculpture's phenomenological priority.

Departing from the *Rovesciare* series and concluding with *Palpebre* (*Eyelids*, 1978), a room-sized charcoal drawing exhibited at the Venice Biennale, this chapter charts Penone's exploration of the complexities of visual and tactile apperception as they relate to the production and reception of artworks. The artist's works are considered alongside other challenges to the stability of vision made by his artistic peers, in order to demonstrate both the relevance of his work to contemporary discourse and the particularity of his contribution. Using aspects of Merleau-Ponty's phenomenology as a framework through which to view these projects, I argue that Penone purposefully uses visual images and objects to undermine the hierarchy between vision and the other senses. His works reveal, instead, the necessary, corporeal imbrication of the senses. Further, Merleau-Ponty's concept of the chiasm, or a crossing over between sight and touch, aids in appraising Penone's early investigation of artistic process and his own identity as an artist. Works exploring the permeable borders demarcated by the eye and the skin are the means through which Penone demonstrates that his identity is the sum of the things he can experience with his senses. The objects and actions through which he works are meant to be more than mere representations of such realizations and experiences. Rather, the artist's persistent, poetic exploration of the haptic is fundamental to recalibrating the viewer's own relationship with the phenomenal world. In these works we begin to glimpse the socio-political and ethical stakes of rejecting the anthropocentrism of modernism.

Peripheral Vision

Mirrors frequently demonstrate the relative instability of artistic authority and the unreliability of vision in the art of the 1960s and 1970s, and much of it was exhibited internationally. Take, for instance, the mirrored cubes of Morris's *Untitled* (1965), intended for Sperone's gallery, or Yayoi Kusama's *Narcissus Garden*, an intervention at the 1966 Venice Biennale in which she critiqued the self-serving art market by endeavouring to sell mirrored orbs to the exhibition's public (figure 2.4).[23] Notable Italian examples include Lucio Fontana's *Ambienti Spaziali*, Luciano Fabro's *Buco* (*Hole*, 1963), and Michelangelo Pistoletto's photographic, polished-steel "mirror paintings" of the early 1960s. In each of these latter cases the mirror used in the exhibition space draws attention to the context of display, reflecting the experience of looking at art, and

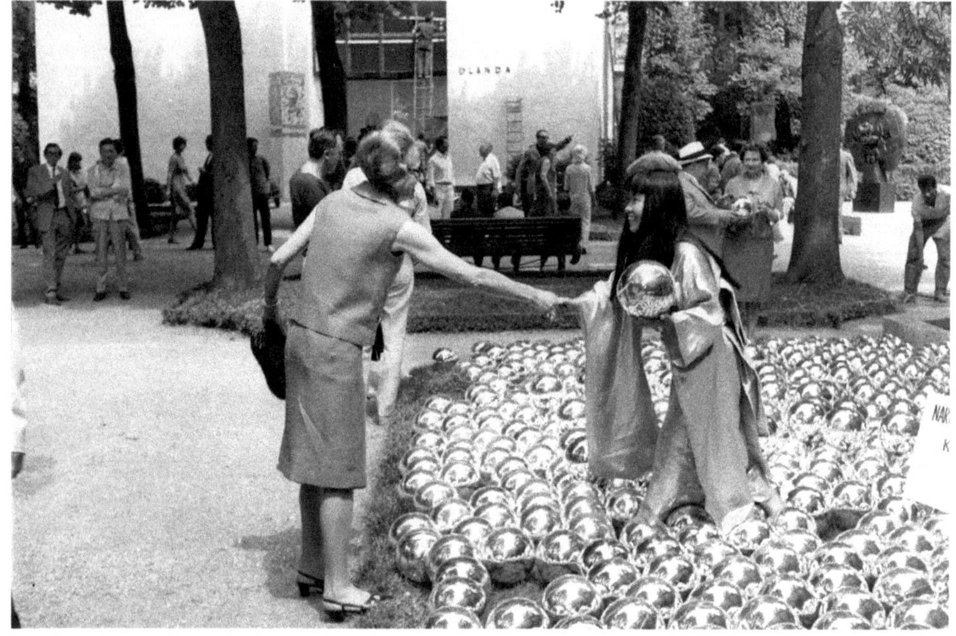

2.4 Yayoi Kusama with *Narcissus Garden* (1966) installed at the 33rd Venice Biennale, Italy, 1966.

making participants of its viewers.[24] Penone's work also does this to an extent; however, the potential of the mirror to interrupt phenomenological space in *Rovesciare* is mediated by its having been photographed. That is, Penone draws attention to the act of seeing without confusing the separation between object and subject. The presumed transparency of the photographic medium in the editioned version of Penone's *Rovesciare* (figure 2.5) tempers the visual conundrum to allow one to reflect upon the experience of viewing an art object, the translation involved in representation, and the syntax of visual communication.

Penone's mirrored eyes share in a critique of vision that was prevalent among his artistic peers, and through such works he partakes of a specifically nuanced way of understanding the interplay between artist and viewer through the visual. American performance artist Joan Jonas's *Mirror Piece I* (1969), performed at Bard College, is perhaps tactically closest to Penone's in its consideration of reception (figure 2.6). In her piece, performers hold oblong mirrors that mostly

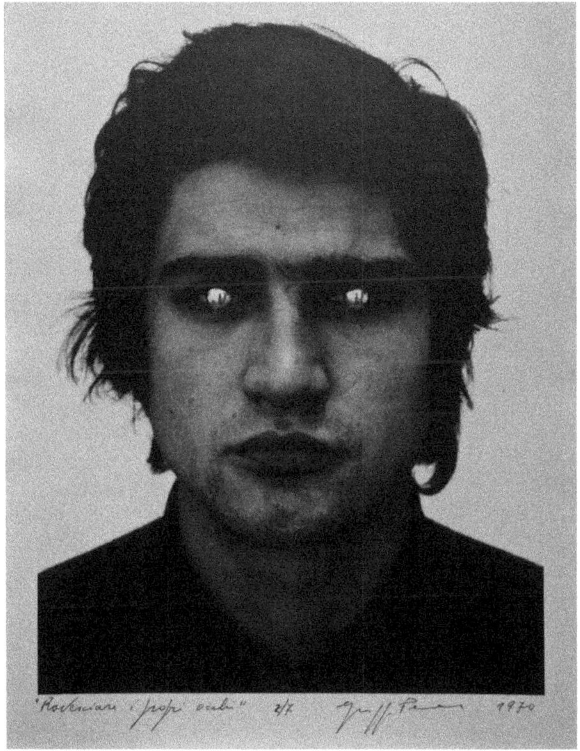

2.5 Giuseppe Penone, *Rovesciare i propri occhi* (*Reversing One's Eyes*), 1970. Gelatin silver print, 39.5 x 29.8 cm.

Photograph: © Archivio Penone

disguise the movements of their bodies. This allows audience members to watch themselves (rather than the performers) reflected in the shifting mirrors. Yet the images shown to them remain beyond their control. Jonas's piece is performed *for* an audience, just as Penone's photograph is *for* the viewer, and indeed the uncanny effect produced by each relies on the instability created within its narrowly defined viewing matrix.

Although Penone shared the use of mirrors with many contemporaries, the photographic aspect of his *Rovesciare* creates an effect of seeing the artist simultaneously with that which he would have seen. This unsettling experience of double vision also calls to mind the debates about the primacy of vision that had engaged surrealist artists forty

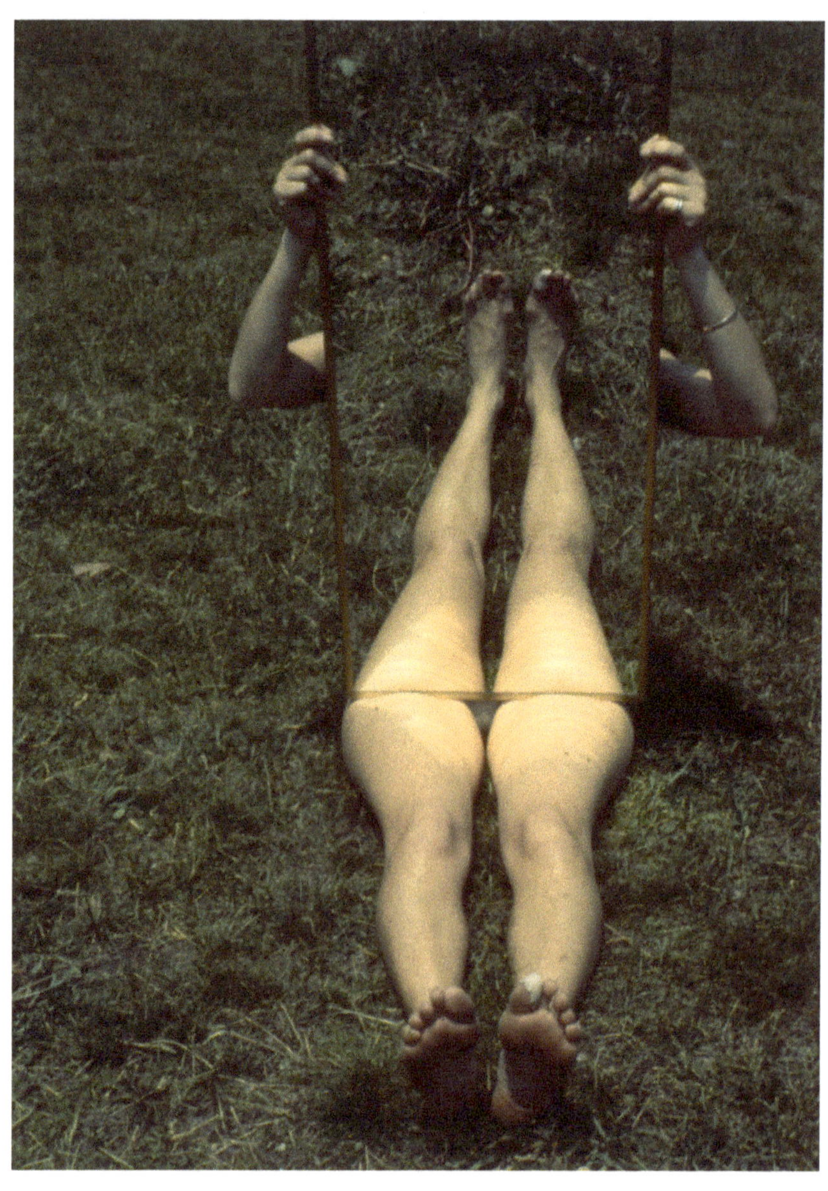

2.6 Joan Jonas, *Mirror Piece I*, 1969. Chromogenic print, 40 x 20¼ in.

Photograph: Joan Jonas © 2021 Joan Jonas / Artists Rights Society, New York. Courtesy of the artist and Gavin Brown's Enterprise, New York / Rome

years earlier.[25] For instance, the artists around André Breton waded through the writer's contradictory claims about the remaining potential of painting, searching for a means to interrogate the visual. In his 1928 pamphlet *Surrealism and Painting*, Breton argues against representations of the external world, to which the "primitive eye" offers more immediate access, but nevertheless makes a place for surrealist painting of the internal state: "The plastic work of art, in order to respond to the undisputed necessity of thoroughly revising all real values, will either refer to a *purely interior model*, or cease to exist."[26] Readings of psychoanalysis and dream analysis led to the frequent depictions of eyes, mirrors, and windows in painted works of the period as a means to indicate the world beyond the visible, the conscious, and the rational.[27]

René Magritte's painting *Le Faux Miroir* (*The False Mirror*, 1929) begs comparison to Penone's *Rovesciare*. Painted during the brief period of the Belgian artist's residence in Paris, the canvas depicts a single large eye, with an azure-blue iris dotted with fluffy white clouds and anchored by a flat black pupil. The painting has been read as demarcating the limits of optical authority, enacting a complex viewing condition for the viewer, who looks at the painted eye and at what the title connotes is a reflection in the iris.[28] Magritte seems to be challenging the notion that an artist simply reflects the world objectively. The eye in his painting is presented as a tool used by the artist, and the idea that artistic vision is neutral here proves to be false. Rather, vision always operates alongside other senses, all co-ordinated in a human subject with individual experience, ideas, and desires. Like Magritte's painting, Penone's *Rovesciare* series explores the role of the artist by contrasting the objectivity of a reflection and the subjectivity of human vision. Penone's photographs and slide projections further challenge the exceptionalism of artistic vision because they show his eyes as part of his own body, rather than as fragmentary, anonymous, and isolated by a tight focus.

This embodied aspect of Penone's investigation of vision and its connection to surrealist notions of artistic subjectivity come into clearer focus when his work is compared to the Belgian artist's *Je ne vois pas la [femme] cachée dans la forêt* (*I Do Not See the [Woman] Hidden in the Forest*, 1929) published in the final issue of *La Revolution Surrealiste* (figure 2.7). Here sixteen photo-automat prints of Magritte and other male surrealists – Breton, Luis Buñuel, Max Ernst, Salvador Dali, and others – each with closed eyelids, surround Magritte's painting of a nude woman and the eponymous text.[29] Though separated by four decades, Magritte's and Penone's works share a tactical

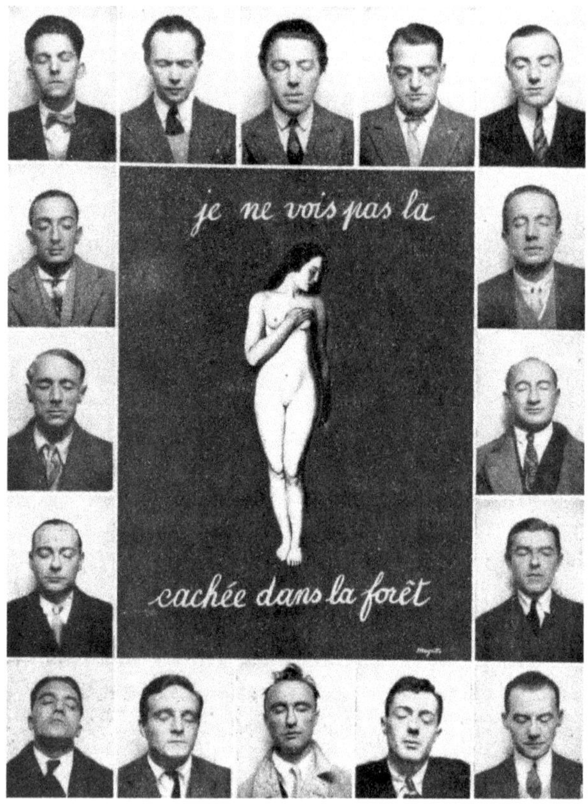

2.7 René Magritte, *Je ne vois pas la [femme] cachée dans la forêt* (*I Do Not See the [Woman] Hidden in the Forest*), 1929. Photoreproduction of surrealist portraits surrounding a photograph of Magritte's *La femme cachée*, published in *La Révolution Surréaliste*, no. 12, 15 December 1929.

approach. Both use photographic or automatic images of the unseeing artist to privilege the viewer as omniscient, while simultaneously suggesting that there is something the viewer does not and indeed cannot see. They both signify an internal world through their photographic images of the artist (or artists) who does not see with his eyes. Magritte refers to the subconscious mind and its desires, whereas Penone links the absence of sight to the embodied multisensory experience of the artist.

Penone's claims for the re-embodiment of vision through the *Rovesciare* photographs and slide projections align even more closely with the ideas of Georges Bataille, who openly challenged Breton's surrealism as substituting the religious imagery of historical painting with equally reified "surrealist imagery." Indeed, the artists around George Bataille maintained a rigorous distrust of sight and rejected the supplanting of the complexities of experience with fixed representations.[30] In his writings Bataille called for art of encounters with the real, terrifyingly unembellished conditions of life.[31] Photography, with its claims to objective, mechanical reflection of the external world, was a favourite medium of this branch of surrealism because doublings, gaps, and other seemingly impossible images could destabilize one's trust in vision and the external world.[32] Penone's use of photography in *Rovesciare* similarly exploits the medium's presumed transparency but undermines it in a new way: more than just a rejection of the hierarchy between artist and viewer, or the conscious over the subconscious mind, the gaps it creates between lived experience and reproduction demonstrate the embodied nature of vision.[33]

Spatial Sight

Penone's *Rovesciare* images short-circuit and redirect the way the brain has been conditioned to manage the embodied aspect of human vision, specifically as it relates to the viewing of artworks. In these photographs and slide projections the viewer sees simultaneously what is behind and what is in front of the photographed figure, creating a rupture that is based on a disembodied experience of sight. Put simply, it does not conform to the way in which humans have learned to see beyond the limitations and peculiarities of their 180-degree, bifocal visual faculties. Moreover, sight creates the spatial awareness in which one's body takes up a position. "When we close our eyes," the artist writes, "our contact with the world is limited to the wrapping of our body. With them open, the identity of our wrapping arrives as far as we can see."[34] Penone here suggests that the temporarily sightless body seems more physically present and distinct. When we open our eyes, however, the reach of the senses extends beyond the physical limitations of our body to a far-off horizon. The mirrored lenses that Penone wears in these photographs therefore underscore the physicality of sight, breaking the illusion of sight's freedom from the body. His images present a distinct challenge to Cartesian logic by reintegrating vision (and the visual experience of artworks) with the body's other senses.

Penone also uses the mirrored lenses as a means to literalize the inextricable connection between the internal and external aspects of experience.[35] One's eyes communicate internal, psychological states across spatial divides, and they also take in information from the external world. The notion that the eyes initiate communication as much as they receive it links his reflected-vision experiments to phenomenological understandings of objects and spaces as being constructed through one's perception of them. That is, the thing perceived is both a material fact and a perceptual construction. More importantly, Penone's photographic exploration of embodied sight attests that the visible traces left by the body are constitutive of space in so far as space is what the body can perceive from its limited position and with its fractured sensory apparatus.

Penone followed these initial contact lens experiments with manifested vision projected into the real space of the body. When he was invited to contribute to the 1970 Tokyo Biennale, the theme of which was *Between Man and Matter*, Penone created a network of small (5 cm in diameter) round mirrors, sparingly installed on the pegboard walls of the gallery as well as on trees outside the building and other surfaces throughout the surrounding park.[36] Titled *Demagnetizzazione di una stanza* (*Demagnetization of a Room*, 1970), the web of lenses was more conceptual than perceptual because most of the tiny mirrors were spaced too far from each other to actually enact a visual dialogue (figure 2.8). As the title suggests, the reflective surfaces created a disturbance in the visual field, rather than an easy alignment.

A significant number of artists associated with Arte povera were included in this exhibition, in a period recognition of the connections between the approaches of Japanese and Italian artists of this same generation.[37] Penone arrived in Tokyo a few days before Mario Merz and Zorio, the rest of the Torinese contingent, because the organizers were concerned that his work's engagement of the municipal park might cause technical or administrative difficulties. Despite the luxury of each artist being assigned his or her own gallery room, a few aspects of the exhibition space at the Tokyo Metropolitan Art Gallery challenged the experimental practices of some of the young artists, including the fact that nothing could be applied or adhered to the building's pegboard walls that might damage their surface. Merz's Fibonacci LED panels, Daniel Buren's pasted paper stripes, Sol LeWitt's wall drawings, and Richard Serra's proposed molten-lead works each had to be altered to accommodate this restriction.[38] Jannis Kounellis completely abandoned his initial ideas and ended up blocking the door to his room in an artistic act born of frustration. Penone's

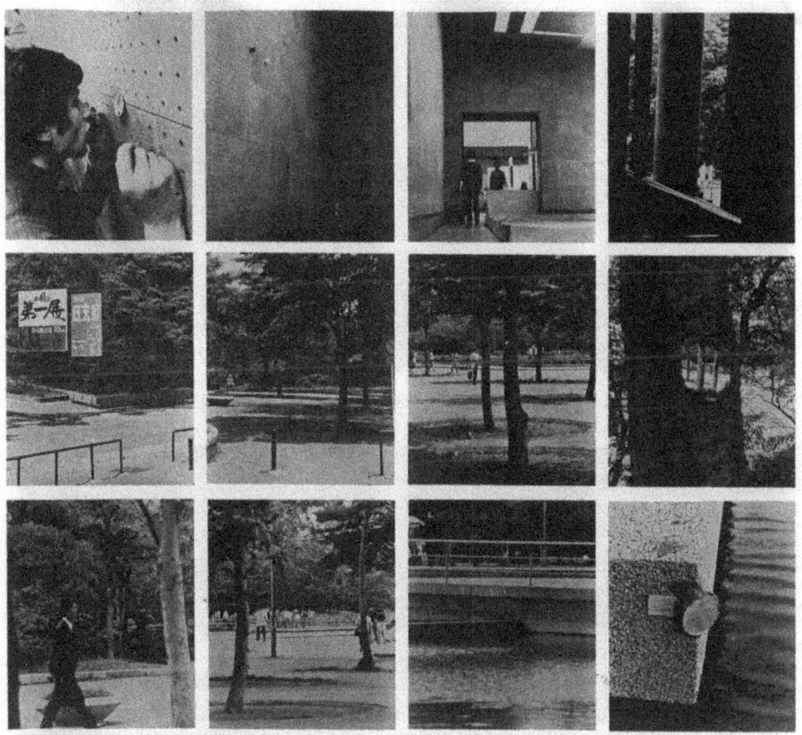

2.8 Giuseppe Penone, *Demagnetizzazione di una stanza* (*Demagnetization of a Room*), 1970. Installation views as printed in Yusuke Nakahara, [Raccolta degli scritti], vol. 5 (Tokyo: Gendaikikashitsu Publishers, 2011), xi.

Photograph: © Archivio Penone

work, however, was nimble from the start and was installed without much difficulty.

Like much of the art in *Between Man and Matter*, Penone's project emphasized the conceptual and embodied aspects of perception over the representational and visual, a bent that irritated some critics. In one of the exhibition reviews of the show, *Art International* critic Joseph Love declared Penone the "worst offender" in a show that amounted to "an almost total deprivation of the sensuous and formal considerations that have been the staple of art since Sumer and Shang China."[39] Finding solace only in the material-forward works by artists like Carl Andre, Barry Le Va, and Robert Morris, the critic ranted against the bulk of the show's forty artists: "To leave so much to the imagination of the audience is simple evasion of the artist's responsibility."[40] As with much reactionary criticism, Love's analysis formulated the show's success as a failure: Penone's work was precisely aimed at making the audience provide the link between these mirrors. The external conditions of the installation were intentionally not enough to produce meaning by themselves (the mirrors did not reflect each other in any observable way); rather, it was the movement of the body through space and the viewer's reflection on that experience that connected the two co-ordinated parts. Since each viewer came to the work from a different perceptual horizon, the artist's responsibility, and perhaps his only option, was to create the circumstances for the experience. Penone's disturbance of the visual field through these mirrors established the conditions necessary to evaluate the cognitive work of deciphering sense perceptions. These "gaps" called attention to the system through which sense perceptions are organized.

Such visualization of phenomenological space and spatialization of visual experience reveal Penone's engagement in the same complex thinking about sense perception and subjectivity that one reads in Merleau-Ponty's seminal *Phenomenology of Perception*, a book published in 1945 and translated into Italian in 1961.[41] In the chapter "The Theory of the Body Is Already a Theory of Perception," Merleau-Ponty posits the body as a co-ordination of stimuli, opening the essay with the following statement: "Our own body is in the world as the heart is in the organism: it keeps the visible spectacle constantly alive, it breathes life into it and sustains it inwardly, and with it forms a system."[42] For him, the interior experience of the body and its physical being in the world are distinct, yet connected fluidly through sensory perception and the language used to describe these sensations. It is through externalization that the internal is made explicit.

Sculptures are just such a fluid externalization of internal experience: they have their own language and internal referents (they create a world of their own), yet they also share the physical space of their audience. By refusing to give the viewer a whole image or experience, Penone's Tokyo installation succeeded in creating a direct, dematerialized work, one in which the viewer could not bear the work of making meaning from the visual data alone. Instead, as if in dialogue with Merleau-Ponty, the work's meaning had to be engaged from the point of view of a body in space. Merleau-Ponty argues that the mind's ability to draw upon the body's experience (its ability to connect the various sensory stimuli into the concept of a unified body) is what gives the viewer access to the concept of a space or an object. Specifically, he writes: "The thing, and the world, are given to me along with the parts of my body, not by any 'natural geometry,' but in a living connection comparable, or rather identical, with that existing between the part of my body itself."[43] Penone's specific use of mirrors in *Demagnetization of a Space* and other early works is central to his developing discourse about the interconnection of the internal and the external, as well as the crossover between the visual and the tactile. Moreover, these mirrors prompt the viewer to differentiate between a purely visual reflected image and a multisensual, even sculptural, experience of the body as an object in space.

In his 1960 essay "Eye and Mind," Merleau-Ponty considers the role of mirrors in art as a tool or technical object that underscores the artifice of representation. For him, the representation of these tools in a visual work constitutes "a figured philosophy of vision" or an "iconography" of vision central to the work of visual artists. That is, a painted mirror demonstrates the mirror as technical device, and within the logic of representation it constitutes a theory of vision that posits the eye as a tool through which humans construct and communicate the perceived world. He submits that the "round eye of the mirror," frequently seen in Dutch paintings, is a sort of artist's wink at the viewer, an artificial eye that acknowledges the mechanical reflexivity of seeing and seen at work in the picture.[44] Jan van Eyck's *Arnolfini Portrait* (1434), for example, emphasizes this by the distinctly convex shape of the mirror at the painting's centre, reading as an eye that captures the social encounter of the painting's subjects with the painter himself.[45]

Recalling works that unmask the dynamics inherent in visual representation, Merleau-Ponty argues: "Artists have often mused upon mirrors because beneath this 'mechanical trick,' they recognized, just as they did in the case of the trick of perspective, the metamorphosis of seeing and seen which defines both our flesh and the painter's vocation."[46] Therefore, for Merleau-Ponty, such flourishes of painterly skill also interrogate the space of the viewer – by their failure to actually reflect his or her space – and they describe the work of an artist who reconstructs his or her perceptions in a visually digestible form.[47] The visual tradition of such iconography is harnessed in Penone's early works with mirrors. The key distinction, in his works, is that the interrogation of the viewer's space is demonstrated, rather than represented. In *Demagnetization of a Room* specifically, the artist demonstrates the visual aspects of spatial experience, extending to the viewer the delay he experienced in *Rovesciare*. By placing mirrors throughout the galleries and park space, Penone focuses the viewer's immediate attention to the act of looking. These mirrors bring the internal operation of sight onto the surface, sparking an awareness of the way one's senses are used to navigate experience of a work and of a space. Indeed, the artist later remarked that the point of departure for such works was recognizing the way the body is both a means to receive external stimuli from the world and the primary vehicle through which one projects out into the world.[48] In these works he begins to investigate the reciprocal aspects of sensory apparatuses.

At the Body's Borders

Penone's Tokyo installation and his *Rovesciare* photographs parallel other experiments with mirrors, photographs, and panes of glass (begun as early as 1968) that more explicitly probe the translation of visual and tactile perception through depictions of his own skin. Among the earliest is a concave mirror set in either a stream or an earthen wall, into which the artist inserts his hand or arm, visually "transferring" his skin to another surface and perceptibly dislocating and fracturing the body (figure 2.9). Penone photographically documented these 1968 experiments, which ultimately led to a number of finished works gathered under the series title *Svolgere la propria pelle* (*To Unroll One's Skin*, 1968–72). In one example from the series, Penone photographed each of his ten fingertips pressed against a transparent pane of glass and then mounted the photographic emulsions on a mirrored ground.[49] The effect, for the viewer, is that each little fingertip is the only part in which the mirror is truly clear, creating little round "eyes" out of the sensitive instruments of his touch. The artist combines his skin and photography in this distinct way – to problematize transparency and indexicality – in a number of other works in the series. Such skin-based works investigate the fundamental relationship between vision and touch: What does it look like to touch something? Or, even more fundamentally, what does touch look like?

Penone's visualizations of his own skin, with their doublings and disruption of the body, again recall surrealist precedents, as well as Michel Foucault's musings on the mirror's disembodying effects: "It is from the mirror that I find myself absent from the place where I am, as long as I see myself there."[50] While some of Penone's works of the period used mirrors to create this effect of dislocation, he made other transparencies through a tape-and-powder-transfer process and exhibited them as backlit images on neon panels or adhered to

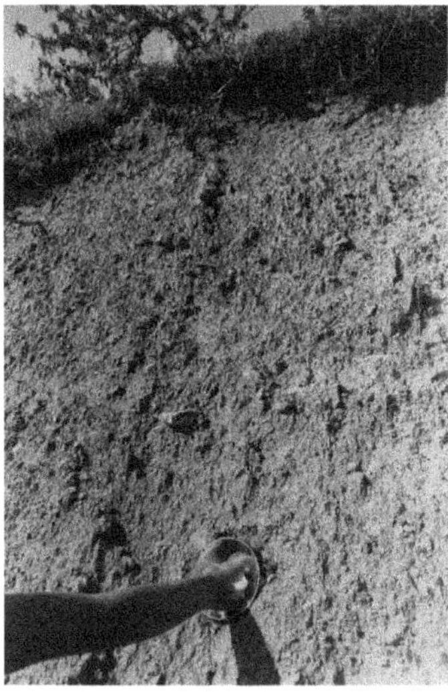

2.9 Giuseppe Penone, *Svolgere la propria pelle sul muro – mano* (*To Unroll One's Skin on the Wall – Hand*), 1968. Concave mirror, 10 cm diameter (approx.).

Photograph: © Archivio Penone

panes of glass. In a 1973 interview with critic Mirella Bandini, Penone maintained that the fingertips pressed on glass created a situation in which the glass and the photographic surface visually collapsed, marking a division as well as fluidity "between reality and its reflection, therefore, its image."[51] Displaying these photographic images on transparent or reflective surfaces effectively allowed a visual merger of the image with the substrate, to the extent that it appeared as if a layer of the skin had been cast off from the body, like the moulting of a snake.

This impulse was especially apparent in his second solo show, at Sperone in the autumn of 1971. Here the artist exhibited grids of tiny photographs as well as some photo collages (figure 2.10). The grids record an action in which Penone photographed every inch of his skin through a small piece of glass, roughly the dimensions of a microscope slide (figure 2.11). The images just exceed the size of the glass, so the viewer simultaneously looks through the slide and sees it as an object against the skin. Within the logic of these photographs the surface of the photograph and the surface of the glass pane collapse, but not completely:

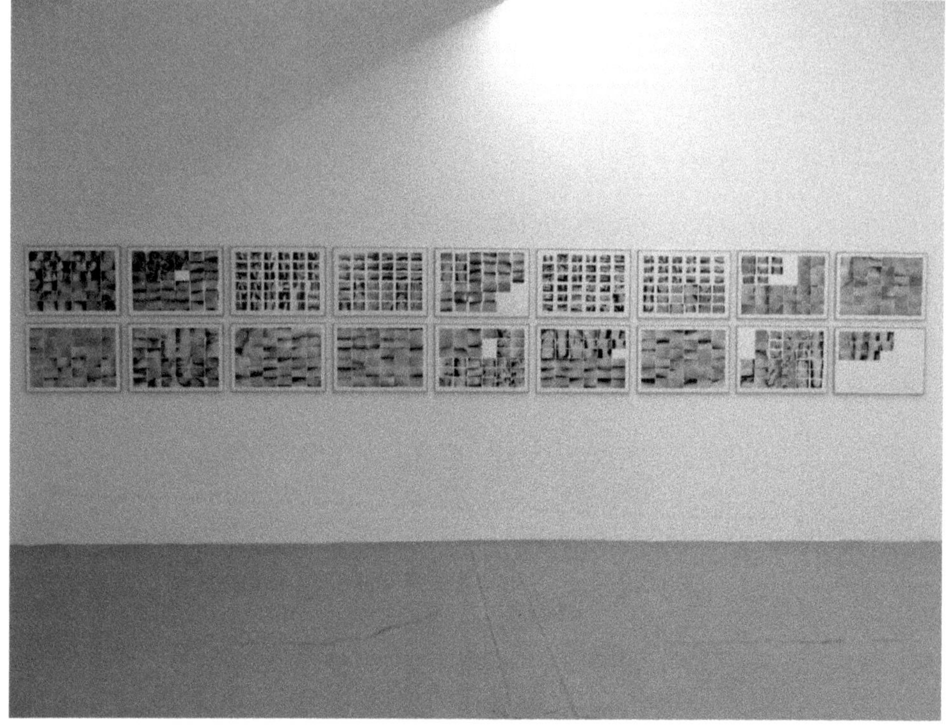

2.10 Giuseppe Penone, installation view of *Svolgere la propria pelle* (*To Unroll One's Skin*), 1970. 607 gelatin silver photographs (10.5 x 7 cm each) in eighteen panels (53.5 x 73.5 x 2.5 cm each).

Photograph: © Archivio Penone

they act as a screen or second lens through which we see the body, and at the same time they read as an object that stands between our body and the body depicted.

The photographic grids, also titled *To Unroll One's Skin*, were published in an artist's book designed by Franco Mello that accompanied the exhibition. Flipping through the full-bleed pages, one can see that the distinctions among substrates and surfaces are further eroded. Through the glass, the camera lens, and perhaps most importantly the pages – which have, for the viewer, a tactile coincidence with the thickness of skin – the artist is revealed in six small images at a time. On one page are depicted his forehead, the back of an ear, the front of said ear, the top of a cheek, and each eyebrow. Without respect to the body's

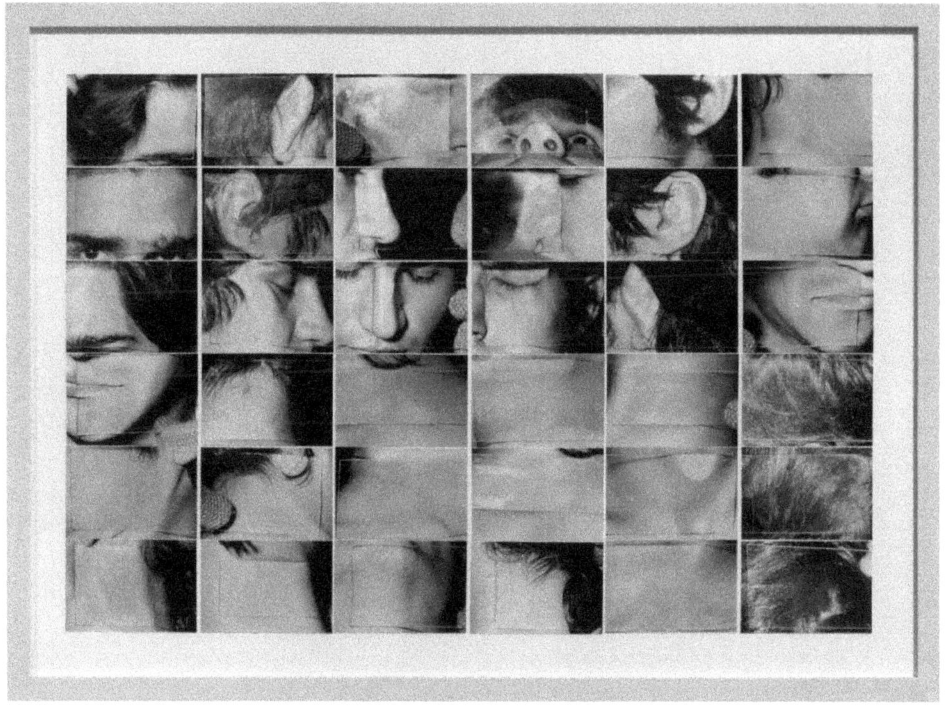

2.11 Giuseppe Penone, *Svolgere la propria pelle* (*To Unroll One's Skin*), 1970 (detail). Thirty-six of 607 gelatin silver photographs (10.5 x 7 cm each) in eighteen panels (53.5 x 73.5 x 2.5 cm each).

Photograph: © Archivio Penone

organization, the facing page shows three images of an ankle and three more of the toes of the artist's left foot. Some images are easy to assign to familiar body parts – be they banal or intimate – while other grids are almost entirely without incident: in the muted grisaille of the photographs, large swaths of flesh are unrecognizable, save a few freckles, hairs, or creases.

The visual registration of the body's tactile frontier in this project seems to mock an analytical and optical approach to knowledge. That the artist also included in the series similarly derived images of his dog, published in the catalogue for Achille Bonito Oliva's 1971 exhibition *Pèrsona*, testifies to the considered absurdity of the gesture (figure 2.12).[52] Penone's methodical approach to his own body is replete with detailed images; indeed, it is hypervisual, with inked

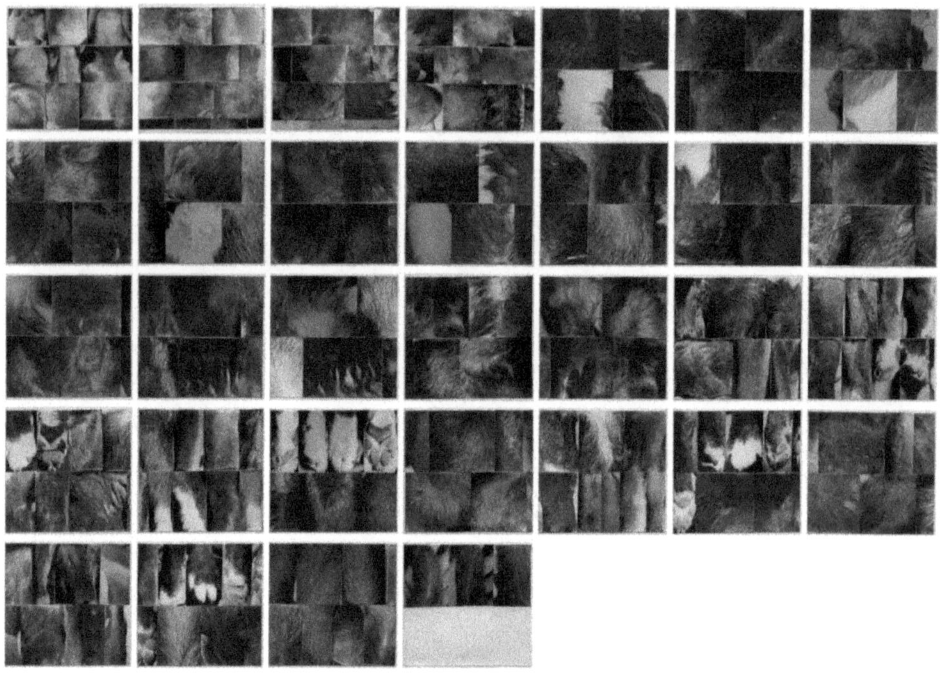

2.12 Giuseppe Penone, *Svolgere la propria pelle – cane* (*To Unroll One's Skin – Dog*), 1970. Black-and-white prints on thirty-two pages (20 x 21.5 cm each).

Photograph: © Archivio Penone

registration marks guiding the careful survey of the body's surface. Yet this experiment purposefully fails to yield any useful information on the nature of human experience or personal identity. The collected images in the photographic grids are visually accurate – their number and variety suggesting a scientific completeness – yet they fall short of a holistic experience of what it means to wear that fleshy covering or to be that individual in the world.[53] Instead these images raise questions: What does it feel like to be inside that body? How is that different from the information I receive from the photographs? Even, perhaps, what is a body? These questions are the same ones that permeate the philosophy of phenomenology. One need only think of Husserl's rumination on the divide between objectness of other bodies and that of one's own body: "My body is the only one of them that is not just a body but precisely an animate organism."[54] A similar conclusion is gleaned from engagement with Penone's unrolled-skin series.

For the 1972 *Documenta 5* exhibition, Penone actualized this experience in the real space of the viewer by adhering a translucent grid of pressure-print images to the real windows of the exhibition space (figure 2.13).[55] The work originated through a process in which the artist coated his skin with powdered pigment to create image impressions that could be lifted off with adhesive tapes, which were later photographed and printed as transparencies. If the multiple transfers somewhat obscure the process involved, the poetic aim of the installation tactic is easily, if unsettlingly, grasped: the gallery becomes a body, and the viewer is perceptually placed within that skin – at once structurally familiar, yet not one's own – as if putting on a stranger's garment.[56] This uncanny condition and its insistent disorder spark a self-consciousness of the border between inside and outside. That is, one's view of the world, like the visual access to the spaces beyond the gallery, is conditional; it must be accessed through the membrane of skin.

Trini referred to *Documenta 5* as the first big exhibition that privileged the function of the viewer over that of the artist.[57] For the critic, a work like Penone's must have been understood as part of the foregrounding of social communication. Though subtle, the work interrogates the permeable border between the individual and the world, and it prompts the viewer to consider whether the latter can be known by any means other than individual sensory experience. Here photography's transparency is literalized, but the fullness of experience relies on a conceptual leap between the visual, externalized, or unrolled skin and one's own, felt, internal experience of inhabiting such a mortal wrapper.

Penone also engages the fluid intermingling of sight and touch through collages that use both "straight" photographs and body impressions in their final form. In the sub-series sometimes titled *Coincidenza d'immagine* (*Coincidence of Image*, c. 1970), examples of this tactic include a photograph of his outstretched arm, collaged with a translucent piece of paper bearing an inked print of the same arm (figure 2.14). This produces a visually compelling misalignment, prompting the viewer to consider the distinctions between two forms of indexical representation. Melding together two registers in a single image, the artist probes the relative impact of indexicality in ways that connect with the prevalent discourses of the era and simultaneously distinguish his project from others of his artistic generation.

Penone's *Unroll One's Skin* series echoes aspects of Mel Bochner's photo-project *Actual Size* (1968–9), in which the American artist

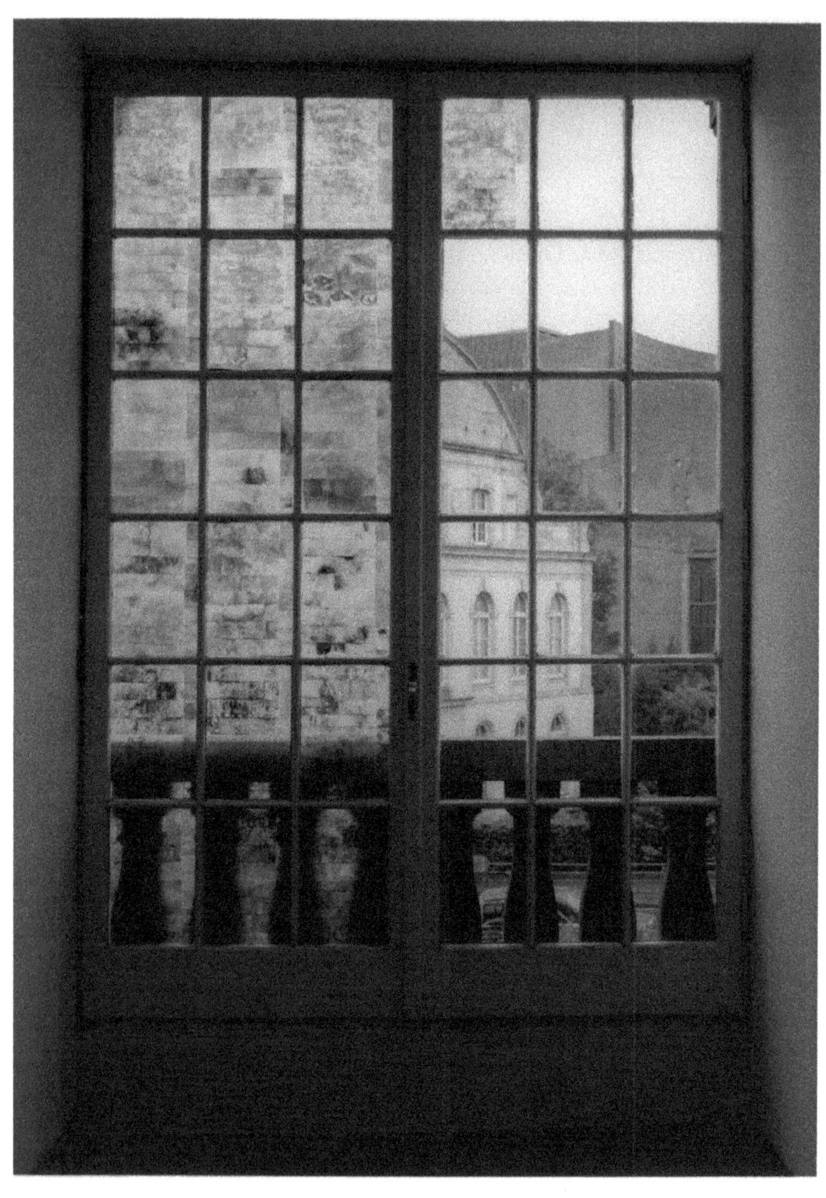

2.13 Giuseppe Penone, *Svolgere la propria pelle – finestra* (*To Unroll One's Skin – Window*), 1972. Installation view at *Documenta 5*, Museum Fridericianum, Kassel, Germany.

Photograph: Paolo Mussat Sartor, © Paolo Mussat Sartor

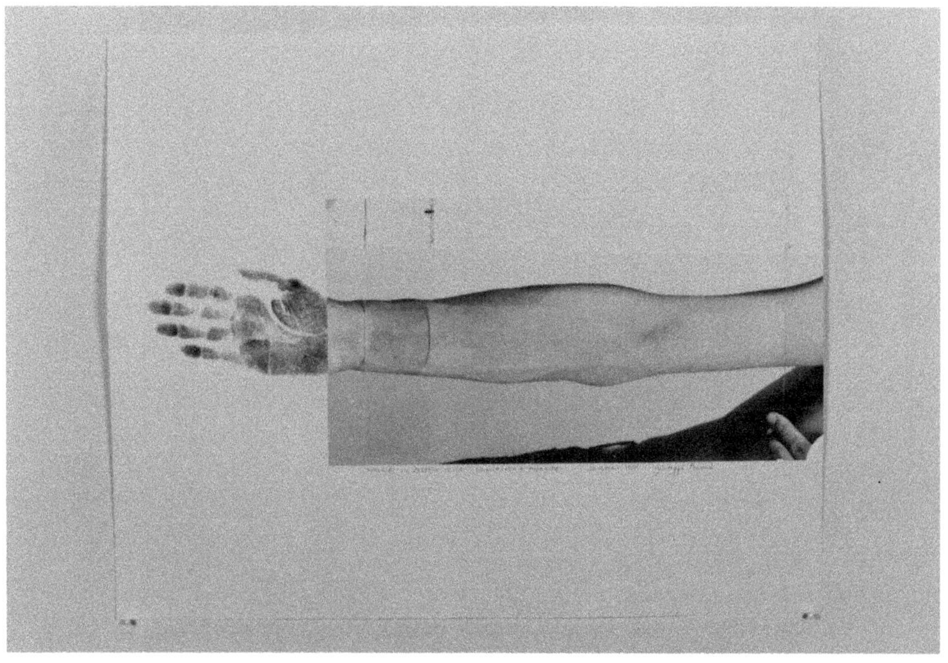

2.14 Giuseppe Penone, *Svolgere la propria pelle: Coincidenza d' immagine – 12 giugno 1970* (*To Unroll One's Skin: Coincidence of Image – 12 June 1970*). Gelatin silver print and ink on paper, 54.5 x 70 cm.

Photograph: © Archivio Penone

photographed parts of his body next to a written measurement and had the image printed at full scale.[58] Bochner's gesture connoted photography's limitations in relation to the body. Penone's eighteen-panel photographic catalogue of his own skin and subsequent works went further, pursuing production and installation tactics that engaged multiple means of indexing traces of corporeal presence. Using photography and body prints together – the coincidence of two forms of capturing the body – led Penone to a more profound investigation into the orders of representation *through* photography.[59] In *To Unroll One's Skin: Coincidence of Image – 12 June 1970* the photograph's indexicality is the product of light bounced off the arm and captured through a lens on sensitized paper. The body print results from the direct transfer of ink or powdered pigments on the surface of the arm to the surface of the paper. That is, in the latter, not only is the body captured visually, but it acts as an instrument or tool: its boundaries are defined at the many points of the skin's contact with the other surface.

In Penone's works the sense of "that has been," which Roland Barthes famously ascribed to photographs, is forcibly distinguished from the transparency indicated by the body print.[60] In order to see the collaged parts as referring to a unified body, the viewer has to reconcile two orders of indexicality. The first is derived from a learned response, its intelligibility more theoretical because it requires having had some reflection on photography's mechanisms. The second is raw and immediate, based on the common knowledge of the body through one's own skin and the traces of presence one encounters every day. In a 2012 interview, art historian Benjamin Buchloh asked Penone about the importance of indexicality in his practice. The artist responded that he was interested in prints (imprints) because they were the most democratic types of images, but they were also contradictory ones. That is, they are marks that every human makes; yet, perhaps because of their ubiquity, they are considered dirty, so people are always wiping them away. He noted: "I use [the index] in the idea of flattening, reconsidering the possibility of working on a phenomenology, while taking hold of the reality of nature and thinking about the most simple images we make, which belong to everyone."[61] Combining these accessible, yet equivocal marks in a single image makes it plain to viewers that perception is equally fragmentary and conditional.

In the spring of 1973 Penone examined these different orders of indexicality in a more plastic or sculptural form by exhibiting discrete plaster casts of his chest and of his right foot. Installed in a darkened space, each was illuminated by projection of a colour slide depicting that same body part. In *Torace* (*Thorax,* 1972) one can see that the coincidence of these two types of "prints" resulted in an eerily lifelike fragment, here chillingly excised from the body's overall system (figure 2.15). At the time, curator Jean-Christophe Amman argued that Penone's combined casts and slides work together as positive and negative volume in order to arrive at "the smallest space of interpretation not extended by an arbitrary construction."[62] That is, while both are "indexes" (non-arbitrary constructions), they are both only partial. The plaster casts are the closest physical surrogates of the body, and the photographs are the most compelling visual images of the body.[63] Conflated in the exhibition space, physical and visual indexicality are again revealed to be fragmentary, and, even when brought together, they create an incomplete surrogate of the living body.

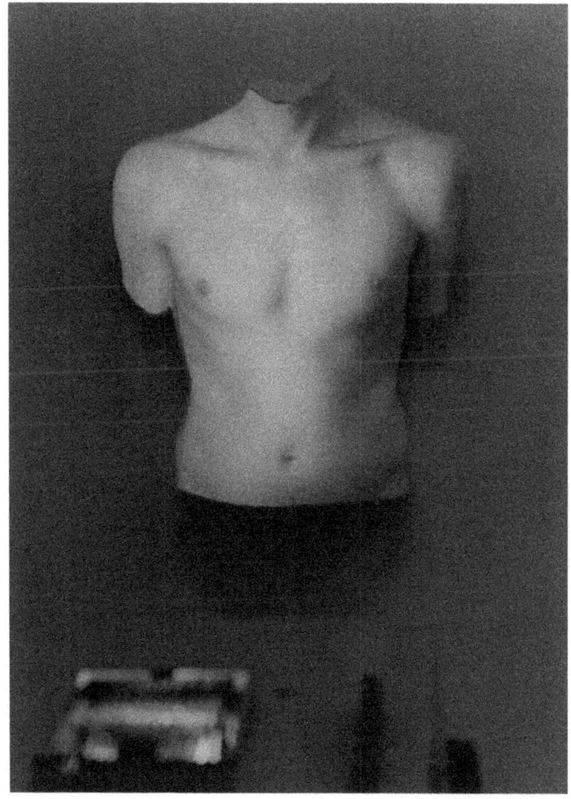

2.15 Giuseppe Penone, *Torace* (*Thorax*), 1972. Plaster cast and slide projection. Installation view at Galleria Franco Toselli, Milan, 1973.

Photograph: Paolo Mussat Sartor, © Paolo Mussat Sartor

The fluidity between visual and tactile stimuli in *Thorax* again recalls the ancient Greek notion of the haptic. Simultaneously, they engage a more contemporaneous concept: the chiasm, proposed by Merleau-Ponty. In *Eye and Mind* (1961) and *The Visible and the Invisible* (1964), Merleau-Ponty introduced the term *chiasm* to describe the mind's ability to create a concept for an invisible physical sensation – a function essential to being: "A human body is present when, between the seer and the visible, between touching and touched, between one eye and the other, between hand and hand, a kind of crossover occurs, when the spark of the sensing/sensible is lit."[64] Merleau-Ponty refigures the body and mind as two sides of the same being, brought together by the workings of the senses, as opposed to a Cartesian model, in which the body is present only because a soul can conceive of it.

In his working notes for the posthumously published "The Interwining – The Chiasm," the philosopher offered numerous further reflections on the impossibility of the separation of mind and body, arguing for a reconceptualization of the body as *flesh*, which, apart from the term's literal meaning, he described as "the sensible in the twofold sense of what one senses and what senses."[65] This formulation – of the flesh as the site in which the sensible world and that in which senses are unified – can be extrapolated to assert that presence is incomprehensible without the co-ordination of not just eye and mind, or skin and mind. Rather, it emerges through the body's engagement with the things of the world, with which it is coextensive. The self is produced and reciprocally produces the other through a carnal network of sensory apperception.[66] Penone's photographic exploration of skin, as well as his body prints and plaster casts, attempts to locate the spark of self-knowledge enacted by the chiasm. These images and objects born of the body's physical limits allow the tenuous non-space of sensory border crossings to take a palpable form.

Marcel Duchamp theorized a similar tautological conundrum of inseparable difference, which he named "infra-thin." It is a quality for which he gave examples – the odour of cigar smoke mingled with the scent of the smoker's breath, the warmth of a seat recently vacated, and the difference between two objects cast from the same mould – but which one could never really define.[67] Read through Duchamp's concept, all of the indexical body prints, fingerprints, and plaster casts that frequently appear in Penone's works of the 1970s could be considered infra-thin in the sense that they are visual documentation of the twinned acts of touching and of being touched.[68] In a 2003 interview, Penone and curator Catherine de Zegher discussed Duchamp's 1920 work *Dust Breeding*, and the artist noted that Duchamp's concept of infra-thin in this work interested him, both as a means to describe something minute and in the way it connoted a social compulsion to erase the traces of touch that were considered dirty.[69] In his 2012 conversation with Buchloh, Penone further testified to the importance of Duchamp as an artistic precursor. When Buchloh asked the artist to choose between Duchamp and the Italian metaphysical painter Giorgio de Chirico, Penone responded that he would chose Duchamp, without a doubt.[70]

Several of Penone's 1970s works focus exclusively on artistic touch through meditation on the skin, and are arguably investigations of the entwined nature of the skin as both receptor and matrix. If the nature

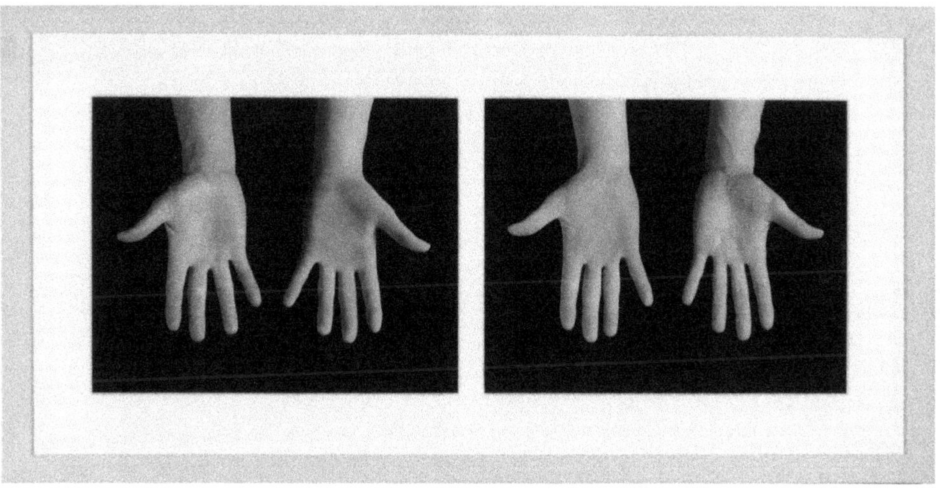

2.16 Giuseppe Penone, *Guanti: La pelle della mano sinistra indossata dalla mano destra* (*Gloves: The Skin of the Left Hand Worn by the Right Hand*), 1972. Colour photograph on aluminum; two elements, 38 x 48 cm each, 62 x 123.5 cm (with frame).

Photograph: Paolo Pellion di Persano, © Archivio Penone

of touch could be ascertained, then it might provide new insight into the complex formation of artistic subjectivity. In *Guanti* (*Gloves*, 1972), for instance, the defining boundary marked by the skin is probed in yet another photographic documentation. Here the artist records an action in which he coated his left hand with a thin layer of liquid latex and pressed it to his right hand. Once dried, the left, latex-covered hand bore the imprint of the right hand embedded in its surface, making it an exact fit or "glove" for the right hand (figure 2.16). The photographic documentation of the experiment presents a visual puzzle to its viewers, who might struggle to identify why the image of the two hands is uncanny.

For the artist, however, the twinning of his two hands was primarily a tactile experience, one that challenged the image of his body's limits and the independence of its constituent parts. At the time, Penone wrote a detailed description of his experience during the action.

> When I put my hands together, the marks on the skin of my right hand were embedded in the marks on the skin of my left hand. The state of complete adherence without hollow spaces gave me the sensation that

> both hands were smooth, without fingerprints, without marks. My hands, sunken one in the other, were a single body, and the thought of pulling them apart was unlikely, no less unnatural than thinking of detaching one nostril from the other. My right hand by acting, feeling, and touching, had created the negative of its skin, which my left hand by acting, feeling, and touching, had put on.[71]

These written notes reveal that the experiment created an unsettling tactile experience for the artist, whose altered hands fit together so seamlessly that they challenged his mind's ability to interpret the sensory information transmitted by the skin. It created a situation akin to sensory deprivation. This potentially complicates one's subjectivity because when the body schema to which one is accustomed falls away, so does one's image of the world. Much of Penone's work of the late 1970s, especially that in which skin is both the means of making a mark and the boundary that defines the difference between self and world, partakes of a notion similar to Merleau-Ponty's chiasm and Duchamp's infra-thin.

Finally, John Dewey's theories of experience – which were critical to the intellectual milieu of Turin in the 1950s and 1960s – give further texture to Merleau-Ponty's concept of the chiasm and to a reading of Penone's investigation of the skin as simultaneously conditional and conditioning.[72] The American philosopher's theory of aesthetics relied on an acknowledgment of the foundational import of encountering one's environment through the fragile border of sensory organs. He writes: "No creature lives merely under its skin; its subcutaneous organs are a means of connection with what lies beyond its bodily frame, and to which, in order to live, it must adjust itself, by accommodation and defense but also by conquest."[73] For Dewey, awareness of the skin as at times accommodating, at others defensive, would be central to understanding one's own being in the world, one's own subjectivity. Reading Penone's works through Dewey's concept of the skin as a living boundary, it becomes clear that what is at stake is not merely the overturning of ocularcentrism but the very structure of experience as a binary relationship between subject and object. Therefore, these artworks might indicate more than just the ontology of sculpture; they might also point to the very nature of being.

Seeing Through Closed Eyelids

In the late 1970s Penone began to investigate the eyelid as a means to probe the formative distinction between the interior and the exterior of the body. The eyelid provides a natural example of the body's

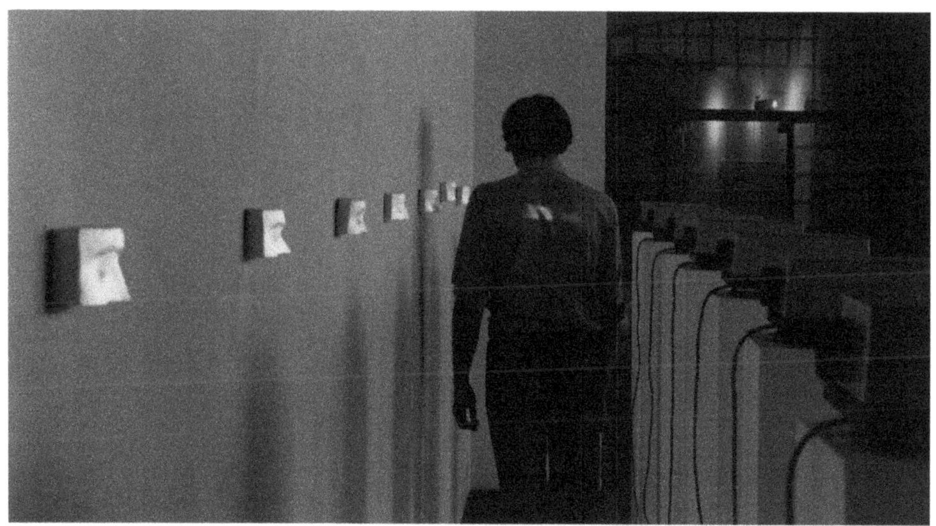

2.17 Giuseppe Penone, *Guardare l'aria – Occhi* (*To Look at Air – Eyes*), 1976. Plaster casts, hair, and slide projections. Installation view at Galleria Nuovi Strumenti, Brescia, 1976.

Photograph: Paolo Mussat Sartor, © Paolo Mussat Sartor

indescribable, perhaps infra-thin, integration. To see one's own eyelids directly, not in a reflection or in a representation, the eyelid must be closed, thus denying sight as it is usually conceived. The eyelid is also the only thing that can comfortably touch the eye; not only is one accustomed to this touch, but it is welcomed as physically and psychologically protective. The eyelid, therefore, is an icon of the distinctions between sight and touch and, simultaneously, a symbol of their inseparability.

In 1976 Penone exhibited a row of plaster casts with slide projections, this time of facial fragments lit by slides of closed eyes (figure 2.17). In a departure from the earlier casts of his own body, here the facial fragments represent an array of different individuals, including the artist's wife, Dina Carrara; his brother, Giovanni; his teaching assistant Gianni Sedda; and the gallerists Tucci Russo and Giorgio Persano; as well as fellow artists Gilberto Zorio and Giovanni Anselmo.[74] This lineup constituted a sort of group portrait of his colleagues in the Turin art scene, not unlike Magritte's 1929 collage of the Surrealists around Breton. However, here the closed eyes of Penone's haunting fragments denote a separation that is, critically, *both* physical and psychological.

The impact of these works owes to the artist's tautological doubling of indexical representation, which would seem to bolster physical and psychological presence, but instead surprisingly denotes absence. The plaster casts are positives. That is, they are not the moulds that had direct contact with the body, but surrogates of the body's exterior made from those matrices. Thus, although chalky and visually distinct from the experience of skin, they provide a trace of the body through their fragmentary volumes. This cannot but recall the pre-photographic death-mask tradition.[75] When Penone projects photographic images onto the surfaces, he visually returns colour to the flesh, if not signs of life to the body. Yet, despite this doubly indexical representation of an eye, each remains closed, blocked by its natural veil, and therefore each subject is closed within an interior world that is never visually accessible to the viewer or to the other subjects of the casts. The eyelid here is infra-thin, in the sense that it denotes the state of both fullness and the very emptiness that invites itself to be filled.[76] By the closing of one's eyes, identity moves inside the body and becomes less a part of the outside world. At the same time, one's own body becomes more physically present.

Penone literalized the means by which the skin defines both visible and invisible spaces of the body, in a number of works in which he transferred impressions of his skin onto the walls of the exhibition space with charcoal drawings. Of particular note is his installation at the 1978 Venice Biennale, where he made enlarged drawings of impressions taken from his eyelids, confirming that this particular patch of skin, more than any other, constituted one's subjectivity in space. *Palpebre* (*Eyelids*, 1977) is a suite of graphite-and-charcoal drawings that transfer the eyelid's wrinkly surface to the four walls of the gallery (figure 2.18). Through this installation tactic, Penone transformed the room into a virtual body, even more so than the photographic emulsions on windowpanes did at *Documenta 5*. That is, since the eyelid is the only part of the skin one can view *from the inside*, it is more familiar than the experience of looking through the impressions of the artist's skin made from various other areas of his body. However, as noted, one can only "see" the eyelids when they are closed, when sight is theoretically denied. An eyelid is both part of the instrument of vision and a limit to it. This apparent contradiction models the central paradox of the cross-over between touch and vision at the foundations of subjectivity, perceptual space, and sculpture. Simultaneously visible and invisible, opaque and translucent, the eyelid is an ideal example of the body's manifestation of this irresolute dialectic.

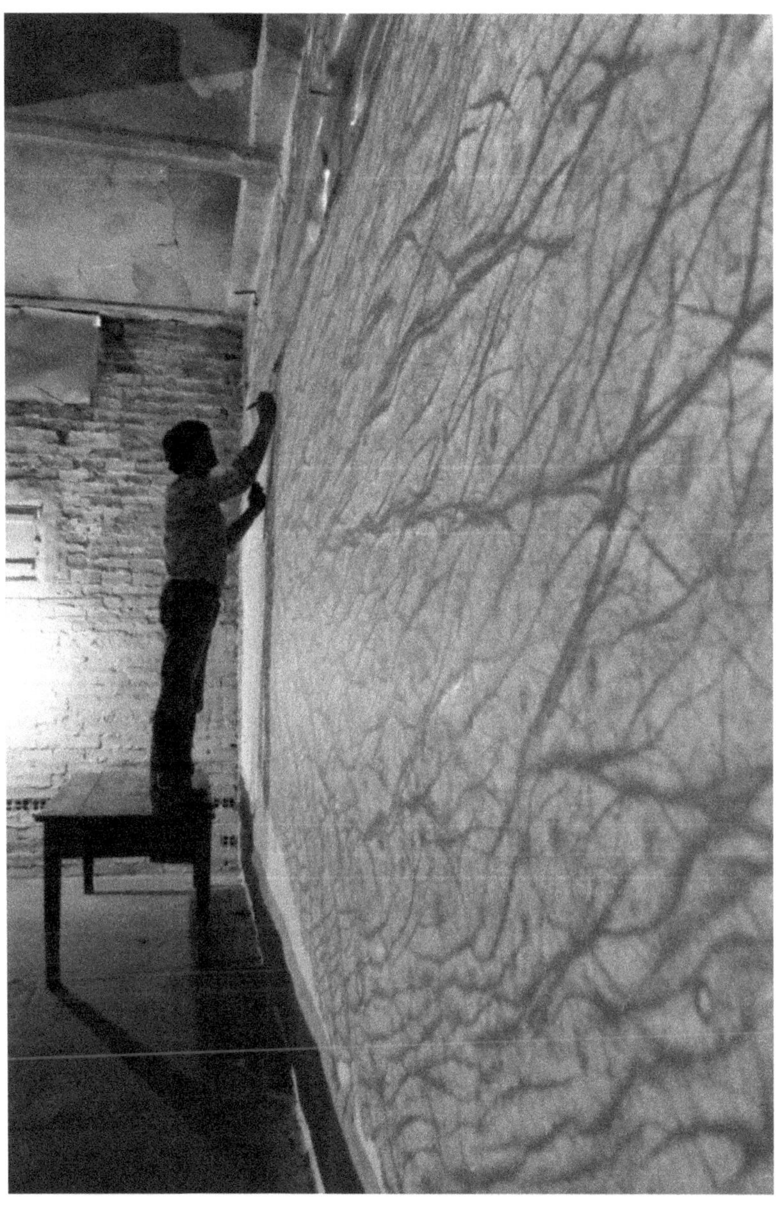

2.18 Giuseppe Penone, *Palpebre* (*Eyelids*), 1977. Charcoal on paper, mounted on canvas, plaster; two elements of 200 x 1,000 cm each. Photographic documentation in the artist's studio, 1977.

Photograph: Dina Carrara, © Archivio Penone

Like the *Rovesciare* images, which are the product of a very physical process, the eyelid drawings made for Venice were not arrived at easily. For however much it seems to be an automatic image, indeed one might argue it is the ur-image – the first thing one sees *in utero* is one's own still-closed eyelids – the creation of this work was painstakingly physical for the artist. The scale is monumental, and the careful and exact movement of first pencil, then charcoal, over the purposefully rough or "toothy" paper required intense concentration for long stretches of time. It demonstrates that even a hyper-visual image like an eyelid in fact relies upon touch and requires the mind's ability to conceive of the materiality of the body.

It is precisely the play between the automatic image (pure sensory information) and the consciously, laboriously made one (a concept formed through experience) that lies at the heart of Penone's theorization of artistic subjectivity in these works. His reorientation from vision to touch is not just anti-Cartesian but also anti-anthropocentric in a way that connects his work to the suspicions placed on vision by surrealism, as well as to the conceptual, if unnamable, implications of Duchamp's readymade. Penone's body prints, plaster casts, and indexical drawings of the 1970s literalize the counterpoint between sensory information and concept that Merleau-Ponty argues is necessary for presence. Through such works Penone demonstrates that the perceptive subjectivity at the core of artistic identity comes into being through the fluid co-ordination of the visual and the tactile.

In his writings, which often verge on poetry, Penone proposed the notion of seeing through closed eyelids as a means to tie the relationship between sense and concept, as well as sight and touch, to his pursuit of sculpture as a discipline:

> Eyelids closed, the exact definition of limits and space of thought reflect the notion of one's body in space.
>
> Eyelids closed, a definition of the fullness of a sculpture as opposed to the emptiness of seeing …
>
> Seeing though closed eyelids.
>
> Expansion of a ridiculously small point.
>
> Eyelids closed have the same great, vital importance as a foot set on the ground.[77]

Read in relation to the works of the 1970s, this paradoxical concept creates a mental image that aptly describes the complex fluidity among the distinct senses. Therefore, "seeing through closed eyelids" stakes a claim on the fundamental way in which sculpture's address to the body in phenomenological space creates a haptic experience that is more direct than that traditionally associated with purely visual, representational art.[78] Photography and body impressions – making automatic images, marks, and forms – allowed Penone to follow this line of inquiry about the nature of artistic activity to a certain point. But, if an investigation of the nature of sculpture was at stake, then he had to find a way to make this legible though the language of objects as well.

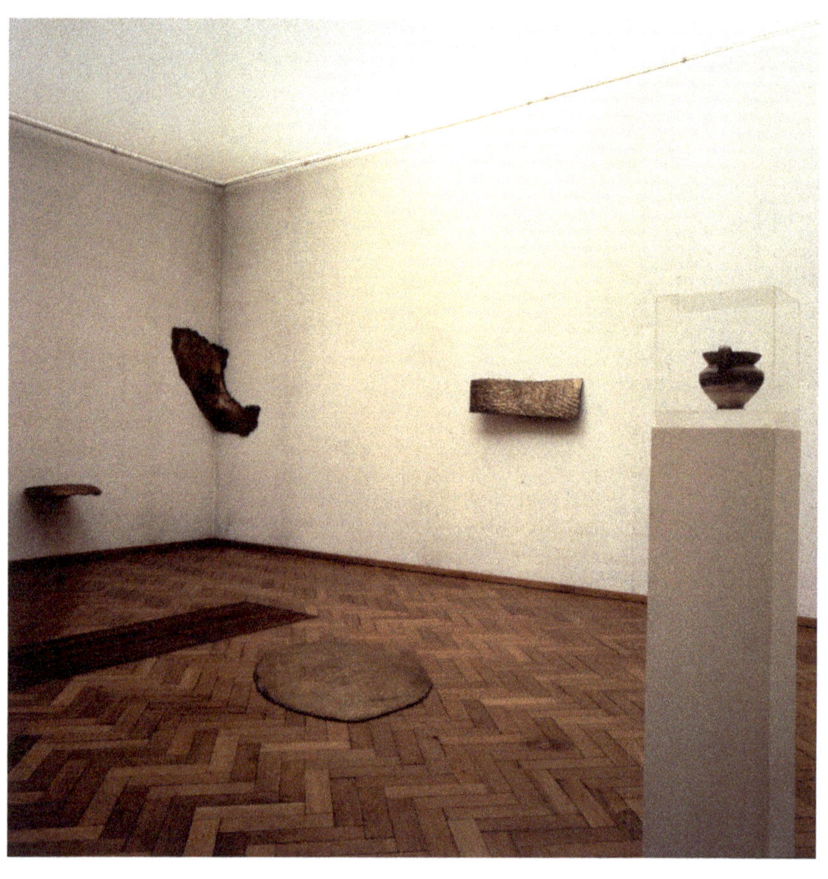

3.1 Giuseppe Penone, *Vaso* (*Vase*), 1975. Excavated vase, four bronze elements, dimensions variable. Installation view at Stedelijk Museum, Amsterdam, 1980.

Photograph: Paolo Mussat Sartor, © Paolo Mussat Sartor

3

Radical Reciprocity: Passive Sculptor / Active Material

The succession of contacts, of gestures, impressed on a plastic material defines content and determines form. The traces of the fingers become idea channels for the flow of fluids. They bring the image closer to the configuration and structure of a plant ... The clay that fixes or memorizes the action, retains the imprint, solidifies the trace of fluid, and makes the sculptor's work a plant.

– Giuseppe Penone, in Germano Celant, *Arte Povera=Art Povera*

Try this: With palms facing each other, press your hands flat against each other and try to determine which hand is doing the touching. Can you separate the feeling in your right hand from that in your left? Touch something else: the pages of this book, the keyboard of your laptop, the surface on which you sit. Consider the resistance of the other material to your touch and try to divorce the sensation of what the paper *feels like* from the tickle of the paper against your skin. Such "dividing" is a difficult task. Alternatively, the fact that your hand does not lose its definition and merge with the paper (or fabric, wood, metal, etc.) is due to this division, to the way your body preserves its integrity. It also owes to the material maintaining its own structure, effectively pressing back against your skin. Depending on the coincidence of physical make-up and formal organization, however, some materials can break through the barrier of the skin – think of a smooth piece of sea glass versus a shard of a broken window. At the same time, a human hand can easily breach the surface tension of other substances, like a pool of water, a pile of loose sand, or a lump of soft clay. When we touch something, we initiate a complex interplay between active and passive aspects of the body's sensory systems. Given the marvellous invisibility of such brain-body transactions, material agency in such human-thing relationships is often taken for granted.

In Penone's work an embodied negotiation of the material world emerges as one cornerstone of a theory of sculpture in which touch carries as much weight as sight does. As argued in chapter 2, this corresponds with a diverse collection of philosophical approaches to understanding experience, which submit that human subjectivity is formed through a process of identification with and rejection of the things we see and touch. From Descartes to Duchamp, and from Dewey to Merleau-Ponty, it has been argued that humans actively create an internal sense of self through the interpolation of external stimuli or in relation to a set of given conditions. From his earliest mature works, however, Penone further problematizes these theories, recasting the formative relationship between his body and matter in ways that de-emphasize the human side of that equation to favour the agency of the material.

For instance, inasmuch as the artist actively intervenes in the growth of trees in his 1968 *Maritime Alps* series, the living trees also dynamically react and adapt to the passive vestiges of the artist's touch. In the various body prints and plaster casts made by Penone throughout the 1970s, the images result from the body having been pressed onto or into the material and from the material's ability to resist breaking apart at his touch. Building upon the argument that Penone's works reject the Cartesian foundations of modernism and instead recast human subjectivity through phenomenological experience, this chapter further demonstrates that such subject formation is not merely the result of a human actor appropriating passive objects; rather, it emerges through a negotiation between the body and things in which both have agency. In numerous works of the late 1970s Penone employed soft materials like wax, clay, and live plants to differentiate those parts of the sculptor's work that are active from those that are passive. If touch is one of the foundations of Penone's concept of sculpture, then problematizing agency in the infra-thin dimension between the touching body (the artist) and the dynamic things of the world (the materials) emerges as an important feature of his project.

In his works of the mid- to late 1970s, a conceptual wrestling with the reciprocity of touch comes together with new tactical approaches to underscoring the traces of touch. For instance, in *Vaso* (*Vase*, 1975) Penone exhibited a vase on a pedestal and several large, abstract bronze forms that either rested on the floor or cantilevered from the wall (figure 3.1).

Human and material interpolation is the subject of this installation, in which the artist uses casting to investigate an antique vessel from the point of view of its material testimony to the artist's body and labour. Traditionally, a vase like this is celebrated for aesthetic pleasure or studied for its ethnographic value. For example, the form of the vessel, the iconography of its decoration, or material traces left inside might provide new insights into the customs and values of a past human civilization. Penone sidelines such anthropological or archaeological approaches and instead underscores the fundamental idea that, before a vase reveals data about the culture in which it was made, the exterior surface of the vase is first the negative space of an individual potter's hands. That is, the handmade object is foremost an index of the artist's body.

To make the bygone body of the vase's maker as present to the viewer as the object itself, Penone made wax casts of the pot, trapping subtle grooves left centuries ago. He then enlarged these and cast them in bronze, lending both visibility and durability to the delicate, incidental marks. The original maker of the vase may not have intentionally left his or her fingerprints in the clay and in fact may have attempted to efface them through finishing and decoration. Nevertheless, traces of the material's encounter with corporeal forces remained and could not be completely divorced from the vase as an aesthetic or useful object. Penone's investigation testifies to the points of contact between the material and a human hand or a wielded tool. In particular, the artist positioned this antique vase in terms of the body when he described vases as things designed to substitute for what the hands could not hold.[1] Indexing the ancient potter's fingerprints also serves to underscore the reciprocal aspects of artistic making and the changing metrics by which one values individual artistic labour.

The bronze-cast elements of Penone's *Vase* further demonstrate this principle because they are passive matrices that might remake the solid of his own hands. The wax used to pick up the old, incidental fingerprints in the clay also captured the impressions of Penone's fingers on the opposite side. Here distinctions between inside and outside, or touching and touched, are again reversed. Later, when the partial wax casts were translated into bronze, traces of both ancient potter and contemporary sculptor were equalized, touching each other over centuries through a tangle of human and material encounters. Penone's *Vase* contrasts such traces of the body with the object of artistic labour. He exhibited the enlarged bronze "sherds" alongside the appropriated antique vase itself to unite further comparisons between the two. Is one of these objects, one matrix of touches, more valuable than another because the artist is nameable, because the fingerprints are intentional, or because it enters into a different economy of artistic making? *Vase* underscores the way in which both touch and its reversibility are inherent in the material processes of forming things, as well as the way in which bodies are pressed into economies of successive touches, of different registers of labour. In fact, in the way it records the hands of its maker, *Vase* demonstrates that all human-made objects are the bearers of the incidental labours of touch. Contextualizing *Vase* and other works that similarly foreground the reciprocity between the human body and the material world proves the relevance of such artistic experiments to the philosophy of phenomenology. It also indicates the way in which forms can hold and communicate theoretical concepts without recourse to written language.

In this same period Penone devised several projects that proceeded from the point of view that a material or force of nature beyond the artist's hand was actively engaged in the works' making. Such works compel viewers to consider familiar objects and processes from the point of view of the things themselves. It may seem strange to talk about materials and things having a point of view, not to mention agency, but this is precisely the kind of expanded thinking that Penone's works engender. Levelling the hierarchy between subject and object through a focus on forces, traces, and the reversibility of touch offers a way to conceive of a non-anthropocentric relationship between humans and their environment. Through the reciprocity of touch modelled in his work, Penone proposes a relationship in which subjectivity is distributed across human-thing interactions, in which both take on active and passive roles at given moments in the relationship. Works that give form to the force of air, take shape organically, or conflate the processes of sculpture with the flow of a river make visible the often-invisible agency of things.

In particular, many of Penone's works demonstrate the material to be active, either instead of the artist or in concert with him, prefiguring non-anthropocentric approaches to anthropology in their synthetic way of thinking about the multivalent, discursive relationship between humans and things. This chapter thus employs the twenty-first-century recasting of thing theory, in particular its use in recent anthropology.[2] These anthropological models demonstrate the interconnectedness of humans and the material world by considering the relationship from the point of view of the material (Ian Hodder), and, more importantly, they reveal the relationship to be non-binary (Philippe Descola). These concepts are not introduced here as a *new* new materialism; rather, they serve to provide language to describe the complex dependences and dependencies between humans and things, humans and other humans, things and other things. Indeed, borrowing the language of this anthropological vein of critical theory allows a focus on Penone's materials without falling back on the trope of "poor materials" that has plagued so much of the scholarship on Arte povera.[3] Instead, the non-hierarchical, reciprocal relationships between humans and things that are evident in much of Penone's art emerge as a demonstration of the ways in which art can act as a distributed cognitive engine because it uses the external world to help us organize and understand our internal thoughts.

This chapter also proposes that Penone's exploration of intersubjective agency in the late 1970s is paradigmatic of some of the most radical reconsiderations of society that emerged at the same moment. Many accounts of the artist's work read its social impact as ecological in the most basic sense: it demonstrates the impact of humans on the natural world. Penone's critical examination of artistic agency through natural forms and materials does more than this. By recasting the relationship between artist and matter as reciprocal, his works give tangible form to the socio-political context from which they arose, namely the profound connections between Italian labour and social theories of the mid-1970s. While Penone's works are certainly not aimed at being overtly political, the way in which they overturn a closed, binary way of thinking about the artist-material relationship has the potential to shift one's view radically, beyond the scope of aesthetics. Could one, for instance, think of one of the automobiles made by local giants FIAT or Lancia as bearing perceptible, if infra-thin, traces of its workers' bodies? Surely these same bodies were physically marked by their interaction with the materials and processes of their industry in ways that came to define their very beings. This aspect of Penone's socio-political context is read through the contemporaneous Italian development of *biopolitics*, a term first used by Michel Foucault to describe the power relations at the intersection of bodies and politics in society, and represented here by the writings of Roberto Esposito.[4]

In Penone's work, sculpture is proposed as a tool to visualize the body's fundamentally entangled relationship with the material world. Highlighting this entanglement through consideration of material agency challenges the anthropocentric logic that dominates the modernist aesthetic and its contemporary socio-economic discourses. If indeed "humans think through material things," as some critical theorists and anthropologists argue, then Penone's work demonstrates that sculpture is best equipped to access this radical approach to materiality because of the way it meets us in our phenomenological space. When his works refigure the relationship between the sculptor's internal, conceptual drive and his external, material production as one of negotiation, rather than domination, they lay bare the radical potential of seeing the world through new eyes.

Breathing as Sculpture

In 1972 Penone photographed a lop-sided tree in Sardinia, the thrust of its trunk and branches having been pressed into a near-horizontal posture by the constant force of the Mediterranean winds. The snapshot recalls a drawing made by the artist four years earlier in which he imagined an ocarina – a folk wind instrument popularized in nineteenth-century Italy – channelling wind through its terracotta form to sculpt a tree with an invisible force that might also be audible (figure 3.2). In both the photograph and the drawing, alteration to a tree's physical form is the result of air interacting with solid materials in ways that can be visibly and perhaps audibly perceived. The interplay of the visible and the invisible previously explored through sight and touch takes on a new resonance here because air really only becomes palpable through the tension created when it encounters other forces and elements. Thus, in the case of air, the fluidity between subject and object, or between actor and acted upon, is harder to pin down when we are talking about non-human things acting on each other – wind and tree – but easier to understand when made analogous to human breath forced through an instrument. In its categorization as breath, air is no longer positioned as an external thing. Rather, it becomes human, regularly entering and exiting the body – even seeming to be produced by it – often without much notice. As breath, air lubricates the relationship between the body and the world.

Penone's exploration of the physical and metaphoric attributes of breath allows for a deepening consideration of the relationship between artist and material as reciprocal and responsive. In 1977 Penone attempted to make a photographic record of this essential, yet hardly visible material by blowing on white powder and snapping images of the ephemeral clouds thus produced. Over the next several years he drew many plans for giving breath a variety of more solid, plastic forms (figure 3.3). Each of the realized works in the *Soffio* or *Breath* series distinctly manifests the vital movement of breath across

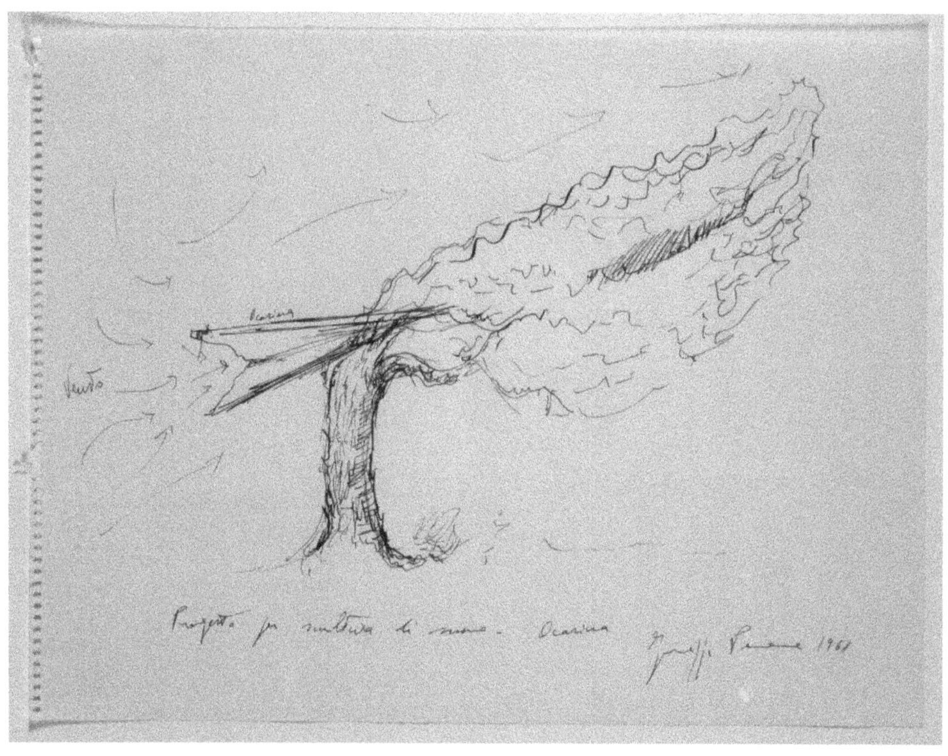

3.2 Giuseppe Penone, *Progetto per scultura di suono – Ocarina* (*Plan for Sound Sculpture – Ocarina*), 1968. China-ink on paper, 30 x 40 cm.

Photograph: Paolo Pellion di Persano, © Archivio Penone

the body's boundaries by giving perceptible form to air that is otherwise disregarded or unperceived. Through its confluence with the body and raw materials in this series, air is perceptible simultaneously as a substance and as a shaping force, problematizing the breath-body divide.

The most enduring example is *Soffi di creta* (*Clay Breaths*, 1978): a series of nine bulbous forms that document in terracotta the volume, shape, and force of an exhalation (figure 3.4). From one point of view the sculptures' smooth swollen bodies, narrow necks, and flanged mouths lend them the appearance of large, undecorated pelike or other antique vessels.[5] A tendency to anthropomorphize objects is already evident in art historians' use of terms derived from the human

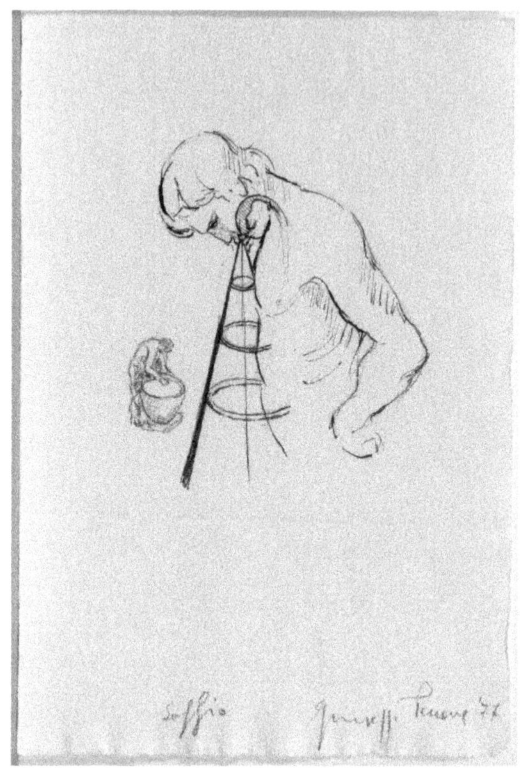

3.3 Giuseppe Penone, *Soffio* (*Breath*), 1977. Graphite and China-ink on paper, 29 x 19.6 cm.

Photograph: © Archivio Penone

form to describe the parts of classical pottery: *foot, body, neck, shoulder, mouth,* and *lip*. Penone has noted that such vessels were used by ancient societies as sepulchres, to preserve the material remains of the body and its important organs for an imagined afterlife.[6] Such correspondences are initially reinforced by the stature of his own sculptures (148 centimetres, or nearly 5 feet, tall). Moreover, Penone's *Clay Breath* sculptures make the connection explicit by interrupting the classical symmetry of one side with a deep vertical gash on the other side that registers the artist's full-scale figure pressed into the material (figure 3.5).

Like his body prints and plaster casts of the mid-1970s, these works partially map the exterior of the body's surface, but they also track

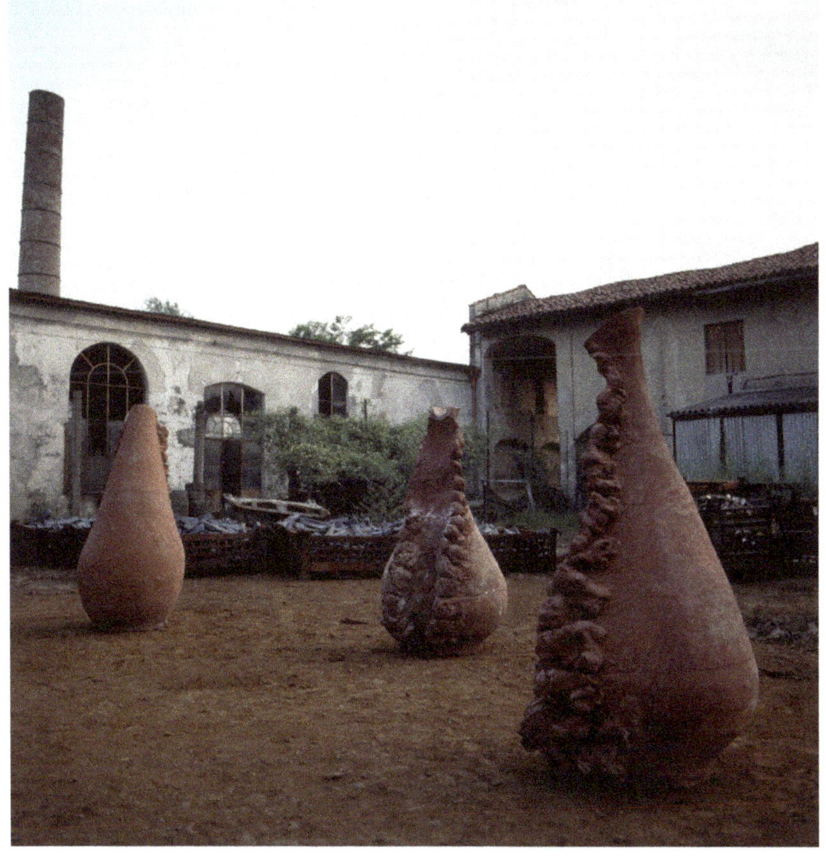

3.4 Giuseppe Penone, *Soffi di creta* (*Clay Breaths*), 1978. Fired clay; three elements, 148 x 72 x 65 cm each. Photographic documentation of works in progress at Castellamonte factory, 1978.

Photograph: Paolo Mussat Sartor, © Paolo Mussat Sartor

its interior space. Penone's formal approach here is trifold: each terracotta sculpture is an index of the space around the body, a plastic realization of the force of an exhaled breath, and the externalization of the negative space inside the body. As matrices of the body's interior volume and exterior surface, these sculptures are precisely *not* bodies but the spaces around and inside an absent body. Further, the turbulent ripples and swirls of clay that frame the body impression

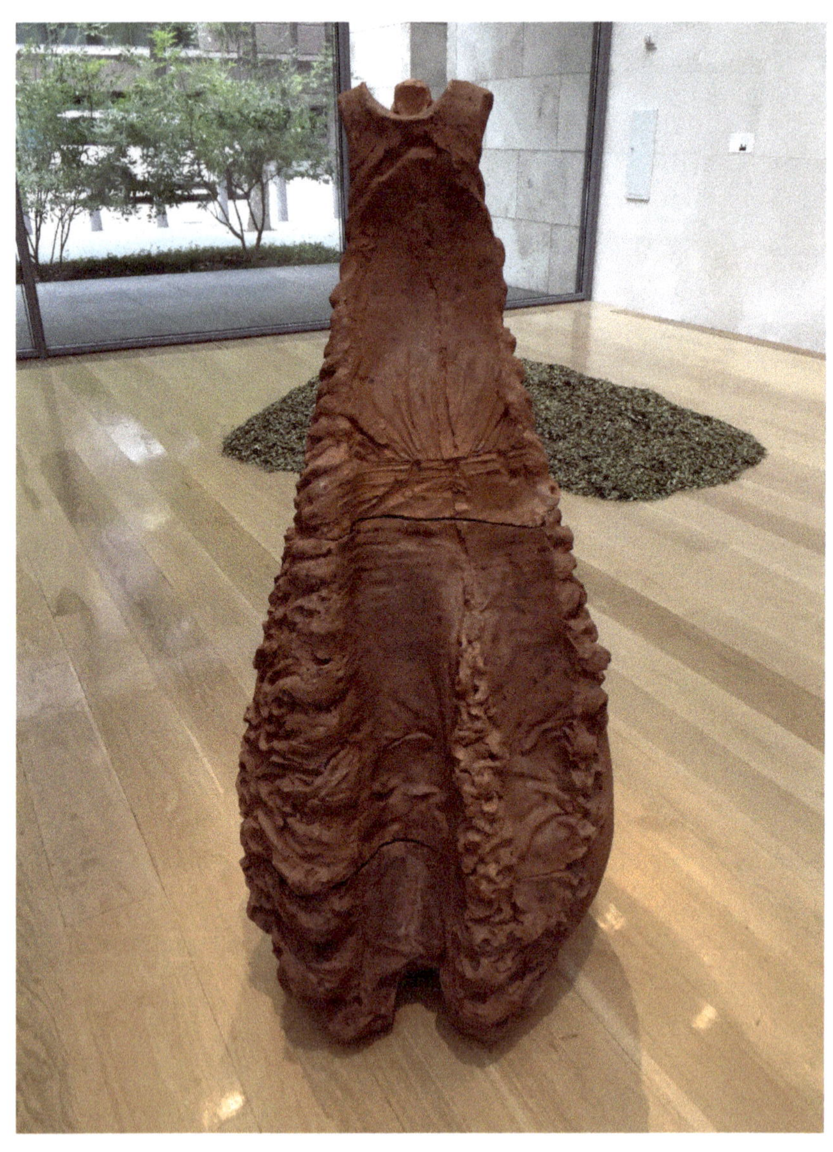

3.5 Giuseppe Penone, *Soffio di creta 3* (*Clay Breath 3*), 1978. Fired clay, 148 x 72 x 65 cm (overall).

Photograph: © Elizabeth Mangini

on each form connote the force and direction of air that has exited the body. In the context of the artist's investigation of the nature of artistic making, these enigmatic objects highlight the fluidity between internal and external experience, between the conceptual and the physical, between the artist and the material, and between active and passive states.

As they evoke the formal tropes of classical vases, the *Clay Breath* sculptures also bring to mind the ancient connotations of working with clay, including many human origin stories that have been told through the medium of clay or earth. The Judaeo-Christian god creates man from dust, the Egyptian god Khnum is represented as a potter at the wheel, and the Qur'an cites man's creation from clay, to name just a few pertinent examples. In these mythologies the human body is considered a vessel that holds air.[7] Penone probed the mythological dimensions of clay and air in his own writings, noting, for instance, that while Prometheus was said to have shaped humans from mud and water, it was Athena who "blew the breath of life into them."[8] This material duality initially seems to reinforce a fundamental divergence of the interior experience of the body from its outward-facing physical form. However, Penone's work with clay and breath is as far from emphasizing such a split as it is from recasting the artist as a divine creator. Instead, through multiple orders of making gathered in a single work, Penone's *Clay Breath* sculptures propose the figure of the potter as a mediator who marshals the specific forces at work in the formation of a pot to bring about a convergence of internal and external form that is fluid, complex, and inextricably connected.[9] Thus the historical reciprocity of clay and air mediated by the body recalls Merleau-Ponty's argument that externalization makes the internal explicit; it models the ineffable link between the artist's concept and its material execution.[10]

In the context of 1970s European art, the historical divide between external form (the art object) and internal experience (or expression) found in Merleau-Ponty or the clay-based origin stories might equally be read as modelling the postmodern debates about artistic identity that came to light in the 1972 *Documenta* exhibition. Is the artist someone who shapes matter with the hands, or, as Duchamp once argued about the fictional creator of his infamous porcelain *Fountain*, is the artist someone who creates a new thought for an object?[11] In Italy one of the chief investigators of this object-concept or interior-exterior split was Piero Manzoni (1933–63), whose kaolin (clay) *Achrome* paintings have been claimed to be a means to "put an end to the inferior ranking of the object with respect to the subject."[12] At the same time that his tautological "paintings" eschewed image in favour of objective materiality, Manzoni nurtured a similarly closed loop of subjectivity through that which the body produces: excrement, blood, fingerprints, and breath. His infamous *Merda d'artista* (*Artist's Shit*, 1961), in which he canned ninety tins of his own excrement, shares both the shock value and the conceptual sentiment about the artistic production of Duchamp's urinal-cum-fountain. Both elder artists also employed breath as a material through which to address the intangible, auratic value of art.

In Latin the word for *breath* is the same as that for *spirit*, making it an ideal topic to investigate in relation to the ongoing debates about objecthood versus expression in twentieth-century art. Duchamp's blown-glass *50 cc of Paris Air* (1919) and Manzoni's *Fiato d'artista* (*Artist's Breath*, 1960) are prime examples of breath as an artistic material. Manzoni's artist-inflated balloons, also known as *Corpi d'aria* (*Bodies of Air*), are important precedents for Penone's subsequent breath project (figure 3.6). Inflated, these buoyant works have a sculptural and even a kinetic presence, but, as children disappointingly realize in the wake of a birthday party or a trip to the zoo, such balloons do not remain inflated for long. Ultimately, Manzoni's work documents the folly of trying to capture the metaphysical in an object: a brittle, deflated splotch of latex is pinned down on a wooden board, with a brass label indicating the air that clearly is no longer present (figure 3.7). It is a relic of the theology that separates mind and body, one that, with its calculatedly pathetic form, criticizes the possibility of a split between the two. Like Duchamp's and Manzoni's approaches, Penone's reconfiguration of the relationship between the interiority of subjectivity and the possibility of its externalization through artistic production is both tied to the artist's body and separate from his identity. His *Clay Breath* works present a powerful re-evaluation of the body schema as a thing in the world and the container of his subjectivity, in ways that resonate with the complexity of perceptual experience over the dialectical impasses brought by reason alone.

In his tall terracotta objects Penone records the body in three distinct ways, which together work to undermine the subject-object binary, replacing it with a non-teleological network of active and passive encounters as well as ongoing exchanges between interior and exterior. In each sculpture three horizontal seams testify to the process of the object's manufacture. On one side the smooth bowl-like exterior bears the incidental imprints of the artist's hands, which actively shaped the iconic form of each object from a mental image. As seen in *Vase*, this

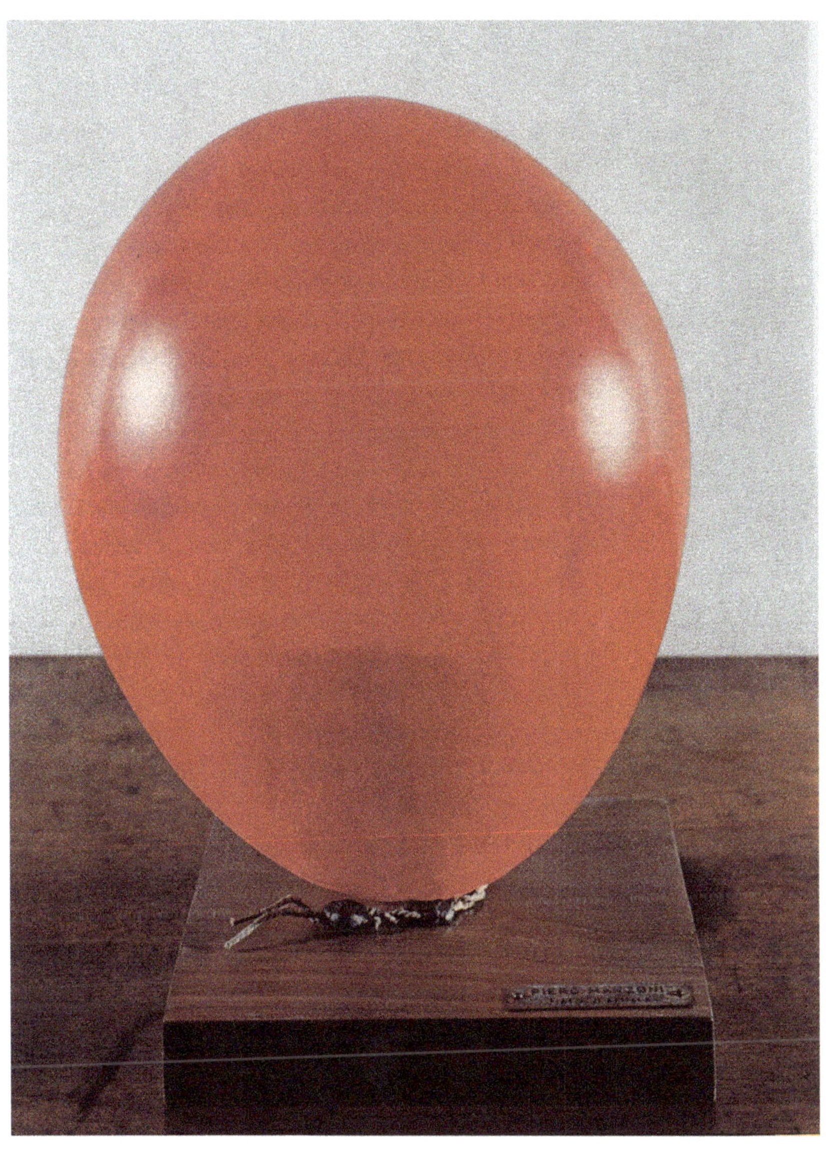

3.6 Piero Manzoni, *Fiato d'artista* (*Artist's Breath*), 1960. Balloon, rope, lead seals, and bronze plaque on wooden base, 35 x 180 x 185 cm.

Photograph: Courtesy Fondazione Piero Manzoni

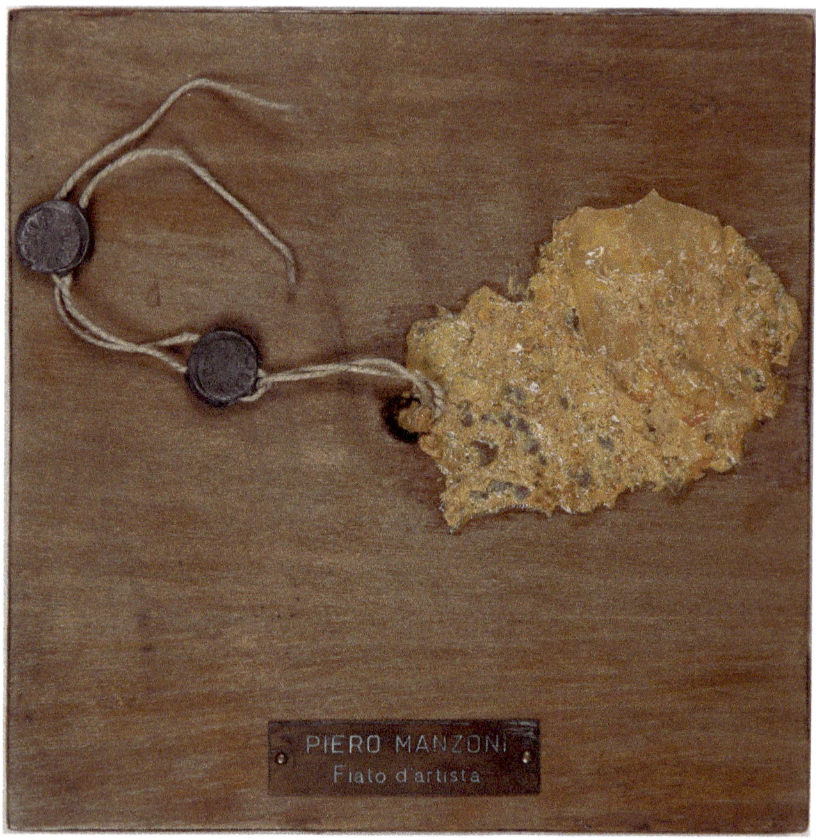

3.7 Piero Manzoni, *Fiato d'artista* (*Artist's Breath*), 1960. Balloon, rope, lead seals, and bronze plaque on wooden base, 35 x 180 x 185 cm.

Photograph: Courtesy Fondazione Piero Manzoni

simultaneity between process and image models the persistent fluidity between form and concept. At the same time, on the reverse side the artist's clothed body has been passively recorded by means of a plaster cast that was pressed into the wet clay. Although recognizable as a human figure, this mark plainly indexes the body's exterior as a collection of surfaces and textures, rather than an idealized, unified form. The ripples that signify both gesture and the force of exhaled air mediate between the iconographic and the indexical marks. Together these are the kind of inscriptions to which we are accustomed, authenticating the artist's active and passive roles in his making of the work. It is only when the viewer closely inspects the impressions of the artist's body that the sculptures reveal their third and most radical mode of communication, eliciting an involuntary response through their indexing of the body's *interior*.

A corporeal communication with the viewer occurs when they recognize that the "head" of a work like *Clay Breath 3* is not merely a concave impression of his face; rather, a strange, solid form projects from where the mouth should be (figure 3.8). This abject protrusion might elicit nausea when it becomes evident that this is a cast of the inside of the artist's mouth.[13] For the viewer, recognition of this form produces a sympathetic sense of heaviness against the tongue or perhaps a reflexive gag, upon imagining plaster filling the mouth. Responses to such forms are not entirely considered; rather they are at least partially automatic. As soon as the form is recognized, the viewer's body responds of its own accord. Thus, the terracotta sculptures of this series probe the invisibility of an internal function against the visibility of the body's surface, breaching the boundary of the viewer's body, too, through a sympathetic response to its disruption.[14]

Penone doubles down on breath as a means to investigate the intricate and often-reciprocal interaction between material forces, by again engaging the viewer's body along with his own in *Soffio di foglie* (*Breath of Leaves*, 1979) (figure 3.9). In this work the artist lies atop a large pile of leaves mounded on the floor and exhales, leaving an unmistakable indentation in the shape of a human figure and a "breath bubble" of displaced vegetal mass when he stands up. The gesture is quite simple and emphatically passive: the artist rests, he succumbs to gravity, and he is "just" breathing. The leaves actively respond to the moving air and the friction of the accumulated mass, and they settle down in a new arrangement.[15] In Penone's *Breath of Leaves*, however, his body and its exhalation of air are not merely represented through visible traces of the artist's actions. Indeed, this installation also actively uses breath, engaging the viewer's respiration to breach the border marked by skin. Here Penone extends the experience of the transgressive nature of breath – the way it links the interior and exterior of the body – through its connection with scent. When a viewer encounters the work in an empty gallery, their body stirs the still air, which in turn carries the herbal scent of the drying leaves to their nose, stimulating the sense of smell as the air travels to the lungs. Further, by choosing fragrant leaves like box and myrtle, Penone ensures that the air takes on a perceptual thickness that illuminates the viewer's body: they instantly become aware of their movement and their breath.[16] The

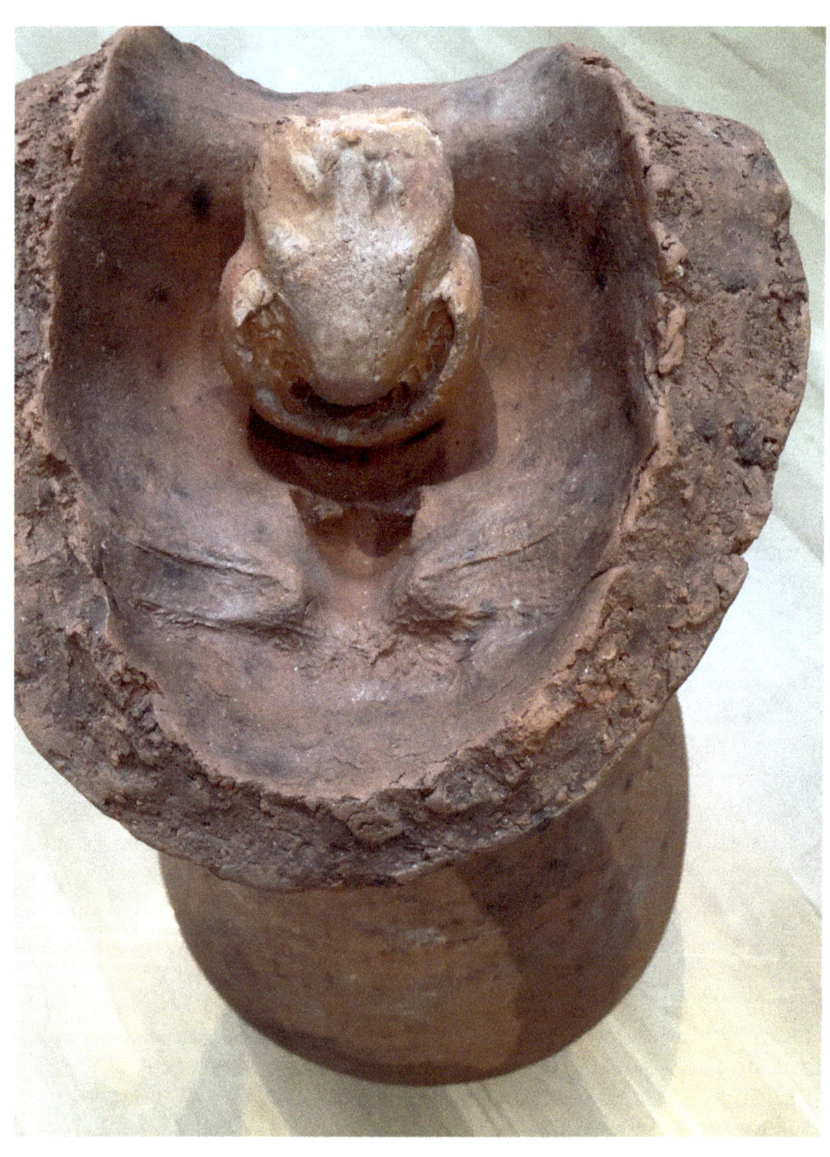

3.8 Giuseppe Penone, *Soffio di creta 3* (*Clay Breath 3*), detail, 1978. Fired clay, 148 x 72 x 65 cm (overall).

Photograph: © Elizabeth Mangini

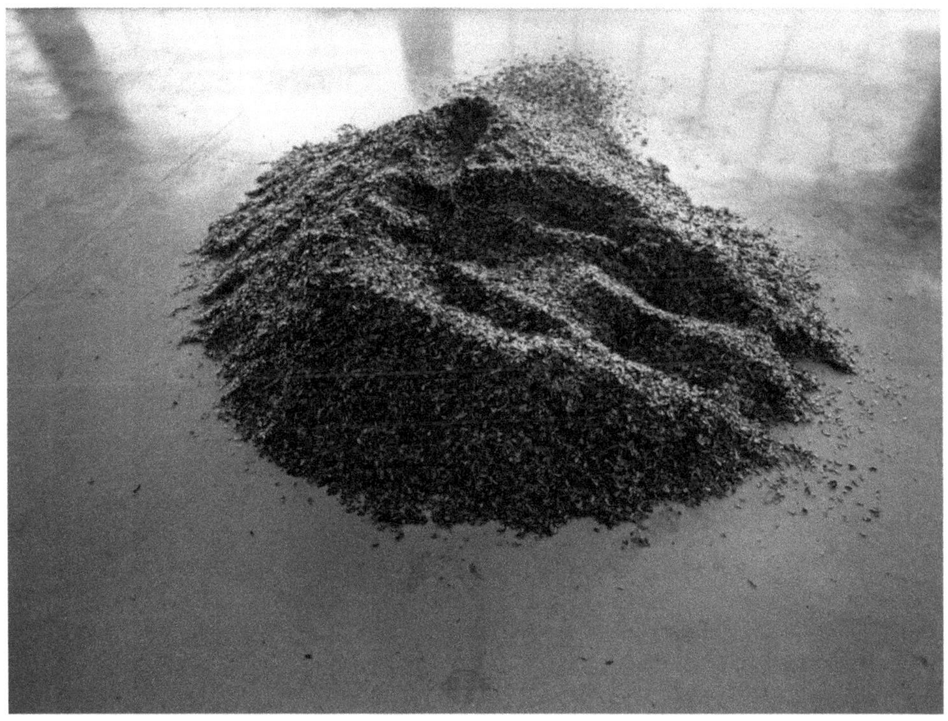

3.9 Giuseppe Penone, *Soffio di foglie* (*Breath of Leaves*), 1979. Box tree leaves, dimensions variable. Installation view of the work in the artist's studio, c. 1979.

Photograph: © Archivio Penone

invisible matter moving between one body and another becomes perceptible through breath.

Quite apart from the metaphysical connotations of breath as the fluid of life, the inherently dual modes of respiration make it an ideal means to address the complexity of the body as subject and object, because breath is both active and passive. Of all the body's essential functions, breathing is one that is controlled by two separate areas of the brain and two different sets of nerves. Under normal conditions, respiration is autonomic or involuntary and continuous. However, it can also be conscious and somatic, or controlled by the body, when one chooses to focus on it. (Consider the difference between how you breathe when you are sleeping versus when you are exercising or meditating.) Breathing relies on a network of muscles not proper to the lungs, because the latter have no skeletal muscles of their own. Instead, the movement of the diaphragm, ribcage, and abdominal muscles create the conditions in which air can enter and be expelled from the lungs. Fundamentally, breathing is a complex network of actions and reactions. It is both active and passive. In Penone's work we must therefore read breath as more than a nod to ancient theology or popular physiology. "Breathing," Penone wrote in 1977, "is automatic, involuntary sculpture, that brings us closer to osmosis with things."[17] For him, breath models the continuity and ambiguity of a non-hierarchical relationship between subject and object.

Sowing as Sculpture

In the catalogue for the artist's 1978 show at the Kunstmuseum Folkswang in Essen, Germany, in which the *Breath* works featured prominently, Celant links Penone's art and its identification with nature to his childhood in an agricultural community, which "built its cultural development on primitive thought."[18] He argues that Penone's writings, too, prove that the work partakes of a conscious mythological context in which "interior and exterior, soul and body, water and vase, feminine and masculine, unite pleasantly, in honor of the Great Mother."[19] Celant here identifies the project's attempt to overcome dialectic opposition through the adoption of what might be considered premodern perspectives. However poetic this "unification" of self and world in a personification of nature may be, it also is an overly simplistic way of describing the effect. This attempt to distinguish the works of Penone from those of American land artists like Nancy Holt, Dennis Oppenheim, and Robert Smithson risks overshadowing the more complex, intersubjective aspects of the Italian artist's oeuvre. Conversely, when Celant suggests that Penone is renewing the archetypes and mythological forms of a distinctly European history, he eclipses the contemporary, cosmopolitan context of the making and reception of Penone's works.

The proper socio-historical context of Penone's project is not only the farms of Garessio but also the city of Turin, which is at once an industrial centre of labourers and migrants and the historical home of the Italian monarchy. The city holds these two identities simultaneously, just as Penone's works test the rhetorical opposition between nature and culture as a theoretical and linguistic construct. Indeed, in an interview with Celant, Penone seemingly refutes the reductive opposition between nature and culture through which the critic contextualized his art.

> On close examination even the image of the factory makes reference to that of the field. Take assembly lines: the lines parallel one another just like the furrows of a ploughed field … There's a millennial quality in this way of thinking, and I want to preserve it. Our culture has separated one way of thinking from the other, the human being from nature. I don't believe such a clear distinction can be drawn; there is human material and there are materials called stone and wood, which together make up cities, railroads and streets, riverbeds and mountains. From a cosmic point of view the difference between them is irrelevant.[20]

For Penone, then, segregations between rural and urban, artistic work and factory labour, the "natural" wood of a tree and the "cultural" timber used to build a house or make a sculpture are, like wind and breath – false distinctions. Instead, the ways in which many of his works emphasize the agency of materials over that of the artist can be read as challenges to such binaries and, on a larger scale, to the concept of human society as being rooted in the struggle for domination over one another and over the natural world.

In one of his most radical examples of deference to materials Penone brought the intersection of sculptural work and agricultural labour to the foreground. He buried plaster casts of parts of his face and head in a patch of earth where potatoes had been sown. It followed that the seedlings nearest the fragmentary casts grew in relation to these forms, moulding themselves into vegetables with the form of a human nose, an ear, a mouth, or a closed eyelid (figure 3.10). Of the sixty casts he buried, only five of them resulted in potatoes that bore recognizable facial features.[21] The artist then cast these five altered tubers in bronze, and exhibited them together with conventional potatoes. In a period image by Paolo Mussat Sartor, a photographer with whom Penone and other Arte povera artists often collaborated, two full crates of potatoes are propped up against a stone street curb (figure 3.11). At first glance this image resembles a snapshot taken at an open-air market or an impromptu roadside produce stand, the likes of which are frequently seen throughout Italy as intrepid farmers truck in their wares and set up on street corners to sell nuts, citrus, or other delicacies. In a black-and-white photograph such as this, it is only the faint glints of light reflecting off five of the topmost potatoes in the crate on the right that attract the eye and give a clue to the difference of these tubers from the rest of the harvest. Still, it is only upon close scrutiny of the vegetables that the lumpy bumps of *these* five potatoes reveal their human features.

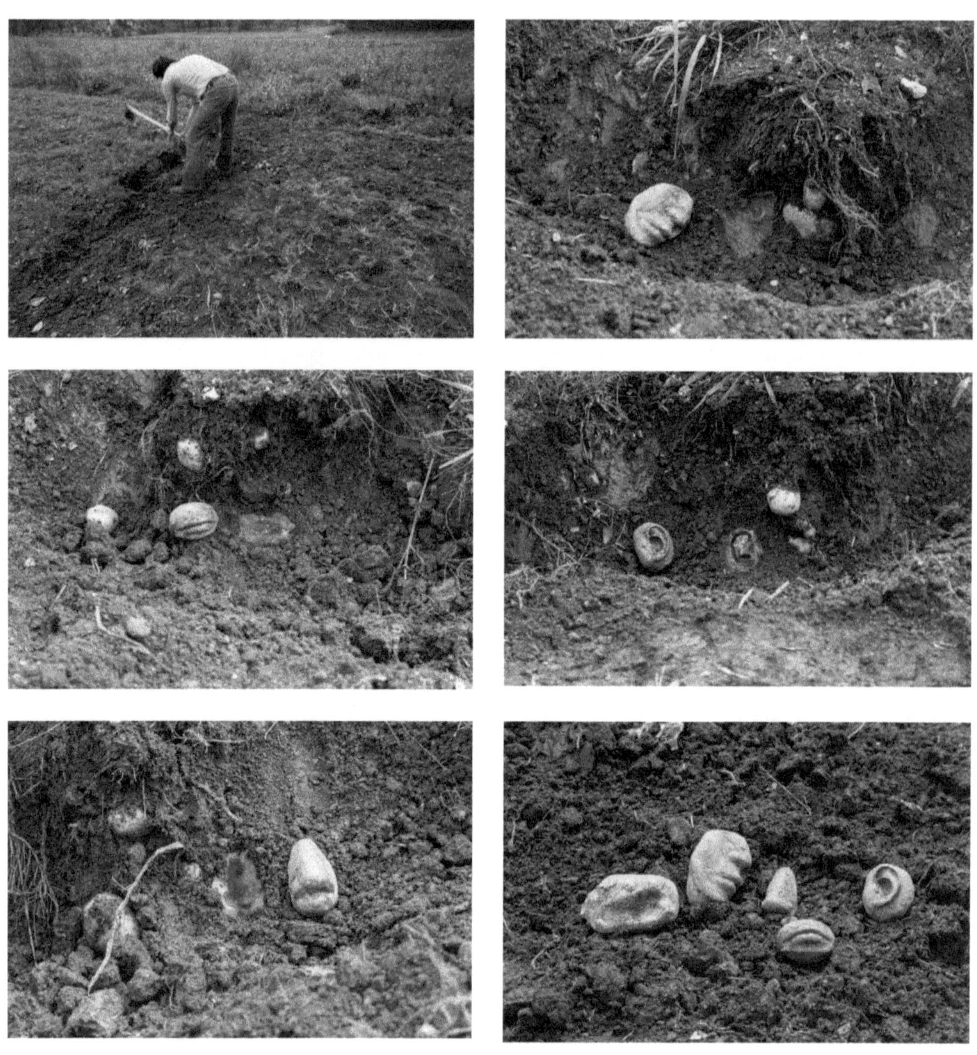

3.10 Giuseppe Penone, *Patate* (*Potatoes*), 1977.
Documentation of work in progress, Garessio.

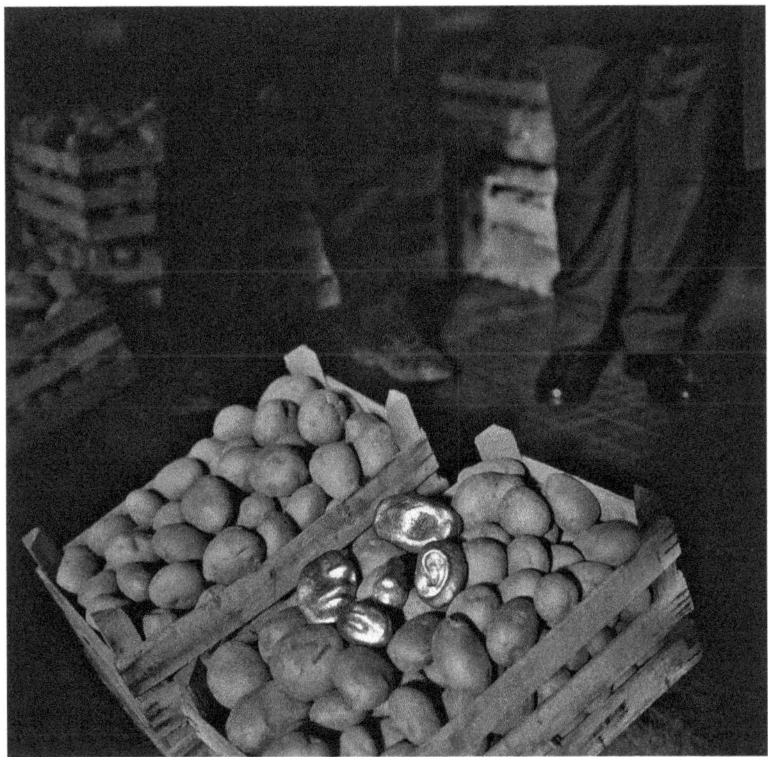

3.11 Giuseppe Penone, *Patate* (*Potatoes*), 1977. Five bronze elements, potatoes, dimensions variable. Documentary photograph of installation, c. 1978.

Photograph: Paolo Mussat Sartor, © Paolo Mussat Sartor

Although this image of the work known simply as *Patate* (*Potatoes*, 1977) is clearly a set up for the purposes of the photograph, the initial installation of the sculptures in a more conventional art context, Paul Maenz's Cologne gallery in 1978, followed the same logic, with the crates building a connotation of everyday encounters, which were nonetheless made strange by their relocation to an art gallery. In later exhibitions *Potatoes* has been shown with the five bronzes distributed throughout a much looser pile of potatoes, which were heaped directly on the floor (figure 3.12). This removed some of the subtext implied by the crates but further emphasized the sculptures' status as a part within a whole. When these piles are encountered in person, especially when an exhibition has been on view for a while, the differences between bronze

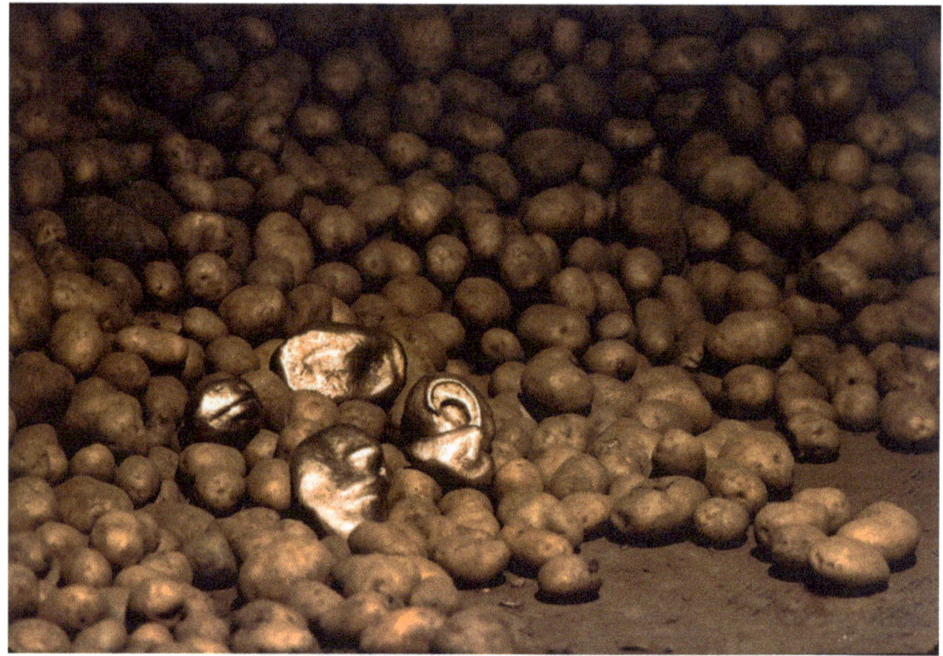

3.12 Giuseppe Penone, *Patate* (*Potatoes*), 1977.
Potatoes, five bronze elements, dimensions variable.

Photograph: © Archivio Penone

and potato begin to recede. The "real" potatoes start to shrivel and turn green under the skin as they oxidize, making them less distinguishable from the bronzes, which also lose some lustre and change colour with age. Mixing the bronze-cast potatoes with fresh vegetables encourages comparison between the natural and the cultural: all of the potatoes have non-geometric lumps, dimples, and protrusions, which document encounters with the forces of other objects like roots or stones. Together they emphasize the way in which any organic matter takes form in relation to its conditions. In this work the organic process comes to the fore, and the viewer is invited to inhabit the material perspective of the plant.

From one point of view, the fact of the potatoes taking on distinctly human features might be considered to anthropomorphize the natural world; Penone's *Potatoes* would seem to confirm the casual and even absurd way in which we often perceive human characteristics in animals, plants, and things. Yet, when the work is imagined from the viewpoint of the *material*, this is merely what happens in most figurative

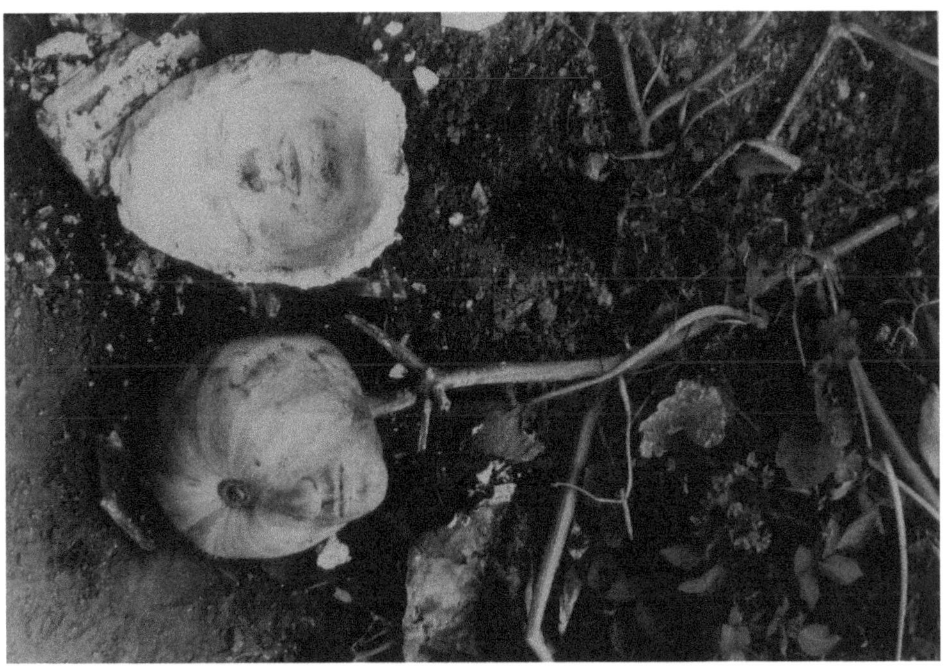

3.13 Giuseppe Penone, *Zucche* (*Pumpkins, or Squashes*), 1978–9. Photographic documentation of work in progress, 1978–9.

Photograph: Dina Carrara, © Archivio Penone

sculpture: a raw material is carved, moulded, or otherwise shaped into a form, which traditionally foregrounds human features. What is revolutionary in *Potatoes* is that the material is simultaneously a passive receptacle of the artist's intervention and an active agent by its own growth. The tubers take their shape underground, in the dark, where the artist cannot see them until they are fully formed. In this case, the artist sows and harvests the artwork, but the material does the actual "sculpting" while Penone is not looking or even present. The work of making is thus shared by the artist and the material, each occupying active and passive roles throughout different stages of its manifestation. Even after the artist casts the altered potatoes in bronze, the resulting sculptural objects continue to change and to oxidize apart from the artist's direct control.

Penone continued this investigation into the agency of things by allowing a squash to grow in a plaster cast of the artist's entire head, the soft fruit slowly adopting his full facial features and hardening into a vegetal skin (figures 3.13 and 3.14).[22] The resulting form, replete with

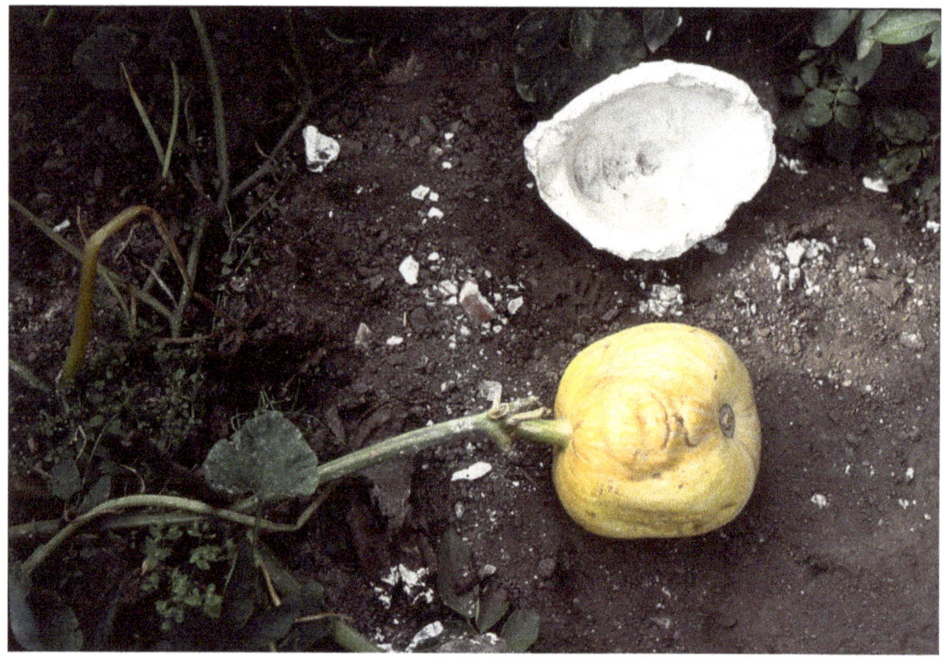

3.14 Giuseppe Penone, *Zucche* (*Pumpkins, or Squashes*), 1978–9. Photographic documentation of work in progress, 1978–9.

Photograph: Dina Carrara, © Archivio Penone

stem and leaves, was cast in bronze, continuing the same back and forth between active and passive stages of the work's iteration seen in *Potatoes*. The work *Zucche IV* (*Pumpkins IV, or Squashes IV,* 1978–9) takes Penone's investigation of artistic labour into new territory (figure 3.15).[23] Since these *Zucche* are more legible as self-portraiture than works like *Clay Breath* or *Potatoes*, they turn the reflection back on Penone himself: What is a sculptor? Which of his actions and reactions give rise to form? It is also a potential play on words (evidence of a subtle humour that pervades many of Penone's works): in Italian a *zucca* (pumpkin or squash) is often metaphorically substituted for one's head. For example, the saying *avere sale in zucca* (to have salt in one's pumpkin) means to have common sense. Specifically, *zucca* usually refers to someone with a bald head, potentially linking Penone's squash self-portrait to a historical precedent in Italian sculpture: Donatello's marble statue of the balding Old Testament prophet

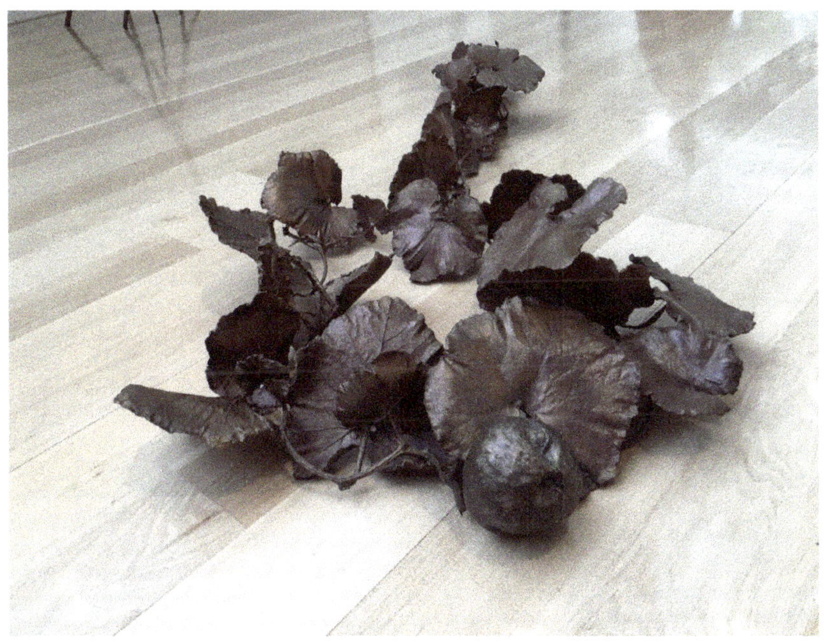

3.15 Giuseppe Penone, *Zucche IV* (*Pumpkins IV, or Squashes IV*), 1978–9. Bronze, 130 x 80 x 40 cm.

Photograph: Elizabeth Mangini

Habakkuk, affectionately known since its artist's own time as *Lo Zuccone* (*The Pumpkin Head*, 1425–36) (figure 3.16).

The Renaissance sculpture, initially made for the Florentine Duomo, is considered by scholars to be a consummate example of fifteenth-century admiration for antiquity. It is a taut combination of formal economy and verisimilitude: the figure's dramatically bulging eyes, furrowed brow, and parted lips with bared teeth are balanced by the softness of exquisitely flowing marble robes. Giorgio Vasari, one of the work's first critics, apocryphally claimed that while making the work, Donatello repeatedly implored it to speak to him.[24] Later scholars have admired the work for more than its dramatic realism, however, focusing instead on the way in which it demonstrates the fundamental values of sculpture at the time of its making. Daniel Zolli, for example, writing in a recent catalogue on Donatello's work for the Florentine cathedral, notes that the artist left unrefined tool marks, clearly visible

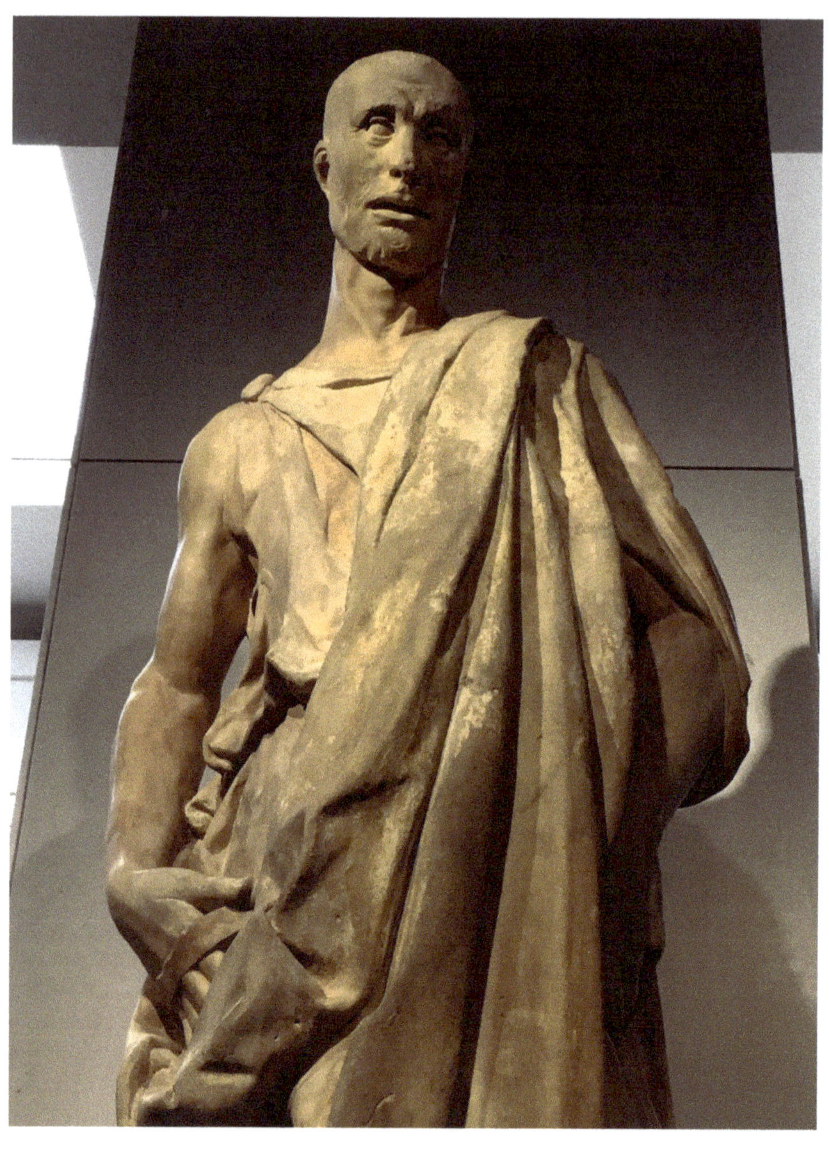

3.16 Donatello, *The Prophet Habakkuk*, known as *Lo Zuccone*, 1425–36. Marble, 195 x 54 x 38 cm. Installation view at Museo dell'Opera del Duomo, Florence.

Photograph: © 2020 Nicholas Mangini

on the arm, neck, and exposed shoulder of the figure. He argues that the artist's admiration of ancient sculptors was on technical grounds.[25] That is, Donatello's sculpture intentionally displays the marks of its own making and reveals the devices used to heighten the tension of the representation.[26] Therefore his sculpture, which looks ready to speak, actively probes the language of sculpture or the ways in which a sculpture "speaks."

Might we see Penone's *Zucche* as similarly demonstrating the values of sculpture in the 1970s? Among these are indexicality and objectivity, an orientation towards process and materials, and a reconsideration of the physical and conceptual aspects of artistic labour. This work, in particular, skilfully makes visible the process of its own making, continuing a sculptural lineage that for Penone stretches back farther than the tenets of Robert Morris's 1968 "Anti-form" manifesto to the fundamental questions asked of the discipline in the early modern period by such figures as Donatello.[27] In addition, the work's challenge to artistic authority, wrought by highlighting the natural course of organic growth, displays a perspective that connects Penone's work to the nascent post-modern discourses of its time.

Beyond the realm of aesthetics, might Penone's sculptures also point to the values of society at the time of their making? That is, by simultaneously highlighting the natural course of organic growth and reducing the prominence of the artist's hand through casting, Penone's work calls into question the sociological drive to separate from and dominate nature that is at the root of industrial capitalism. By repudiating the presumed ontological distinction between Penone's body and the vegetables, works like *Zucche* and *Potatoes* connect to the non-binary, non-hierarchical ways of thinking that were prevalent in the social theory emerging from the political struggles of the 1960s and 1970s. When critics, such as Trini, were writing about Italian art in the late 1960s, the natural or cultural opposition later ascribed to Arte povera artists like Penone was aimed at shattering such binaries. Moreover, Trini claimed that this attitude was endemic to the artists working in Turin and reflected aspects of the city's contemporaneous social turmoil. "The sense of nature is such that the attitude of the artists towards nature and matter is marked with nonviolence, in contrast with the idea of domination through scientific conquest that Western thought traditionally exercises on these entities."[28] For Trini, the art of the period and its horizontal approach to materials corresponded to the anti-hierarchical aims of the social movements of the era, extending the relevance of artistic thinking about nature and culture to the pressing social issues of the day.

By the late 1970s, Turin was even more politically intense and socially stratified than it had been a decade prior, when Penone had first arrived. The strikes and demonstrations begun by students and spread to the city's many factories had changed in tenor. On the one hand, the seeds of revolution sown in the struggles of the late 1960s had metastasized into a nightmare of extremism and violence on both ends of the political spectrum. On the other hand, the intellectual aspects of the workerist movements of the 1950s–1960s had blossomed into new theoretical approaches like the post-Marxist *Autonomia organizzata* (Organized Autonomy), which proposed to revolutionize class struggle through the collective recognition of sovereignty for each individual. In this climate, which will be sketched more fully in the subsequent chapter, decisions either to take action or to passively resist, to submit to labour or to refuse to work, were real choices with divisive implications. Thus, when Penone rhetorically levels the distinction between industrial work and agricultural work, or when his objects compare his efforts in the studio to those of the farmer in the field, he is wading into the contemporaneous debates about labour.

Indeed the processes of sowing, tending, and harvesting indicate the anonymity of certain forms of labour, in contrast to the singularity ascribed to artistic labours. Penone further employs casting, which is a seemingly objective, indexical mode of artistic production. Making a cast is a way of arriving at a form without the expressive connotations of fine art making, and, simultaneously, it is deeply rooted in sculptural traditions.[29] Penone has called it a way to make a "democratic" image, and his use of natural forms rather than cultural ones redoubles this aspect of accessibility. In works like *Vase, Clay Breath, Potatoes,* and *Zucche*, casting also problematizes the politics of exchange values in relation to human labour. While indirect by comparison to the kinds of political theories and violent actions that pervaded Torinese society during these years, the way in which Penone negotiates his own productive power through casting organic materials can be read as similarly challenging authority on ethical grounds. The latent and poetic connections to Turin's labour movements are legible even in the way one talks about the process of casting: the body *gives* form to the plaster, or a cast is *taken* from a part of the body. In works like *Potatoes* and *Zucche*, the cast partially redistributes to the growing vegetable the locus of agency with regard to form and iconographic meaning. The play between assertion and renunciation of artistic agency represented in the sculptural tradition of casting is precisely what Trini identified as contrasting with the Western ethos of domination. It models, in short, an anti-authoritative, distributed way of understanding society and human experience, arising from a network of associations between bodies and things.

The hierarchic division of persons from things that Penone challenges through such works is not confined to the specificities of labour, be it artistic, agricultural, or industrial. Indeed the power generated by this dichotomy is so pervasive that it can be traced to European society's earliest origins and most enduring forms: the ageless association of war with plunder; Roman law that codified a person as someone with dominion over things and objectified beings; or John Locke's enlightened definition of personhood as ownership over oneself.[30] Italian philosopher Roberto Esposito argues that the only way to unravel the logic of this split, which remains at the root of capitalism, is to approach it from the point of view of the body, which has long oscillated between the seemingly exclusive categories of person and thing. He traces the perpetuation of the divide throughout history and along a rational philosophical lineage from Descartes to Kant. He also offers an alternative trajectory through Spinoza and Vico, who saw reason as a construction, towards Husserl, Merleau-Ponty, and Sartre, whose respective focuses on the perceiving body demonstrated that it could not be reduced to either subject or object.

For Esposito, recognizing that the body binds together humans and things has ethical consequences. He cautions, for instance, that rational models elevating personhood beyond the body always threaten to reduce the body to the station of things. Throughout history this dark side of reason has been appallingly realized in colonialism and slavery, as well as in the Fascist and Nazi policies of the early twentieth century. The strikes and protests pervading Italian society in the 1970s might also be traced to the way in which such rationalism had infected Cold War capitalism, objectifying labouring bodies. Like Michel Foucault, whose writings form the basis for a biopolitical methodology, Esposito recognizes the body as the subject and object of power. It is the point of connection between human beings and things, as well as the point of resistance to the dialectic that has traditionally divided the two.[31] Even altering the way one talks about the body can disrupt this dichotomous paradigm. For instance, when Sartre suggests that it would be proper to say "I exist my body," rather that "my body exists," he argues for a radical and inextricable link between the body and the concept of self.[32] Through their demonstration of the agency of organic matter over artistic intention, artworks like *Pumpkins* and *Potatoes* perform the same shift that Sartre seeks by suggesting the use of *to exist* as a transitory verb. They grow the body as sculpture. The aim of Esposito's account is to foreground the urgency of such alternative perspectives in order to remake the social, economic, and political institutions that are built upon false logic. Seen through this lens, the importance of Penone's work lies in the fact that in probing the ontology of sculpture, he approaches the philosophical split between persons and things from a corporeal, material perspective. His works' material relationship with the body make them physical demonstrations that challenge the illusory separation at the core of modern experience.

Nature as Sculpture

Penone's 1980 retrospective exhibition at the Stedelijk Museum in Amsterdam offered him the chance to consider, holistically, the theoretical aspects of a decade of mature work and to take a new perspective on the fundamental questions of his practice. It included all of the main works discussed in this chapter, as well eight *Alberi* (*Trees*, 1969–75), an exaggerated tool-cum-sculpture called *Zappa* (*Hoe*, 1979), and the contribution to the previous Biennale discussed in chapter 2, *Palpebre* (*Eyelids*, 1978). One thing that must have been clear was the continuous counterpoint between active and passive engagement of the body and material, because after this exhibition Penone began work on a sculpture that clearly refigured the relationship between sculptor and material by directly comparing his own toil to that of nature.

Essere Fiume I (*To Be a River I*, 1981) consists of two nearly identical stones set side by side (figure 3.17).[33] One of the stones was extracted from a river without further alteration. The artist did little to this stone, akin to a readymade, but transfer it from one location to another, or, put another way, he moved it from the natural context of the riverbank to the cultural context of the art gallery. Here is one possible definition of the role of the sculptor: he provides a new concept for a thing or material by shepherding it from one physical and ideological location to another. The object is changed by his most basic interaction with it: inserting it into the discourse of "sculpture" and the economy of the art market. Such Duchampian moves are among the fundamental tenets of international art of the 1960s and 1970s, evident in such salient examples as Richard Long's *Walking* series, Marcel Broodthaers' *Museum of Modern Art*, and Robert Smithson's *Non-sites*. This first stone seems to argue that the work of the sculptor is conceptual, rather than physical. Penone's work, however, is about more than exposing the

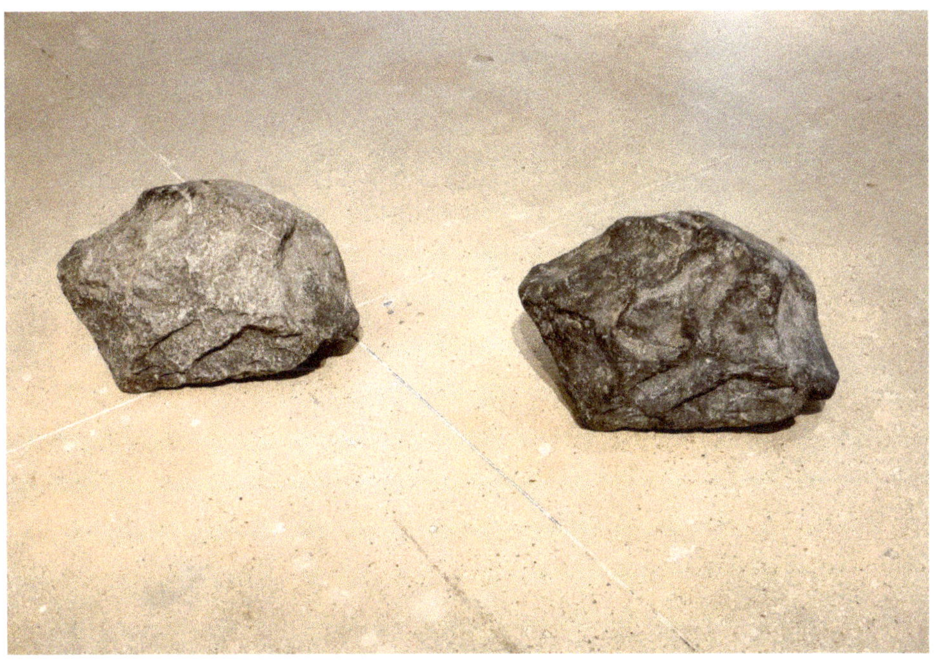

3.17 Giuseppe Penone, *Essere Fiume I* (*To Be a River I*), 1981. Two elements: one river stone, one quarry stone; approx. 40 x 40 x 50 cm each.

Photograph: © Archvio Penone

limiting locations of art's frames or even the fragmentary nature of representation.

To Be a River I, after all, consists of *two* stones, the second of which was painstakingly carved by hand to copy, with the utmost precision, every detail of the first stone. Penone sets them together, in close proximity, to emphasize the difficulty of distinguishing one stone from the other. Thus, the viewer is asked to equate the work of the sculptor with that of the river, and the tools of the sculptor with those of nature. This is tactically similar to Long's *Walking* series but manifestly distinct from the work of Latvian-American artist Vija Celmins, who in 1968 cast several small stones in bronze and painted each to be indistinguishable from its original. By using paint, Celmins demonstrates the way in which artistic intervention can cover up the differences between nature and culture, which nevertheless remain distinct. Penone's work, conversely, reveals the fundamental connection between his artistic labour and natural forces.[34]

To Be a River I posits a physical integration of matter that is contrary to the separation wrought by linguistic structures that separate "persons" from "things," or reality from its representations. The work compels the viewer to recognize the conceptual revolution latent in the material world. If the active work of sculpting the first stone was done by a river – its water flowing over the rock, wearing it down, lobbing all manner of flotsam against its surface for years, centuries, or even millennia – then the sculptor's tools used on the second stone are merely a means to hasten these processes. What is a chisel if not an instrument to widen a crack in the stone faster than many seasons of freezing and thawing would do? A piece of sandpaper is, in essence, a tool that approximates the suspended silt of the river.[35] The discursive composition of *To Be a River I*, with each of its two elements forming the context for the other, highlights the interlocution between the usually separated "natural" and "cultural" processes through which each stone came into form. Exhibiting the two stones together emphasizes the reciprocal link between concept and craft, or persons and things, as well as the confluence of nature with the culture that attempts to replicate its processes.

For Penone, the tension produced by the near inability to distinguish one stone from the other in this work was its most successful aspect because it challenged the false distinction between nature and culture.[36] "To extract a stone sculpted by the river, to travel upstream and discover the exact point from which the stone came and extract another piece of rock from the mountain and duplicate exactly the stone taken from the river is to be the river; producing a stone of stone is perfect sculpture."[37] As he writes, sculpture tautologically confirms the nature of its production as contact between forces that act upon and against each other to varying degrees. Moreover, if one accepts that water has sculpted the stone from the riverbank, then one must also recognize that the stones and silt of the riverbank reciprocally condition the very flow of the river.[38] Not only are the two facets inseparable, but they are entangled in a relationship that also draws in global patterns of weather, human industry and interferences, and encounters with animals, minerals, and vegetables. This kind of thinking may seem obvious, but the "activity" of things is often overlooked until a stone comes loose or a river exceeds its banks. Penone's sculpture offers viewers an opportunity to radically reconsider their place in the material world.

Recently, curator Didier Semin reflected on how Penone's earlier river piece – *Maritime Alps: My Height, the Length of My Arms, My Breadth Set into a Brook* (1967–8, figs. 1.3–5) – reveals the continuity of man and nature. He argues that the action and its documentation invite the viewer to consider that the human body carries the same water as the brook does and is made of the same minerals suspended in it. "It is only by virtue of a tiny percentage of something else that we can look down on that stream with such condescension. It is this percentage that invented the *cogito*, war and the mobile phone."[39] Semin's argument identifies the ways in which Penone's works link the human and the non-human – the artistic and the organic. Like Trini did thirty years before, Semin nods to the social implications of this connection. Ignoring the connections between nature and culture, or amplifying the differences between humans and their surroundings, perpetuates the social and environmental crises of the post-war period. These are challenges that still face us in the twenty-first century, making Penone's work all the more relevant.

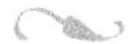

By foregrounding the reciprocity of the relationship between people and things, and by putting the material world on the equal footing with the human body, works like Penone's *Breath*, *Potatoes*, *Zucche*, and *To Be a River I* deny stark oppositions and imbalances of power that on a larger scale might lead to tribalism, conflict, and abuse. This may sound like an exaggeration, especially as Penone often eschews the limitations that direct political readings might place on his work, but the way in which his works break with a binary way of thinking about artistic subjectivity has the potential to revolutionize one's world view beyond the sphere of art. Indeed, as early as 1971 the artist wrote that the political value of any work of art was that it could allow different perspectives on the self and the world: "The ability to identify with or have yourself be identified with the forms and objects that surround us is one of the reasons for the work of art. The work of art is capable of identifying, of encapsulating the values of an individual and indirectly of the society in which the individual participates."[40] Although one rarely finds Penone mentioning politics so directly, here he argues that the ontology of art is at least partially social. Just as Esposito argues for a new philosophical model of personhood through the body interpellated by things, Penone's works and writings suggest that sculptures are things through which humans can think, communicate, and identify. By highlighting the reciprocity of artistic action with the workings of the natural world, his artworks beseech viewers to distribute their thinking across a material world that is their equal.

This critical stance on the impact of Penone's work builds on the biopolitics of Esposito and positions it as prefiguring a particular vein of twenty-first-century thought known as thing theory. Crossing many disciplinary boundaries, from anthropology and art history to psychology and physics, one of the central concepts to emerge from the theories of human-thing relationships is that while modernism posits the individual as dominant over the things of the world, postmodernism takes an anti-anthropocentric position by merit of its refusal to draw such stark binaries between humans and things. One important aspect of many such "neo-materialist" models is that they do not merely invert a naturalist view of human-material relationships (for example, they do not claim that humans are passively shaped by the things of the world); rather they seek to reveal the complex, ongoing intertwining of agency between humans and things. In the eponymous 2001 journal essay that introduced the term *thing theory* as a facet of literary theory, Bill Brown charted the ways in which the effort to rethink "things" could lead one to reimagine the very form of human society. He wrote that the indeterminacy implied by the word "things" meant that they "hover over the threshold between the nameable and the unnameable, the figurable and the unfigurable, the identifiable and the unidentifiable."[41] The ambiguity indicated by the category "things" is valuable because, for Brown, it indexes ways of thinking beyond dominant models.

In his 2005 book *Beyond Nature and Culture*, Philippe Descola also argued against such binaries, denigrating them as relics of the modernist mindset. For him, one of the values of the postmodern was its alignment with permeable boundaries, beyond such narrow limits. He maintained that the nature-culture divide was not universal; rather, it reflected the reductive ethnocentricity of (Western) modernism: "other people's worlds do not revolve around ours."[42] Moving beyond such binary thinking towards uncertainty, ambiguity, and liminality shatters the power relations endemic to the idea of production as the imposition of human will on inert matter. By razing the qualitative discrepancy between the creator and what they produce, such non-binary theoretical models – whether one calls them *thing theory*, *actor network theory*, or *new materialism* – step outside the rigidity of structuralism to open spaces characterized instead by fluidity, dependency, and interpolation.[43]

In an attempt to bridge even these wide theories, Hodder's notion of *entanglement* may be most relevant to reading the complexity of Penone's investigation of human and material interaction. Hodder argues that entanglement avoids subject-object or material-ideal splits because the core of the theory is that everything is mixed together with equivalent values at different times: humans, things, technologies, culture, matter, society, and so on. Most importantly, Hodder upholds that entanglement is not simply a "new materialism," because human-thing dependences and dependencies are embedded within social and historical contexts.[44] Recognizing previously invisible alignments and relationships provides new perspectives on the structures that already govern power and agency.[45]

If one reads Penone's reversals and complications of his own agency in works of the later 1970s as speaking to the kind of entanglement of which Hodder would later write, it allows one to refute the overly biographic readings that have dominated Penone's work since the period in question. Whereas Celant submitted that Penone's attitude towards nature functions as "a recognition of the archetypes and as the unresolved conflict of a primitive phylogeny," applying the concept of entanglement to the natural materials and processes that pervade the artist's work allows an alternative focus on the way in which the agency of things partakes of a distinctly postmodern attitude. The value of reading Penone's work in this manner is not merely to give it new labels. There is an ethics inherent to this integrated understanding of the self and the phenomenal world in that it might affect one's actions in other spheres. Art does not have to focus on a political issue to have a political impact. Like this chapter's initial example of two hands touching, the most groundbreaking sculpture may be a simple demonstration that alters the way we think about something as fundamental as our own bodies.

As do the two stones that form *To Be a River I*, many of Penone's works demonstrate that the actions of humans *and* the actions of things give form to our experiences. The point is not to puzzle out which is the natural stone and which is the worked stone, nor is it to recognize a specific human face in a potato or a pumpkin. Rather, the meaning of such works comes from the ability, acquired through the viewing of the works, to identify the human body, which we know, and a mineral or plant, which is beyond the body, as equally important parts of the material world. Each of these works uses nature to demonstrate that what the artist does is akin to the processes of nature and, simultaneously, that there is something akin to culture in the relationship among the materials and the forces of nature. This point of view both raises the value of nature and de-aggrandizes the status of the artist. In Penone's works of the later 1970s and early 1980s, one's breath is a material, a river is a sculptor, and a sculpture is a plant. His investigation into the entangled relationship between humans and things via the reciprocity of the tactile delineates the fundamentally non-hierarchical, post-structuralist aspect of his working theory of sculpture. In this horizontal, anti-anthropocentric model, one's perspective on the roles of active and passive, and who or indeed what occupies them, is entirely dependent on the perspective through which the work is considered.

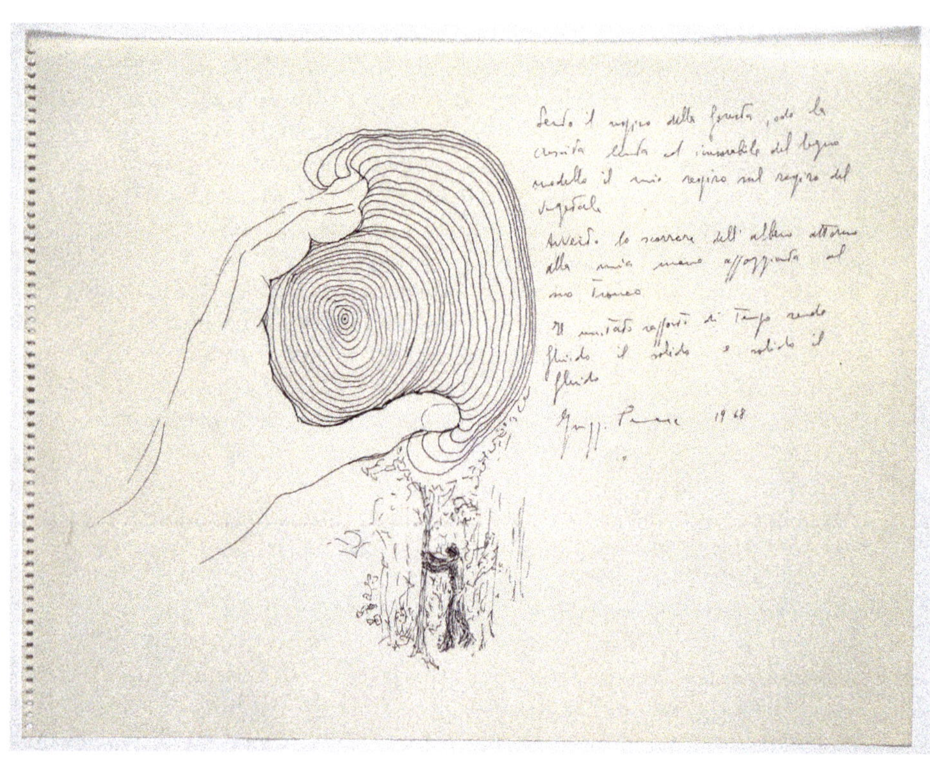

4.1 Giuseppe Penone, *Sento il respiro della foresta (I Hear the Breath of the Forest)*, 1968. China-ink on paper, 30 x 40 cm.

Photograph: © Archivio Penone

4
Tempus Arborus (Tree Time)

Individual things conceive and measure time with their existential, biological rhythms, of formation and existence. The concept of time a butterfly has, or a flower, a tree, an animal, a man, a stone, a mountain, a river, a sea, a continent, an atom, produces the infinite variety of thought and forms of the universe.

– Giuseppe Penone, *Writings*

In a 1968 sketch Penone imagined how one of his *Maritime Alps* actions would appear in the future (figure 4.1). The ink-on-paper drawing presents a cross-section of *It Will Continue to Grow except at That Point* – the tree to which he had recently attached a cast of his hand. The futurity of the projection is visually marked by the depicted growth rings, the distortions of which quantify precisely the number of years that the tree would have been in contact with the surrogate hand. This predictive drawing, titled *Sento il repiro della foresta* (*I Hear the Breath of the Forest*), is heavily inscribed. The handwritten text includes the following line: "*Il mutato rapporto di tempo rende fluido il solido e solido il fluido*" (The altered sense of time renders fluid that which is solid and solid that which is fluid). This notation is evidence that in Penone's ontology of sculpture any solid material can be considered fluid and malleable when viewed over an extended period of time. The artist's work with trees, in particular, hinges on this rumination: they reveal the differences between the familiar rhythms of a human lifespan and the radically different cadences of other types of organic matter.

Penone has persistently wrestled with the ways in which time and temporal perspective affect the structures of experience. This principle spans his entire career, commencing in the artist's rejection of figurative representation, continuing alongside his probing of the tactile over the visual, and maturing in his works' counterpoint between the active and the passive roles of an artist. Seen together, the varied parts of his oeuvre demonstrate that a deep attention to the material aspects of sculpture provides the means through which one can conceptually inhabit alternative temporal perspectives and, accordingly, adopt potentially radical points of view.

In 1972 Penone wrote about the effectiveness of art that provoked conceptual shifts in one's concept of time. It had, he argued, the potential to change one's view of other systems and structures of society: "The condition for better grasping the reality of the growing tree / and its fluidity is a different concept of time. / Our adherence to the tree's action presupposes / a changed interpretation of reality. / This condition projects us into a new imagination, / dense with unusual forms and sensations. / If one of the functions of art is the continuous reinterpretation of reality, / changing the concept of time puts us in a position to revise / and recreate the conditions of the real / and allows us to imagine new forms with new values."[1]

What are the new values to which Penone refers in this text? Why might he have believed that it was critical to adopt a different concept of time at that moment and in that place? One of the main outcomes of the entanglement of the self and the world demonstrated by Penone's projects of the 1960s and 1970s is the ability to imagine the world from alternative points of view – from the perspective of "things." His statement proposes that such a reorientation to the tactile sense, and attention to the activity of the material world, is part of a larger project of challenging the dominant, Western concept of time as well as the structures of social control that flow from it.

Time as the subject and primary motivator of the work of art is seen in much Italian art of the 1960s, from Boetti's *Annual Lamp* to exhibitions like Palazzoli's *Con temp l'azione* (*With Time, Action/Contemplation*). Among the works of Penone's contemporaries, Anselmo's *Senza titolo: Struttura che mangia* (*Untitled: Eating Structure*, 1968) indicates a distinct temporality through its need to be refreshed, or risk the dissolution of its formal tension. Similarly, Zorio's *Senza titolo: Piombi* (*Untitled: Leads, 1969*) changes visible form over time as hydrochloric acid and copper sulfate crystallize on a copper bridge that connects two leaden basins filled with the liquids. It has already been mentioned that Penone exhibited six of the *Maritime Alps* photographs in his first group show at Sperone in May 1969. What is less known about Penone's contribution is that he also stamped the walls with the number "8046," a seemingly random figure, which in fact corresponded to the sum of days the artist had been alive at the time of its inscription on the linocut matrix.[2] The show put the works of Penone in physical proximity to those of other artists of his milieu, and this temporal intervention marked his own distinct position within this generation.

Among the Torinese subset of Arte povera, Penone, Anselmo, and Zorio are precisely those cited by critic Tommaso Trini as being the most adept at extending the duration of the work of art by programming the object to change over time or by devising visible means of marking time through the work. Written in 1973, "Anselmo, Penone, Zorio e le nuove fonte d'energia per il deserto dell'arte" (Anselmo, Penone, Zorio and the new sources of energy in the desert of art) is a repudiation of curator Achille Bonito Oliva over the conspicuous absence of these three artists from his recent exhibition, *Contemporanea*. Trini argues that these artists are essential to contemporaneous conversations because their art provides an experience of space and time that is distinct from that of everyday life.

More subtly, the critic proposes that such works affirm that art can indicate life, or the social realm, through the careful acceptance of its fundamental materiality.[3] Trini claims, essentially, that the way these artists marshal the inherent properties of their materials and use them to anticipate future states and formal possibilities provides new and potentially radical energy to cultural discourse: "It is here then that the solicitations and the stimuli in which Penone, Zorio, and Anselmo work, that they expand in space and time, no longer only metaphorically, subtend the search to bring *new energy to the criticism* of existence (existence of art, existence of truth, no longer split, the conflict is elevated to the level of freedom against necessity). They are not even further on the side of art, but on its material and mental borders, where they reach for new sources of energy such as systematic tensions, revealed contradictions, explicit depreciation – materialized in objects."[4] Trini recognizes these artists' sculptures as radical departures from the ideal, a-temporal traditions of painting. While still distinct from the everyday, their works open up phenomenological time and space by offering views to the socio-cultural conditions of art's making and reception. As the critic asserts, Anselmo, Penone, and Zorio create objects that depart from the individually expressive roles prescribed for art and artist in order to investigate factors, like time, that structure human perception and experience itself.

Art's engagement with human measures of time was, of course, an issue that pervaded many international artistic tendencies of the period. Analysing this tendency in its broader socio-political contexts, art historian Pamela M. Lee argues that a general anxiety over the relative speed of post-war life, brought on by advances in information-age technology, was expressed in art of the 1960s as a crisis of time (fear of, lack of, etc.). Although Lee does not discuss Arte povera in her 2003 book *Chronophobia*, she maintains that the extended duration of much sixties art – ranging from Warhol's experimental films and Op Art to the Minimalist "object" and Kinetic art – results from there being little time to reflect on the present under everyday conditions.[5] Synthesizing the arguments made by prominent critics of the 1960s and 1970s, Lee charts the means by which art can provide the space and time for such reflection by extending the duration of the work.

In particular, Lee's assessment of the Japanese artist On Kawara connects most fruitfully to reading Penone's complex engagement with time as politically and culturally relevant. In Kawara's documentation of lived experience through cultural constructions of time and space, Lee reads the location of historical meaning in the important, combinative play between geohistorical time (slow, almost imperceptible, glacial change), social time (centring on cultures and societies), and individual time (discrete individual events). She argues that the artist responds in the only way that one can in the face of postmodern conditions: "It is an ethic of slowness and commitment, as if to bear unflagging witness to its endlessly accelerating projections."[6] For Kawara, this happens by harnessing civic systems of documentation like newspapers, maps, telegrams, and postal mail. Penone's approach is similarly grounded in his own experience, but it is not connected to social circuits of distribution. Instead, it is characterized by an interpolation of "human time" with natural models like "river time," "stone time," and, most enduringly, "tree time." His tactics reveal a hastening of postmodern velocity as merely one limited, anthropocentric perspective.

Penone's works with trees provide the means to inhabit conceptually the temporality of other organic materials, which, in turn, offers infinite opportunities to reconsider the structures of human experience in other ways. Not unlike the human body, trees carry marks of what they have encountered over time. For the tree such inscription is most often visible (on the trunk, in the rings, by the thrust of its branches), while for the body these marks can remain invisible (psychological, intellectual, and even sensory). In Penone's lexicon of sculpture, the sculptor occupies a position somewhere between these two poles, carrying fleshy scars and invisible psychological indexes of experience and simultaneously making durable marks on the material world through the practice of sculpture. Like other works in his oeuvre, the tree-centred works upend the presumed hierarchy between sculptor and material, reconfiguring it as a complex entanglement of reciprocity, the legibility of which is enhanced by shifts in the temporal frame.

The previous chapters of this book have demonstrated that Penone's art aligns with aspects of phenomenology and its reception in other disciplines. Particular attention has been paid to the way Penone's sculpture engages the body, problematizing the paradox of the modernist dominance of vision and its simultaneous emphasis on gesture. This connects to the writings of Merleau-Ponty, in which vision is always considered perspectival because it is embodied. That is, when one sees an object, one takes up a position in space (sometimes both literally and figuratively) from which to view it, temporarily eliminating other possible perspectives.[7] This projection of the physical onto the visual is what Merleau-Ponty argues constructs, in each case, a "horizon" against which each perception occurs. In relief with such a horizon, an object retains its identity – it seems to be stable – while we investigate it from different perspectives.

Merleau-Ponty's concept of the horizon, however, also implies that because visual perception is embodied, it is not just spatial and haptic but also temporal. Each perspective one takes has duration. It is through the experience of the body as something with a particular time and space (it is not an absolute) that one understands that the world and the objects of the world are also not absolute, fixed, or stable. Rosalind Krauss brings this concept into the realm of art history in her 1977 book *Passages on Modern Sculpture,* in which she argues that one of sculpture's defining characteristics in the late nineteenth and early twentieth centuries was its tension between "time arrested and time passing."[8] For her, the contemporaneous development of modern sculpture, phenomenology, and structural linguistics is meaningful in that it allows three distinct ways to understand the "complex manifestations of a modern sensibility."[9] Her study concludes with a chapter on American sculpture of the 1960s, the obdurate objecthood of which demonstrates the way that any sculpture depends on the viewer's engagement. She argues that the works of artists like Donald Judd, Robert Morris, and Richard Serra, by breaking with the idealism of modernist precepts, provide the means to see that the self is equally fragmentary and conditional.

The present analysis of Penone's works with trees similarly departs from the modernist paradigm, having argued that the contingency of phenomenology extends it towards a postmodern paradigm through its negotiation of self and world from the perspective of things. Merleau-Ponty's writings on the concept of "wild being" offer one possible origin point of this philosophical trajectory. In this late elaboration of his own theories of the spatio-temporal aspects of perception, the philosopher contends that to know the world is to perceive it – as indeed we must – from the inside, from our experience of the world. To know an object, then, one must be immersed in it as animals are, and perhaps as our premodern ancestors were wrapped up in the sensory world. This perspectival dislocation may also mean accepting an object's different registers of temporality. When Penone's sculptures draw together trees and human bodies, they initiate a comparison between one's spatio-temporal knowledge of one's own body and the tree's experience or, more speculatively, its knowledge. In particular, by demonstrating that both registers are constructions when seen from within the perspective of each material body, or on a geological timescale, such works provide access to immersive perspectives on the material world that have the potential to re-establish our ethical engagement with it.

The present chapter explores the extended duration of Penone's tree-centred works as a potentially radical destructuring of the temporal dimensions of perception. Accordingly, it is not continuous with the roughly chronological trajectory of the previous chapters. Rather, it runs parallel to chapters 1–3, and it exceeds them, tracing the evocation of temporal shifts through Penone's work with trees over more than five decades. As is true of many artists, Penone does not just pick up ideas, work with them, and drop them. In fact, his career is marked by its reiterative nature, in which he returns to familiar tactics, imagery, and themes with new energy and continues to push his investigation of the material foundations of sculpture in new directions. Encompassing decades of his work, this chapter therefore allows a view into the depth of Penone's engagement with wood as a material and with trees as a subject.

This focus also offers a view to Penone's investigation of time as simultaneously progressive, continuous, and recursive. That is, his works with time are not just future oriented, ongoing, or archaeological. The fact that each work persists in the time and space of the viewer means that at whatever point in time it is encountered, it indicates a future, a present, and a past. The range must be considered as part of the work, complicating easy readings of Penone's use of natural materials as anti-technological, or the broader idea of Arte povera as an art of "poor materials."[10] It also challenges the rapid consumption of images and objects to which twenty-first-century viewers have become accustomed. Instead, extended encounters, material delays, and continued entreaties to take shifting perspectives through the material and the phenomenological are the means by which Penone constructs his ontology of sculpture and disseminates a radical perspective on the socio-political and ethical potential of conscious human activity.

Autonomous Trees

Penone has continued to make excavated or recovered *Trees* throughout his career, but looking in depth at the formation of the series in its first decades helps us identify its initial concerns. Beginning in 1969 and continuing throughout the 1970s, the temporal interpolation of self and world emerges most clearly through a series of sculptures in which Penone recovers the form of a tree from a beam of wood. These objects mine an infinitely thin distinction between trees as organisms and wood as material. In many such works with trees, the plant is treated as an equivalent to the body, not in an anthropomorphic sense of seeing the body reflected in nature, but rather in the sense of recognizing trees as material equivalents to the human body. A plant is a force, as the artist has remarked, against which he could measure his own agency.[11] At times, the tree-body connection is metaphoric: leaves as the tree's eyes, which absorb light; bark as the tree's skin, which protects its flesh; and sap as the tree's lymphatic fluid, which runs through the organism. In other cases, the relationship between the tree and the body is cast in equally poetic, yet specifically temporal terms that serve to further investigate the material and tactical means of sculpture.

His/Its Being in the Twenty-Second Year of Life at a Fantastic Hour (1969), discussed in this book's introduction, was among the first of what might be described as Penone's recovered-tree sculptures (figure 0.1).[12] This early example also makes explicit the temporal aspect of the subsequent tree sculptures because it reveals the form of the tree as it would have looked at the age that the artist was at the time of its making. This means that if the piece of lumber he selected had thirty-five visible growth rings in its cross-section, the artist carved away the pulp of the outermost thirteen, avoiding the knots left from stunted branches, to arrive at a "tree" with twenty-two growth rings, or an approximation of what the tree looked like when it was twenty-two years old. Thus, the artist and the sculpture would share a certain synchronicity for about a year, at which point the artist would continue to age, and the carved piece of wood would remain frozen in time. Penone devised numerous ways to measure his own life and activity against the age of a tree during the ensuing decade, continuing to "excavate" trees from milled beams or to conflate rubbings of wooden surfaces – parquet floor, decorative panels, raw subfloor – with numbers corresponding to the number of days he had been alive.[13] Through such works Penone began to explore a means to complicate an anthropocentric conception of time by materially and poetically conflating the tree and his own body.

In 1969 he also made *Albero di 4 metri* (*Four-Metre Tree*), two versions of *Albero di 6 metri* (*Six-Metre Tree*), and one *Albero di 8 metri* (*Eight-Metre Tree*). Just as the titles of these works refer to the size of the beam of wood from which each was carved – indeed this is how one might purchase such lumber, by the metre – they also indicate a temporal computation of human labour. That is, the work involved in making these trees depended on the size of the beam, in addition to other factors like the type of wood. This tactic has a distinct resonance with the investigations of art and labour pioneered by Situationist artist Giuseppe Pinot-Gallizio, also working near Turin, who most famously sold his monotyped and gestural paintings by the metre as a critique of artistic aura.[14] With such works, Pinot-Gallizio demonstrated that traditional notions of artistic making and even the expressive connotations of gesture were susceptible to the stultifying reach of industrial capitalism. Penone's early *Trees* similarly juxtapose the artist's conceptual work with the quantitative appraisals of manufacturing.

In 1970 Penone undertook the largest tree that he had until then attempted and charted its coming into form in terms of his own labour. When invited to exhibit at *Aktionsraum 1* in Munich – an alternative space for experimental art founded the previous year by Eva Madelung, Peter Nemetschek, and Alfred Gulden – Penone proposed to make *Albero di dodici metri* (*Twelve-Metre Tree*, 1970).[15] As befitted the unconventional but evocative venue (an empty factory) Penone planned to make the tree on site, its size ultimately determined by maximizing the dimensions of the space in which it would be both made and shown. These self-imposed limits foregrounded the time-based process of making the work and also drew attention to the ways in which the physical and cultural aspects of a space permit certain kinds of labour. In a statement to the German art periodical *Interfunktionen*, Penone related the making of this particular work as the product of his own quantifiable days and work hours, all aimed at reversing and fixing the perception of the temporality of the material: "I will carry out an action, which lasts 15 to 20 days. I'll be returning a wooden board to the days when it was a tree, and to a specific age in the tree's past, which I will determine on site. Every day I work 2 to 4 hours because it is in a space of about 12 x 4 m. On the day when the trunk has again become young, I'll leave."[16] Penone here describes his time as dedicated to making an inert industrial material – a wooden board – regain some of its natural appearance, transfigured again into a "trunk" that has a specific age.

The importance of process begins to unfold in this text and is emphasized by the images printed on the adjoining pages. Of the four

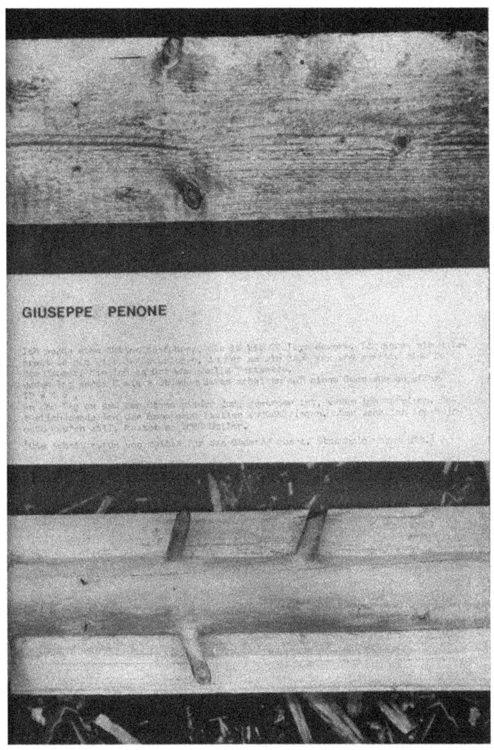

GIUSEPPE PENONE

4.2 Giuseppe Penone, *Albero di dodici metri* (*Twelve-Metre Tree*), 1970 (detail). Wood, 25 x 25 x 1,213 cm. Title page of article on Penone and photo documentation of the work's making at *Aktionsraum 1*, Munich, 1970, published in *Interfunktionen* 5 (1970): 143–6. Original photographs by Peter Nemetschek.

Photograph: Elizabeth Mangini

magazine pages dedicated to Penone's project, only one shows the full finished state of the artwork. The title page of the photo-essay, however, displays details of the before and after states of the work, which are used as a design element framing the artist's statement (figure 4.2). On close inspection one can see two knots in the wood just to the left of the board's midpoint (*above*), which become the branches of the carved tree sculpture (*below*). Rarely do viewers get such a clear, diagrammatic revelation of the journey from beam to tree in the literature on Penone's trees. On the subsequent three pages of images the laborious process required for this transformation comes into sharp focus.

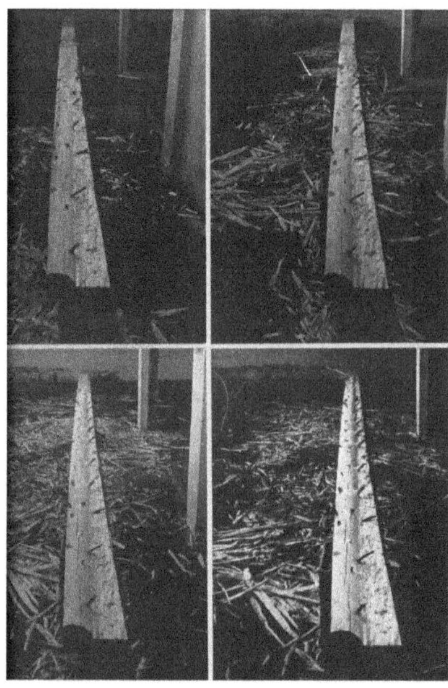

4.3 (above) and 4.4 (opposite) Giuseppe Penone, *Albero di dodici metri* (*Twelve-Metre Tree*), 1970. Wood, 25 x 25 x 1,213 cm. Article on Penone and photo documentation of the work's making at *Aktionsraum 1*, Munich, 1970, published in *Interfunktionen* 5 (1970): 143–6. Original photographs by Peter Nemetschek.

Photograph: Elizabeth Mangini

The next page is a full bleed image of the rectilinear beam (25 x 25 x 1,213 cm) sitting atop four regularly spaced milk crates. (In the far left background of the industrial space, Penone's *Alphabet* photographs appear, tacked on a wall near a microphone and speaker, a reminder of the informality of the combination work and exhibition space.) The facing page in the magazine reprints four individual photographs of the beam at various stages throughout the carving process (figure 4.3). In each panel the "tree" comes further into view, and the floor is increasingly carpeted with wood chips and shavings. Flipping to the fourth page, one sees a final image of the finished *Twelve-Metre Tree* depicted by itself in a sparse industrial room that has been cleared of all tools and remnants of the carving process (figure 4.4). The sculpture is a horizontal monument to the combined labours of the growing tree and the living artist, both labours having now come to an end. The resultant object no longer reads as the same order of thing as the wooden post that, as part of the architecture of the industrial space,

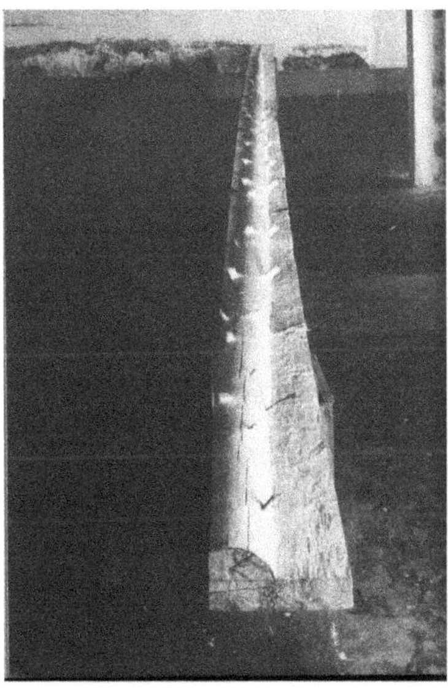

stands sentry at the distant right in all of these images. The serial aspect of these published images of *Twelve-Metre Tree* communicates the importance of the physical, temporal engagement of body and material – that is, the labour – within Penone's developing concept of sculpture, but the object itself carries indicators of the same concerns.

Here Penone's labour effectively documents itself, and it also reveals the tree's past work to overcome and adapt to physical encounters with other organisms, objects, and forces. This is evident in the way the work highlights the sculptural process, as well as in traces of the tree's previous organic life. On first glance the viewer instantly reads a "tree," but on closer inspection it is evident that, as with all the recovered or excavated trees that Penone would make during nearly five decades of his practice, this *Twelve-Metre Tree* does not entirely return to its organic silhouette. The tree as sculpture remains in a state *between* beam and tree. That is, Penone's precise carving allows the viewer to perceive the object fluidly – to read two distinct forms in one object. In the "final" image the surface of the sculpture that faces the ceiling reads as a figure in relief: a smooth trunk and stunted branches rise from a ground that remains rough with visible tool marks. The carved figure may initially appear "natural," but the ground signals the laborious "cultural" process by which this tree was made. Furthermore, except for a small section at the lower left, the sides and bottom of the beam appear to retain right angles, their rectilinear shape forming a frame or base that can only be man-made. Penone also indicates the directionality of the growing plant, which only later became his *Twelve-Metre Tree*, through a slight movement as the core of the trunk shifts from far left to centre near the top. Finally, the tree's growth rings emanate from a centre point within the square surface that faces the camera, along with traces of a stamped or branded number. The growth rings connote a unique organic form in nature, while the number denotes its investiture in an industrial inventory.

Taken together, these signs indicate a conflict between the perception of the "tree" as a living organism and the perception of the wooden beam as inert material. The only resolution can be found in accepting the material and conceptual fluidity of things like trees, wood, and sculptures. That is, over time, this same organic matter has undergone a conceptual transformation: from tree, to wood, and now to an artwork, the material aspect of which the artist catalogues as a "wooden tree." Little attention is paid to this last detail of the work's archival registration, but it is of paramount importance because it points directly to the tautological character of these sculptures. That is, to call something a "wooden tree" seems like a redundancy or a poor translation from Italian to English. In this case, however, communicating through a tautology is precisely what the artist himself later reflected was one of the most powerful ways of working in the late 1960s and early 1970s.[17] Indeed, "wooden trees" like the one made in Munich insist on a conceptual doubling by retaining oppositional traces of both material states and both categorical assumptions – cultural and natural – in a single object.

Penone continued to explore the implications of the wooden-tree tautology throughout the 1970s, when labour issues were in the foreground of Italian politics and society and were especially palpable in Turin. Through these works the artist demonstrated the manner in which sculptures could present new ways of seeing the conflicts around labouring bodies that were omnipresent in the industrial region.[18] When he undertook another large tree sculpture in 1975, *Albero di undici metri* (*Eleven-Metre Tree*), Penone wrote in great detail about the arduous act of making the work (figure 4.5). Here the artist is straightforward about the impact of his choice of the material and the size of this work on the hours it would take him to carve the wooden tree. He also compares the not insignificant measure of his own effort to the vastly different scale of time it took the original tree to produce its form. The viewer, he notes, will consume the sum of these two generative forces in the blink of an eye. In order to give a sense of his own concept of the project, it is necessary to quote Penone at length:

> For 20 days every day, following a laborer's schedule, I work near Garessio, my town, in an abandoned shed; the fact that it is a former sawmill, while accidental, is significant; it is a place for working wood, there I work extracting from a beam, originally 11 meters long, 22 centimeters wide and 10 centimeters thick, the form of a tree that is fossilized within it. Of course everything made of wood was once a tree, and I could just as easily start with a door or a table leg; here I chose a beam because I needed a significant dimension.
>
> Technically, to give it back the appearance of a tree at a specific moment of its plant life, I must first establish where the top is, where the bottom is. I can determine this based on the growth rings, which correspond to the two layers always traceable in the wood, one denser, one softer. The base coincided with the hard, broader layer. From there I begin to dig and it suffices for me to continue scrupulously, following this harder layer, to recover the form of the tree. At this point I not only obtain a form, but I also have retraced the entire growth phenomenon, up to the moment when the hand of man, or who knows, an event of nature, arrested it. However while this process will have taken me about a month and whoever sees the finished work will spend a moment of visual perception, in reality it was originally a very long time. Thus I consider my work in a certain sense like a film sequence, shot in reverse and strongly sped up.
>
> The photographic documentation of its phases, three fundamentally: the initial beam; a moment when the still unfinished tree emerges from the beam; the tree restored to its form, becomes an explicative fundamental support; because for me the work lies in the process related phase, it is the relationship between the real time of growth and the personal time of "stripping away the bark."[19]

Three distinct points can be drawn from Penone's extended description of the project, which is itself only an excerpt of a longer statement. First, the artist considers the work to be invested in the concept of sculpture as a time-based endeavour in the sense of the material having its own temporality. Second, he is positing the sculpture as having a temporal relationship with the viewer who is experiencing the work. Third, the object requires of him an investment of time. This statement reveals his desire to show that the tautological object is distinctly tied to the complex process of the work's making: both the tree's growth and his carving. The perceptible traces of time and labour involved in making the form allowed Penone to frame this work in terms that would be instantly legible in the initial context in which it was received.

Given the recurrence of time and labour in Penone's work, it is worth pausing to consider in greater detail the context of both at the time these first trees were made and the early texts about them were written: in 1960s–1970s Italy. By the mid-1960s the nation's post-war economic recovery was unravelling, and organized labour began responding to the loss of jobs due to decreased demand and increased mechanization. Beginning in the late 1960s and codified in what became known as the "hot autumn" of 1969, the nation experienced a series of massive workers' strikes that threatened to seriously destabilize the economy and, by extension, the governing coalition. Numerous worker groups were formed to demonstrate collective power, and, tragically, violence became a common feature of many of the encounters between protesters and police. In Turin a prime example was the strike at a FIAT factory on 3 July 1969, which turned into a street fight known as the "Battle of Corso Traiano."[20] As many as 500,000 workers went on strike, occupying the city's streets. Before being beaten back by riot police, they set up roadblocks and torched a flatbed truck full of new automobiles leaving the Mirafiori factory.[21] Such clashes displayed a nascent shift in power claimed by Italian workers over their labour. As a highly industrialized city, Turin was central to this story.

By 1974, local, politicized coalitions of workers and intellectuals had largely replaced the influence of the big national unions. That year the widespread Autoreduction movement took hold in Turin, wherein consumers and workers collectively determined to reduce the price of public services. It was a form of protest against the way in which the government was understood to be colluding with large corporations and institutions in opposition to the interests of the labouring classes.[22] The following year, during which Penone made *Eleven-Metre Tree* and wrote the attendant text, was auspicious in the history of Italian post-war labour movements. For one thing, it was the year that former members of *Potere Operaio* – Toni Negri, Franco Pieperno, and Oresete Scalzone – formally initiated *Autonomia organizzata* as an extra-parliamentary group separate from the oversight of the traditional unions. When *Potere Operaio* had dissolved in 1974, these intellectuals and activists split away from a fringe, militarized faction that would later become the far-left terrorist organization the *Brigate Rosse* (Red Brigades).[23] With vastly different tactics, both groups aimed to infiltrate the factory floors of Turin's industrial giants. Time was, of course, central to these debates about labour.

Ownership of time, or autonomy over one's own time, was at the theoretical heart of *Autonomia organizzata* in particular. In his 1979 text "Dreamers of a Productive Life," Paolo Virno prescribes the ways in which autonomy for the labouring body can be achieved by expanding the ways in which time is considered: "Time is not always the empty and abstract index for assigning value, a unit of measure in itself. The simultaneous presence – and the rather haphazard combination – of a work as 'coordination' and 'supervision', together with embryonic elements of countereconomy, submission to the machine, or nomadism among many and various precarious activities, establishes a pluralistic perception of time, a diversified perception deeply marked by the 'space' of the experience."[24] Virno here argues that time is not experienced in the singular. If one accepts a polychronic view such as this, the old constructions of time no longer have power over its distribution and order. This concept – an altered, diversified perception of time, marked by the space of experience – is precisely what Penone's "wooden trees" allow. Penone recalls that the increasing mechanization of the FIAT factory was one of the main points of conflict at the time because each technological advancement not only sped up production but also eliminated the need for human employees.[25] The amplified visibility of the needs of Italian labour and the pressure to produce at speeds that exceed human abilities must be read to provide part of the framework for Penone's early appraisals of artistic labour and time through the tree sculptures. In the context of these debates, Penone's wooden trees underscore the material signs of his own investment of time and toil. Moreover, by conflating his own work with the slow labour of the plant, as well as the anticipated phenomenal time of the sculpture's viewer, Penone, via his recovered trees, returns agency to viewers, who must negotiate this expanded spatio-temporal perspective autonomously.

Forest Solidarity

Through the tautology of the wooden trees Penone offered viewers an opportunity to reconsider the stability of time, to renew one's concept of active work, and to reassess organic self-determination. Formal aspects of individual tree sculptures, as well as the exhibition tactics used for these works, reinforce such diverse and polychronic readings. When *Eleven-Metre Tree* was first shown at Kunstmuseum Lucerne, for instance, it was laid flat on the floor, with its carved surface facing the ceiling.[26] This installation emphasized the sculpture in relief, as a figure on a ground or a solid on a base. More provocatively, in such an

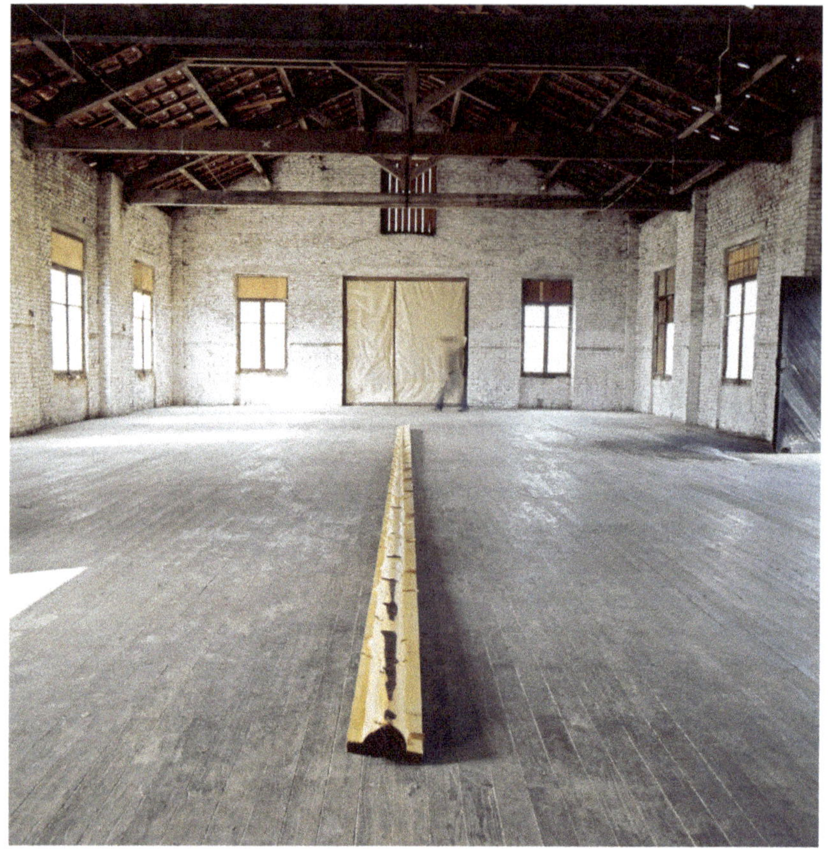

4.5 Giuseppe Penone, *Albero di undici metri* (*Eleven-Metre Tree*), 1975. Fir wood, 1,101 x 20.5 x 12 cm.

Photograph: © Archivio Penone

arrangement the viewer could circumnavigate the sculpture and see the work from different perspectives, thereby being activated as a partner in determining its reception and meaning. This horizontal display is significant because it partially neutralizes the visible traces of the verticality of the organism's growth. Still, the carved trunk is very broad at one end of the eleven-metre measure, while at the other extreme it is slender. Accordingly, the branches are spindly near the narrow end, and more massive near the thick end. The viewer grasps that, despite the horizontal, non-hierarchical installation, the large end is the root end and the narrow one the crown because of their experience that trees in nature grow vertically towards light, being therefore both thicker and older at the base. This formal detail reinforces a pluralistic view of the object as a sculpture *and* as an organism that persisted over time. Through similar means, the formal details of each of Penone's *Trees* indicate fixed moments, and simultaneously they document the fluidity proper to the temporal life of the material. That is, the individual wooden trees bear subtle, individualizing marks of time and experience in their sculptural form.

In 1980 Penone exhibited eight of these early wooden *Trees* together at the Stedelijk Museum in Amsterdam in a way that added further complexity to the counterpoint between human measures of time and vegetal ones. Although the individual sculptures dated from 1969 to 1975, this was the first time he had exhibited them in a group. He also began to use a distinct title for the collective installation: *Ripetere il bosco* (*Repeating the Forest,* 1969–80).[27] An installation view of the exhibition shows eight relief-carved trees propped against the intersection of two walls, so that they emerge from the corner and diagonally traverse the space of the gallery (figure 4.6). This dynamic placement not only visually activates the space but also reinforces the in-between state of these sculptures as simultaneously tree (vertical) and wood (horizontal). The fragility of this material tension – the viewer's tenuous ability to hold onto both concepts at once – is connoted through the palpably precarious state of these large, leaning objects.

Such dialectical oscillations pervade other aspects of the work as well. For instance the title, *Repeating the Forest*, intimates a mechanized approach to artistic labour – as Penone has written, "the forest [is] a slow factory producing wood." Yet, this Fordist aspect is perceptibly contrasted with the individuality of each tree's growth. In the same text he notes that just by looking closely at the knots in a piece of wood, one can tell which side faced the sun, which was battered by the wind, and even whether the tree grew in a crowded forest or an isolated meadow.[28] These details – the thickness of a branch, a slight curve in a section of the trunk – indicate the struggle of the tree within its environment and against other organisms. Formal details might evince the tree's survival of a year of drought, perhaps, or its weathering of a flood. When these individual tree sculptures, realized at different moments, come together as *Repeating the Forest*, they mimic the complex temporality of a forest. The artist notes that people tend to think of the forest as peaceful and still, but even amongst vegetation there is a constant, active struggle for individual survival.[29] The collective

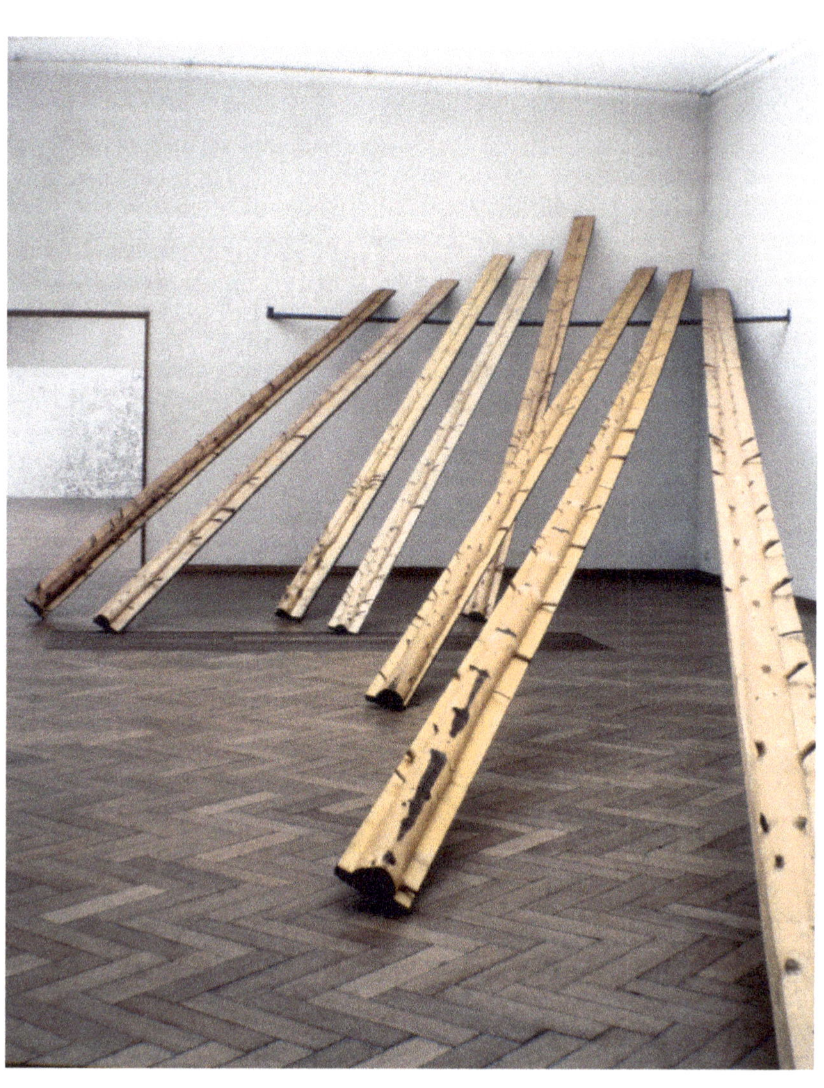

4.6 Giuseppe Penone, *Ripetere il bosco* (*Repeating the Forest*), 1969–80. Dimensions variable. Installation view at Stedelijk Museum, Amsterdam, 1980.

Photograph: © Archivio Penone

installation of Penone's wooden trees reveals the natural sociality of the forest, in which the hand of the sculptor – human labour – is merely one of the many forces with which the tree contends. An encounter with this human-assisted forest prompts viewers to consider, as part of one fluid system, the biological drive of the organic material, the labour of the person who harvested the lumber, and the artistic intervention that enacted a partial return of the natural form. These messages appear concurrently in the unified time of the work's reception, interrupting and superseding the division of nature from culture, and theory from sculpture.

If his forest of wooden trees undermined dialectical structures, Penone also found ways to emphasize the structuring role of time on one's perception through installations of single trees like *Albero di dodici metri verticali* (*Vertical Twelve-Metre Tree*, 1980–1), first exhibited in *Italian Art Now: An American Perspective* at New York's Guggenheim Museum in 1982 (figure 4.7). Announcing its upright position in the title, this larch wood sculpture initiated a group of *Trees* that were not carved in relief. Rather, these examples were partially sculpted in the round, rising out of cubic bases that retain their rectilinear, milled form. Always exhibited standing erect, sometimes in pairs that add up to the stated length, these at first seem to the viewer to emphasize the "natural" figure of the tree over the "cultural" material of the beam.[30] Therefore, Penone had to be more cunning in order to produce the intermediate reading of the work as wooden tree, as both nature and culture.

Displayed in the Guggenheim's sky-lit rotunda, *Vertical Twelve-Metre Tree* was anchored to its thirty-six-inch-high, fifteen-inch-square foundation, yet simultaneously appears to be upside down. Despite the solid foundation provided by the thick base, the work reads as being inverted because the "trunk" has a greater diameter at the top and a smaller diameter at the bottom, where it emerges from the base. That is, Penone carved the beam so that one intuits that the younger part of the wood is near the base, and the older part of the tree is suspended in the air.[31] It therefore appears to be upside down because this is a reversal of the way the tree would be experienced in nature, a point reinforced by the work's installation in a space awash with natural light. In the show's exhibition catalogue the curators claim that Penone's work is a response to the concentric circles of Frank Lloyd Wright's own interplay between the natural and the man-made in the design of the building.[32] Being thicker at the top might seem to mirror the expansion of Wright's spiral, but one's experience-based knowledge of the way a tree grows means that *Twelve-Metre Tree* does not acknowledge the movement of the

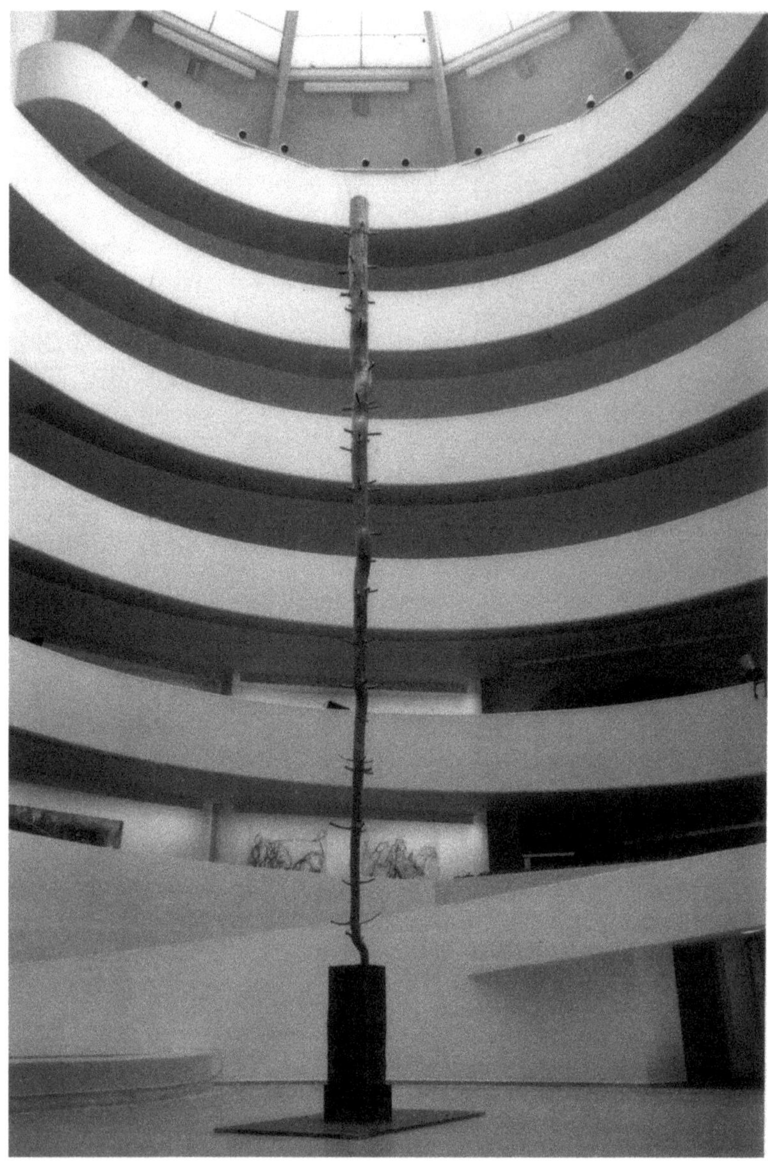

4.7 Giuseppe Penone, *Albero di dodici metri verticali* (*Vertical Twelve-Metre Tree*), 1980. Wood, 1,200 x 50 x 50 cm. Installation view at *Italian Art Now: An American Perspective*, Solomon R. Guggenheim Museum, New York, 1982.

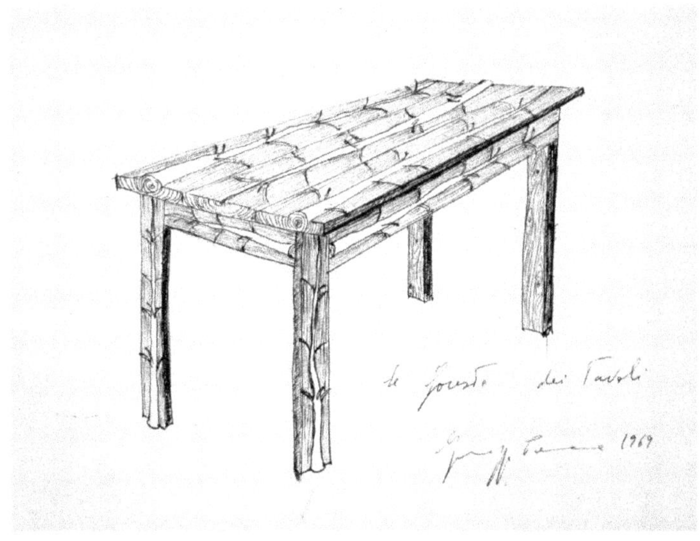

4.8 Giuseppe Penone, *Le foreste dei tavoli* (*The Forests of Tables*), 1969. India ink or China ink and graphite on paper, 24 x 32 cm.

Photograph: © Archivio Penone

spiral towards the skylight; rather it actively works against the building's rise. Penone's work creates a downward vector towards the earth. This is the means by which it communicates its tautological status: this sculpture risks being mistaken for an ordinary tree more than its predecessors do because it is mostly carved in the round, but Penone's clever inversion proclaims it as, resolutely, a wooden tree.

Works like this throw the limits of our embodied perspectives into clear view. Indeed, how many of us regard a two-by-four-inch plank at a hardware store and think about its two ends being different in age? Arguably, we consider even less the variance in age of the two ends of a tabletop, a door, or a floorboard. In sketches like *Le foreste dei tavoli* (*The Forests of Tables*, 1969), an ink-on-paper drawing, the artist imagines the trees hidden within the everyday objects and architectures of our homes (figure 4.8). The drawing allows one to visualize the two states together, another means of challenging the conceptual barrier erected between a living tree and wood as a material. Other drawings of the time make this charmingly explicit, imagining forests of chairs or a roof of trees. They reimagine the spaces humans construct as intimately intertwined with the natural world that these very same constructions aim to sublimate. What is the roof of a house, if not the means to protect one's body by separating a living space from the vagaries of the natural world? Yet, it is often made of the same materials – wood, clay, grass – that it is trying to keep out. More than this, such drawings raise the viewer's awareness of how the structures of human society, its material systems, and its languages actively separate us from connection to the natural world.

Penone dismantles such impediments to a diverse and integrated world view through the *Tree* sculptures, which reveal the latent temporality of sentient organisms within a seemingly lifeless material. Although in the early works of this series Penone often compared the age of the recovered tree to his own age – through their titles or statements about the amount of labour required of his own body – it was in later works like the inverted tree shown at the Guggenheim or in *Le due età dell'albero* (*The Two Ages of the Tree*, 1991) that the form itself brings to the fore the temporal complexity of organic matter (figure 4.9). In *The Two Ages of the Tree* the artist carves away the beam to leave distinct indicators of multiple moments in the life of the tree. Whereas most of the *Tree* sculptures contrast a single core against a horizontal or vertical beam, here an inner trunk appears to emerge from a shroud of its older self, casting it off like a winter coat. Two separate groups of growth rings – two discrete ages of the tree – are held in relief on the milled plank. Just as humans tend to think of their lifetime in phases (infancy, childhood, adolescence, maturity, middle age, retirement, etc.), this tree demonstrates at least four distinct periods of its life (sapling, mature tree, lumber, sculpture). Through the convergence of these diachronic forms in the single moment of its viewing, such a sculpture expands the way the viewer thinks about the lived experiences of other forms of organic matter. This, in turn, provides the opportunity to adopt new perspectives on the material world.

Penone also underscored the contingency of temporal perspective in the 1987 sculpture *Albero fiume* (*River Tree*, 1987) (figure 4.10). This tree, included in a reprised installation of *Repeating the Forest* in 1991 at Turin's Castello di Rivoli, is carved from a massive piece of wood. One quarter of the cubic volume has been removed, revealing a very slight, spindly tree at the centre. In a work like this, the dramatic difference in age from the fragile core of the beam to its thick exterior reinforces

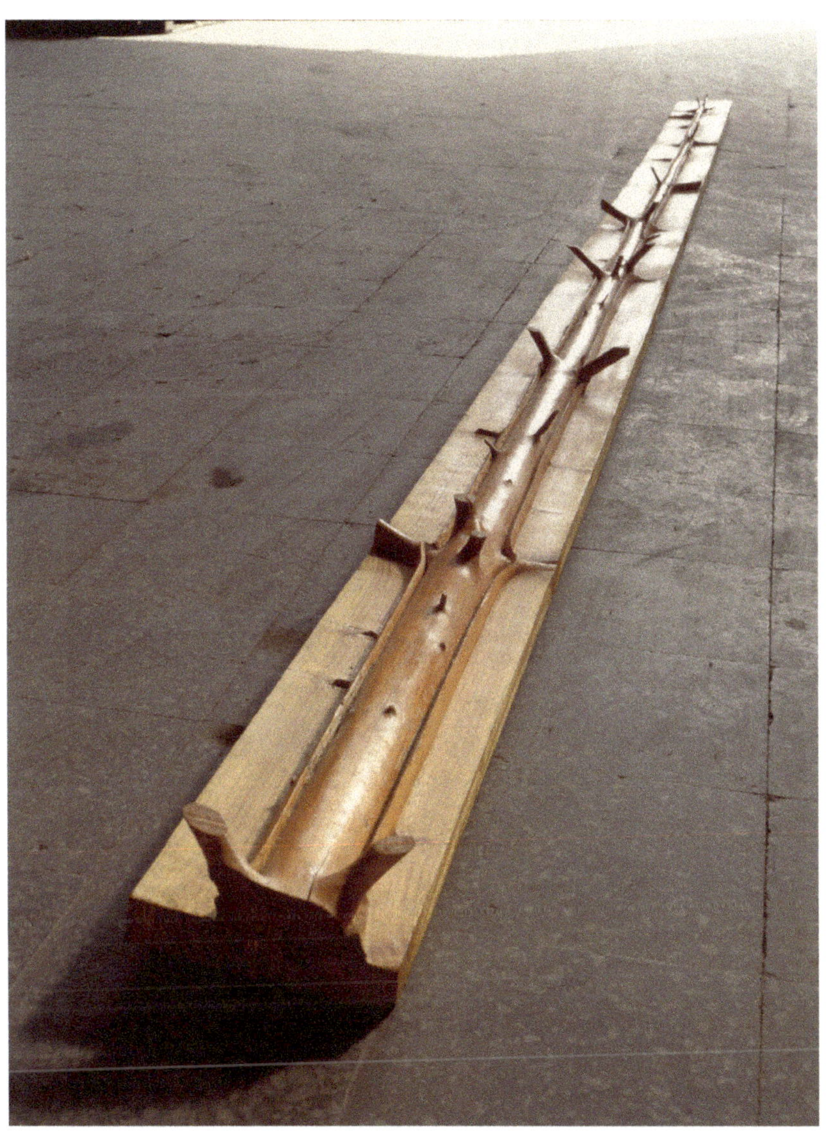

4.9 Giuseppe Penone, *Le due età dell'albero* (*The Two Ages of the Tree*), 1991.
Larch wood, 508 x 19 x 9.5 cm.

Photograph: © Archivio Penone

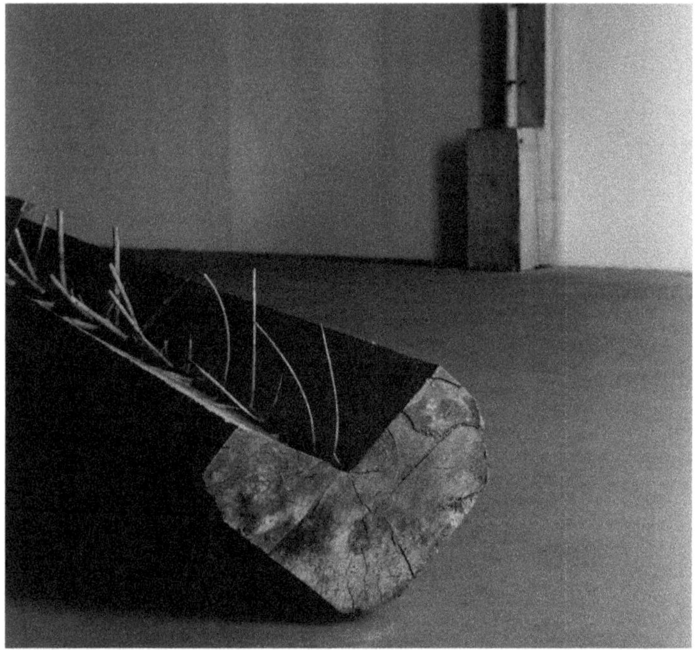

4.10 Giuseppe Penone, *Albero fiume* (*River Tree*), 1987. Wood: two elements, 607 x 42 x 41 cm and 610 x 30 x 30 cm. Installation view at Castello di Rivoli, Turin, 1991, as an element of *Repeating the Forest*, 1969–91.

Photograph: Gérard Rondeau, © Association Gérard Rondeau

a reading of the wood's fluidity when it is considered over time. One has to shift from an anthropocentric timescale – one commensurate with one's own lifetime – to what we might call an "arborcentric" or tree-centred clock in order to reconcile the tiny branches of the carved-out sapling with the colossal trunk from which it now emerges. That these two are part of the same organism requires thinking about the hundreds of years of growth between them. Hence this is a tree in which wood flows like a river through years, decades, and perhaps centuries.

Through these forests of wooden trees, Penone challenges the stability of an anthropocentric world view by exposing the fluidity of solids and, in so doing, invites the viewer to inhabit consciously non-human frames of mind. This broader aspect of the artist's project comes into focus when read through Roberto Esposito's biopolitics and Ian Hodder's argument about the entanglement of humans and things, introduced in chapter 3. Hodder's writings similarly propose that the material world is far less stable than humans tend to think it is. To perceive the fluidity of things requires evaluating them from the perspective of different disciplines, or taking up the point of view of objects themselves. For instance, Hodder argues that while things may appear to be fixed and solid from the point of view of ethnography, an archaeologist like himself regards things to be transient as they break down and transform over millennia.[33] On a smaller scale, humans become regulated and disciplined by things that require care to be maintained (like an art collection), repaired (like a broken pipe), or harvested (like a crop), each in accordance with the specific temporal materiality of the thing. For Hodder, finding ways to recognize the long-term entanglement of humans and things has the potential to raise one's consciousness to ethical considerations of the social, ecological, and cosmic effects of a present action or inaction.[34]

Penone's wooden *Trees* and his collective installations of *Repeating the Forest* critique the partiality and inadequacy of human measures of time by marking the disjunctures that occur at the various points of physical and psychological encounter between a body and a tree. In many of such works the human body and its corporeal timeline are made present through direct correlation to the age of a tree, as well as through the signs of labour or human-hours invested in growing, harvesting, milling, selecting, and carving the wood. The objects themselves conflate the somatic time of the organism in nature with human time, since the artist consistently maintains both the received and the recovered form in the finished object. It is always clear that one is looking at a sculpture – a thing made and mediated – and also something that lived in time and space, not unlike that in which the viewer persists. The slippage between human time and tree time was further emphasized in the mid-1980s when Penone cut down the original *Maritime Alps*. He exhibited these felled trunks as objects, along with the photographs that documented the intersection of their lives with his own (figure 4.11).[35] In later tree-related series, actual entanglement is again catalysed by the incorporation of living plants into his sculptural works, a development through which one can follow the artist's deepening investigation of the differences among tree time, body time, and sculpture time.

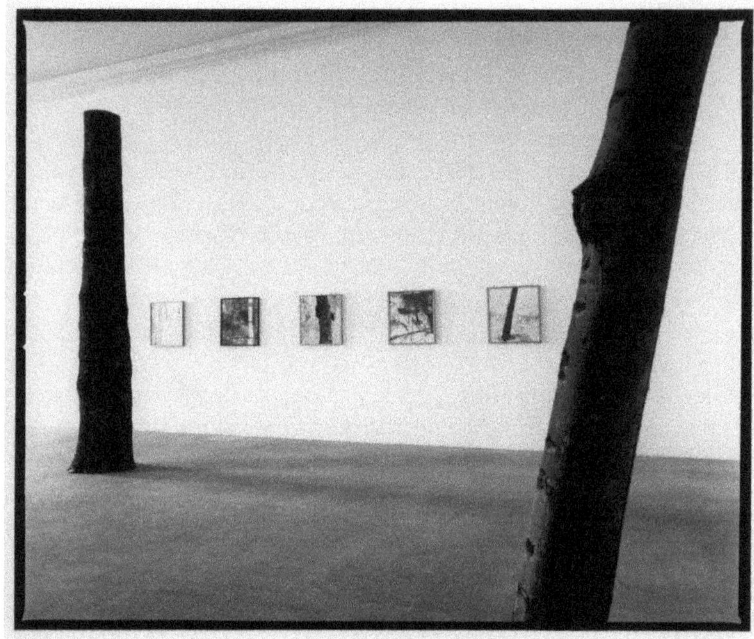

4.11 Felled *Maritime Alps* trees, including detail of *Trattenere 17 anni di crescita (Continuerà a crescere tranne che in quel punto)* (*To Retain 17 Years of Growth (It Will Continue to Grow except at That Point)*), 1968–85. Installation view at Castello di Rivoli, 1991.

Photograph: Gérard Rondeau, © Association Gérard Rondeau

A Vegetal Sculptor

Gesti vegetali (*Vegetal Gestures*, 1980–4) are among the first of the projects in which Penone returned to working within the parameters of the human body and living trees, having not done so since the late 1960s. This series of bronze sculptures make the entanglement of humans and plants even more visible by materially and conceptually conflating human skin with a tree's bark. Marrying the iconographic with the indexical, these works stem from the artist smearing handfuls of clay onto mannequins, registering the minimum contours necessary to be read as a human figure.[36] When later cast in bronze, the surfaces maintained the traces of Penone's gesture: the palpations, swipes, and scrapes of his fingers. Rough and rippled, the bronze bears a distinct

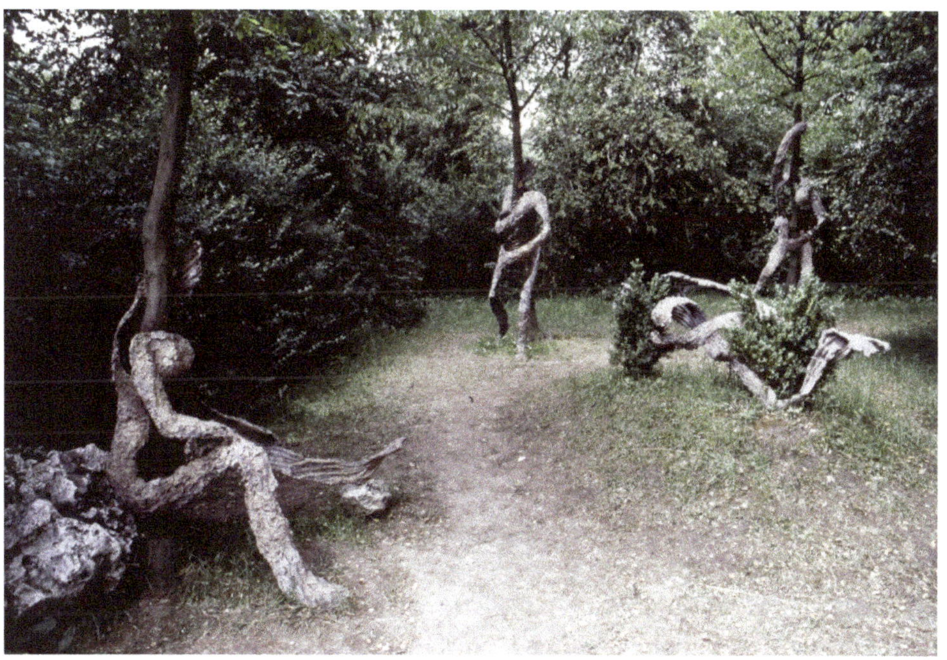

4.12 Giuseppe Penone, *Paesaggio di gesti vegetali* (*Landscape of Vegetal Gestures*), 1983. Installation view at *Skulptur im 20 Jahrhundert*, Merian Park, Basel, 1984.

Photograph: Nanda Lanfranco, © Nanda Lanfranco

visual correspondence to the bark of a tree.[37] The artist emphasizes this aspect by exhibiting the abstracted figures intertwined with potted plants in a gallery or by installing them outdoors among live trees and shrubs.

In the exhibition *Skulptur im 20 Jahrhundert* (*Twentieth-Century Sculpture*), for instance, the contours of three full-scale bronze figures – two standing, one seated – are wrapped around individual trees in Basel's Merian Park: *Paesaggio di gesti vegetali* (*Landscape of Vegetal Gestures*, 1983) (figure 4.12). In the same clearing a fourth bronze appears to stretch out horizontally on the earth, recalling a reclining Venus, intertwining its sinewy limbs between two small shrubs: *Eva* (*Eve*, 1984). In these cases the artist's gesture is solidified in metal, yet by its contraposition with living plants it appears to return to the slow, fluid rhythms of the forest. To be clear, these sculptures are not positioned as heroic in the sense of the human dominating nature through an active gesture;

rather they appear to be submitting to the extenuated temporality of geologic time.

Even when Penone exhibited these figures indoors, as he did in numerous gallery and museum shows throughout the mid-1980s, he intermingled them with living plants in terracotta pots. Period indoor installations at the Castello di Rivoli (1985) and the Musée Grenoble (1986) are notable in this regard because in these cases the works are installed in galleries that contain centuries-old landscape paintings.[38] There, Penone's objects took on an additional theoretical significance, productively contrasting the fundamental differences between painting and sculpture. The limited temporality of a painted landscape, compared to his sculptural forms, was demonstrated by the distinctions between representation and presentation. A landscape, of course, implies a figure even if none is pictured, and that, in turn, means that any landscape painting is frozen in time and is limited to one perspective. Penone's vegetal gestures – bronze objects combined with living plants that require attention and maintenance – persist in the temporal frame of the viewer because of sculpture's occupation of three-dimensional space, which allows the viewer to take up various perspectives on these objects and to perceive changes to the "living" materials over time.

In his writings of the era the artist frequently ruminates on the significance of inhabiting the temporality of the plant through experiments like this: "When one shifts the customary relation of the speeds which is determined only in terms of the function of the speed of our human motion, then our customary ideas of things are also shifted. If one were able to execute one's own motion as slowly as the plants, then, obviously, this would enable the emergence of entirely new unusual forms and pictures."[39] What Penone describes here is a shift in conceptual and temporal frame, catalysed through the work but reaching out into other areas of perception and experience. If one could work like a plant – if one could devise works that have to be lived with, revisited, and experienced over long periods of time in order for their formal and conceptual meaning to come to fruition – then shifts in the very foundations of the way we see the world might ensue. Read in this light, Penone's *Vegetal Gestures* stand as a hinge between early works like *Repeating the Forest* and his later, large-scale public sculptures and were necessary for discovering one of his primary ways of working in the next stage of his career. The tension between movement and stasis, and the way in which the perception of these states shifts over time, became fundamental to the artist's continued pursuit of the temporality of the expanded sculpture throughout the 1980s and beyond.

Invited by curators Klaus Bussman and Kaspar König to participate in the second *Sculpture Projects* exhibition in Münster, Germany, Penone used the occasion to depict the temporal circularity of material entanglements in *Pozzo di Münster* (*Münster Well*, 1987). Here, in a grassy clearing of a public park on the eastern edge of the city, a slender ash tree appears to have been blown over, succumbed to gravity (figure 4.13). The scene is familiar in wooded areas – young trees that have been toppled by storms become, over time, the mulch of the forest floor – but the sight is less typical in a manicured park in a European city. This tree is, of course, a bronze cast made by Penone. On close inspection, one sees that water is slowly emerging from a bifurcation near the base of the trunk (figure 4.14). This juncture is the site of vegetal branching off, and it also bears the imprint of the artist's hand and forearm. In a literal conflation of branch and arm (while *branch* in Italian is *ramo*, its English cognate *braccia* translates to *arm*), water emerges from the fingertips, pools in the palm, and slowly streams down the arm until, near the elbow, it trickles into a circular depression in the ground. This then is a working fountain, which calls upon the tree/body metaphors of his earlier works through means both physical and linguistic, but further explores non-anthropocentric models for conceptualizing duration through the circuitous fluidity of water.

Made a "permanent" installation in 1996, *Münster Well* complicates the narrow binary of nature and culture by revealing the normally invisible circuits of natural systems. By mimicking a natural water cycle – seeping into the earth, being taken up by the roots of a tree or plant, and transpiring back into the atmosphere through leaves – the sculpture makes the distended natural process observable on a human scale of time. Linking the circuitous flow to the already divergent lifespans of a tree and a human body reminds the viewer that both share a need for this precious liquid.[40] Condensed into the limited scope allotted to viewing a sculpture is the suggestion that each drop of water and every molecule of human flesh, bronze, and wooden pulp have been on the earth since its beginning. However unique one feels, each person's individual experience is only a small ripple in the deep well of geological flows. More than an elegiac memento mori or a Romantic reminder of human estrangement from nature, *Münster Well* claims that the very nature of sculpture rests in the creation of moments of pause, of stillness, of pooling within the flow of material entanglements.

The relative stability of sculpture allows ideas like this to become legible, but even such sculptures are still not "permanent" on a geologic or cosmic scale. Penone uses the traditional materials of sculpture – wood, bronze, stone – precisely because, on a human scale, they are stable over time. The physical endurance of sculpture may be uniquely apparent to Italian artists, living amidst the substantive remnants of the various

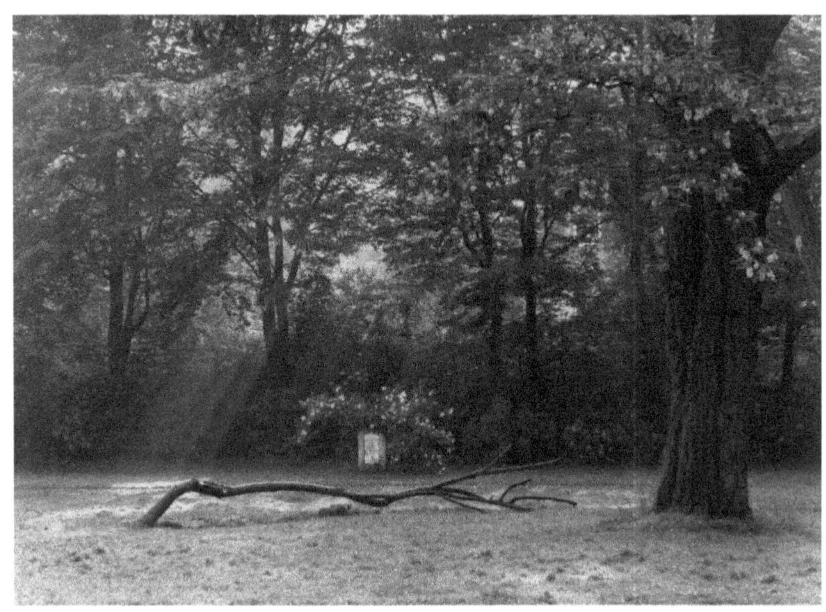

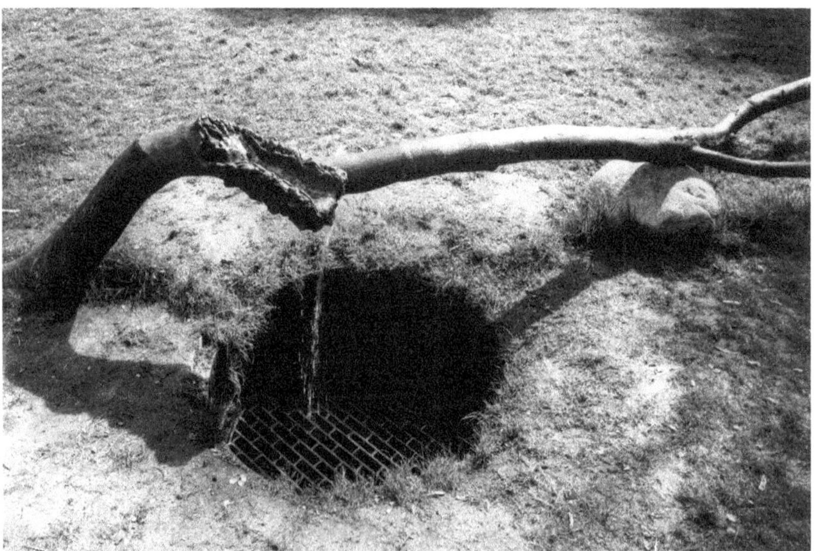

4.13–4.14 Giuseppe Penone, *Pozzo di Münster* (*Münster Well*), 1987. Bronze, water, 100 x 700 x 180 cm. Installation view at Altern Hörster Freidhof, Münster, Germany.

Photographs: Nanda Lanfranco, © Nanda Lanfranco

advanced cultures that have inhabited the Mediterranean peninsula over four millennia. However, that this material stability is also relative is not lost on the artist, both in terms of defining his own actions and in terms of the vegetal or geologic scales of time. Depending on the material he is using, Penone positions his own role as fluid (sculpting wood or stone) or solid (shaping soft clay, or pressing his body into wet plaster). In each case the artist shifts his approach and the scale of his own active and passive states.[41] The relativity of material states and the attendant variability of the role of the artist are borne out over time, in ways that are visible yet subtle.

Perspective Process

Given the prevalence of natural materials and forms in Penone's works, his project is often read as modelling a Romantic longing for a return to Edenic wholeness with nature. However, outdoor works like *Münster Well* harness living landscapes in order to demonstrate the complex entanglement of humans and nature over time.[42] Just as the carved *Trees* that partially emerge from milled beams are best understood through the tautological notion of "wooden trees," the artist's career-defining engagement with natural materials is best understood as maintaining the openness of dialogues and differences, as expanding the possibilities of ways of thinking and seeing. Nowhere is this more evident than in the large-scale outdoor works he began making in the late 1980s. In these works Penone uses trees to investigate the cultural dimensions of landscape by setting up the potential for natural and cultural intertwining over time. In many of these works the complexity of one's estrangement from nature and a desire for restitution within it – of the distance and closeness between humans and nature – is emphasized by their location in superficially natural spaces: the urban and formal gardens of Western Europe.

Like *Münster Well*, Penone's later outdoor works most often inhabit the urban parks of major cities and the most proper of European gardens. In contrast to the private nature of the *Maritime Alps* interventions, these locations occasion a way of thinking about such sculpture as potentially truly public artworks in the sense that they implicate the contemporary viewer in the same way that formal gardens of the sixteenth and seventeenth centuries engaged those for whom they were created. Through these loaded sites the sculptures are conscripted into conversation with concepts of landscape that reflect the cultural logic of these earlier periods, which were ones in which notions of the "public" were in formation.[43] Moreover, the body implied in the tree-body metaphor of these later, public works is no longer the artist's body, but the viewer's. In some cases, this is distinctly due to the way these works

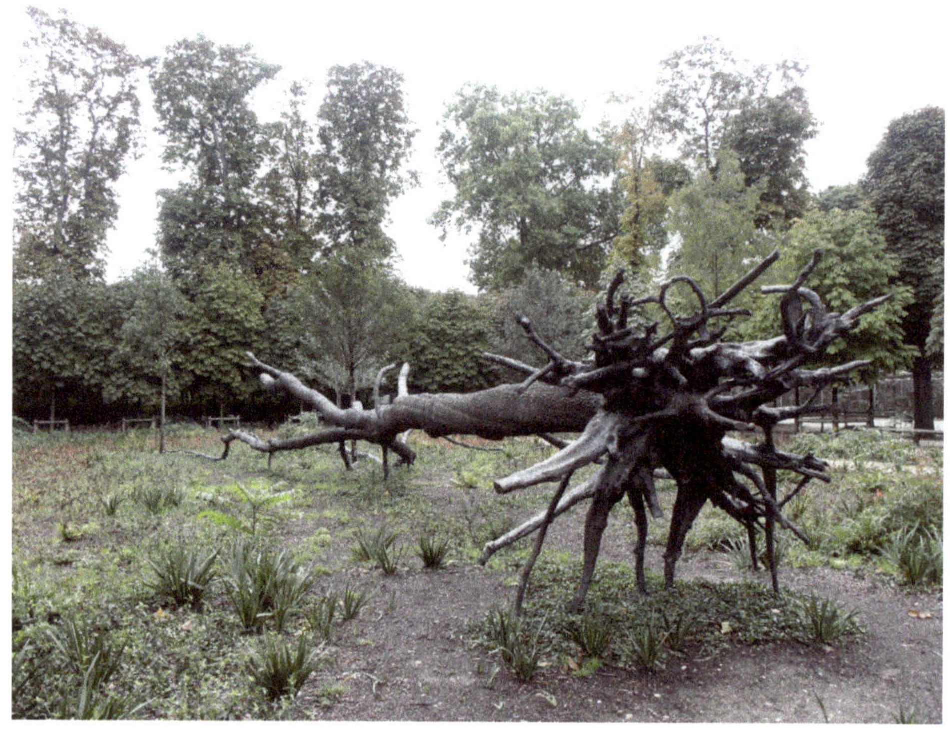

4.15 Giuseppe Penone, *Albero delle vocali* (*Tree of Vowels*), 1999–2000. Bronze and vegetation, 450 x 3,000 x 1,200 cm. Installation view at Jardin des Tuileries, Paris.

Photograph: © Archivio Penone

must be lived with and viewed repeatedly over long periods of time for their meaning to come to fruition.

With *Albero delle vocali* (*Tree of Vowels*, 1999–2000) Penone crafted a sculptural means to demonstrate how experience is conditioned by individual subjectivity, at the same time that it is directed by the forms used to regulate its communication, whether language and grammar, time and clocks, or the formal traditions of landscape architecture. The artist, who taught for decades at the École des Beaux-Arts in Paris, was commissioned to create an installation in the city's Tuileries, one of the most storied gardens in Europe. The work is an intervention: among live specimens planted by the artist a horizontal bronze tree lies with its massive root structure above ground (figure 4.15). The root ball of this apparently toppled tree faces one of the walking paths, while its branches recede away into a wooded area. One's view of the tree is thus highly directed, and, simultaneously, the work is subtly integrated with the living vegetation over time.[44]

The eponymous "vowels" of the tree are reflected in two ways: first, five of the twisting bronze roots subtly form the shape of letters at one end of the sculpture; and second, five different species of living trees have been planted by the artist at the tips of the bronze branches – ash, oak, elm, yew, and poplar. Here, as in some of his earliest outdoor works, like *Alphabet Bread* or *Write, Read, Remember*, the artist invokes language. In *Tree of Vowels* the notations that indicate sound differentiation contrast with a semiotics born of botanical classification. The trees are visually differentiated by the appearance of their leaves, bark, and seeds, which in turn might refer to a diverse range of ecosystems and evolutionary histories. Moreover, different species of trees connote distinct symbolic meanings in mythology, folklore, and popular culture. (Instances of this are too numerous to list, but the peaceful metaphor of "extending an olive branch" or the Edenic parable of the "tree of knowledge" are two easy examples that have persisted over centuries in Judaeo-Christian culture.) Like the written vowels and consonants that allow ideas to be recorded, transferred, and read, references to different species and varieties of trees might be used to communicate ideas. Communicating through any form requires understanding of its constituent symbolic parts, the context in which they are deployed, and grammatical rules, all of which are subject to change over time. A garden is a statement made through a language of vegetation and addressed to the body through sight, sound, smell, touch, and perhaps taste. Meanings emerge from individual plants, as well as the arrangement of plants within a garden's borders, forming a syntax that reveals aspects of the culture in which it was articulated. In a semiotic sense, Penone's sprawling bronze tree is a deictic gesture, the reach of its branches pointing to the live trees as building blocks of potential meaning. The reading of Penone's work thus becomes an invitation to the viewer to apply this same approach to reading the garden itself.

The Tuileries Garden is an ideal locale for investigating the temporal conditionality of experience because it is a palimpsest of land-use and building campaigns through which centuries of French history can be accessed. From Catherine de' Medici's annexation of the site in order to recreate in Paris a verdant bit of her Italian homeland, to its opening as a public park in the aftermath of the 1789 revolution, to Napoleon's filling of the park with statuary from his conquests, to the Nazi's use of the Jeu de Paume building to store looted art, this garden – which was built upon medieval tile workshops, or *tuileries* – exemplifies how land yields to the demands of changing cultures and ideas. Penone's massive bronze tree models this: it is visible in the present, but its recumbent form melancholically recalls a storied past and intimates a new future that will be written, at least in part, by the affects of time and the elements on the bronze, as well as by the growth of the five trees planted alongside it.

A number of Penone's later outdoor sculptural installations take on the densely layered spaces of European Baroque gardens. For instance, in addition to the Tuileries installation, he had a temporary exhibition at the crowning jewel of Louis XIV's reign, Versailles, the elaborate gardens of which were designed by André Le Nôtre. The latter's grandfather had created the Tuileries for Catherine de' Medici, and Le Nôtre himself redesigned the Parisian garden for Louis XIV before the court moved to Versailles. More significantly, Penone installed a long-term program of fourteen sculptures in the restored gardens of Piedmont's Reggia di Venaria Reale, the original design of which is rumoured to have been prompted by Carlo Emanuele II di Savoia's envy of his first cousin Louis XIV. Located within such highly charged, extremely cultivated spaces, Penone's sculptures ask the viewer to consider what a garden's design can tell us about the philosophy of the culture that created it, and, further, to ask, What does maintaining or restoring these places do to us and to our ways of seeing, perceiving, and knowing the physical world?[45] Gardens, as the artist has noted, are spaces where humans intervene in nature for means that are no longer tied to survival, agriculture, or economics. Rather, they are constructed in accordance with aesthetic, cultural, and symbolic values.[46] They are reflections of thought, not indications of physical needs. How then can one read Penone's interventions at storied sites like the Tuileries, Florence's Forte Belvedere (*L'ombra del bronzo*, 2002), La Venaria Reale (*Il giardino delle sculture fluide*, 2003–7), and the palatial gardens at Versailles (various works, 2013) as staging an encounter between central philosophical models of the late twentieth and early twenty-first centuries and those of the sixteenth and seventeenth centuries?[47] Perhaps they are not so different as one might expect.

In his study of Le Nôtre, historian Allen Weiss argues that the French gardener and landscape architect for Versailles anticipates Merleau-Ponty's critique of Cartesianism through the ever-changing perspectives offered by his Baroque gardens. That is, the fact that these gardens are designed to be walked through reveals a philosophical intuition about the instability of vision. Weiss argues that in Le Nôtre's gardens "the object, or the scene, is perpetually unstable, perceptually rich, significatively ambiguous – all due to the radical perspectivalism of our existence."[48] When set in such landscapes that imply specific viewers and distinct historical moments, Penone's outdoor sculptures similarly work to remind us of the limits of our perspective by offering glimpses of something beyond our temporally bound ability to perceive. If we take Weiss's assessment of Le Nôtre's designs to mean that the architect anticipated anti-ocularcentrism, then it is clear that, at Versailles and the gardens it inspired at La Reggia di Venaria Reale, Penone's works recall the philosophical concepts underlying the original garden designs and simultaneously reframe these models from a postmodern perspective. That is, these historic sites grant the artist an ideal context through which to explore and challenge the metaphysical divide between nature and culture. Further, Penone's works at these regal estates bring their symbolic expressions of infinity back to a human scale, demonstrating that experience is always partial because it is limited by embodied perspectives and their attendant temporal scales.

As part of a year-long celebration of the four-hundredth anniversary of Le Nôtre's 1613 birth, Penone exhibited twenty-three works at Versailles, each carefully considered in terms of the spatial context of its installation.[49] Many were reprises of outdoor works he had previously installed elsewhere, including *Elevazione* (*Elevation*, 2001), a long-term installation in Rotterdam, and various works from the series *Idee di pietra (Ideas of Stone,* 2003–11). This had the visual effect of turning the segmented spaces of Le Nôtre's garden into temporary outdoor gallery spaces – green cubes rather than white ones – which limited the integration of the artist's works with their setting. Yet a few works still opened a dialogue with the current landscape and its four centuries of cultivation and sculptural programs. For instance, it is well known that the gardens at Versailles are oriented in concert with the apparent movement of the sun, which seems to rise over the chateau and set at the far western reaches of the garden. The sculptural figure of Apollo, the sun god of Greek antiquity, is literally central to this garden, his gilded figure rising from the central pool on a four-horsedrawn chariot. The iconographic use of this mythological figure was transparent propaganda: the right of Louis XIV, the Roi Soleil, to rule France was posited to be as natural and inevitable as the movements of the cosmos. This heavily symbolic landscape and its hyperbolic paeans to the cultural value of solar light provide an apt back-drop for some of Penone's tree-based sculptural interventions (figure 4.16).

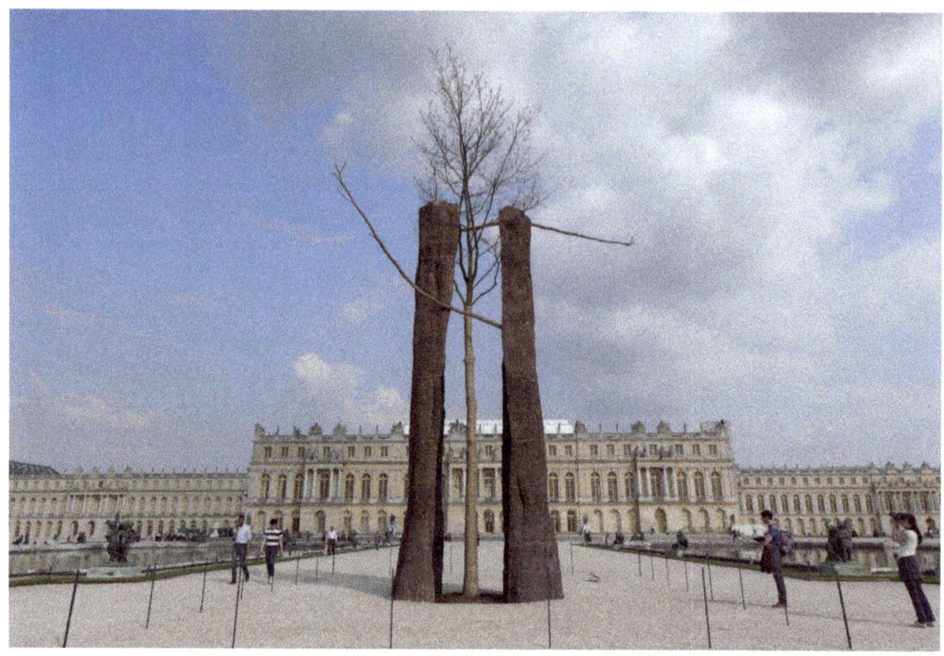

4.16 Giuseppe Penone, *Tra scorza e scorza* (*Between Bark and Bark*), 2007. Installation view of *Giuseppe Penone* at Château de Versailles, 2013.

Photograph: © Archivio Penone

Contrary to the artifice of Versailles's gardens and their constructed illusion of monarchal divinity, Penone's works like *Spazio di luce* (*Space of Light*, 2008), *Le foglie delle radici* (*The Leaves of the Roots*, 2011), and *Albero folgorato* (*Thunderstruck Tree*, 2012) emphasize the material relationship between the garden and the sun through the non-mythologized figures of trees. They do this even while using some of the same materials as those associated with the Baroque palace. For instance, the golden interiors of works like *Space of Light* and *Thunderstruck Tree* intimate the opulent excesses of the palace décor, yet these reflective surfaces here represent the way in which a tree can be considered to be made of light (figure 4.17). A tree's flesh and its form are quite literally produced by its reaching towards the sun and synthesizing its rays. Although monumental, Penone's arboreal sculptures critically oppose Versailles's seventeenth-century program by revealing the aesthetic structures already present in nature, not those that reflect human vanities. As artworks, they are at once grand cultural gestures and humble acquiescence to natural

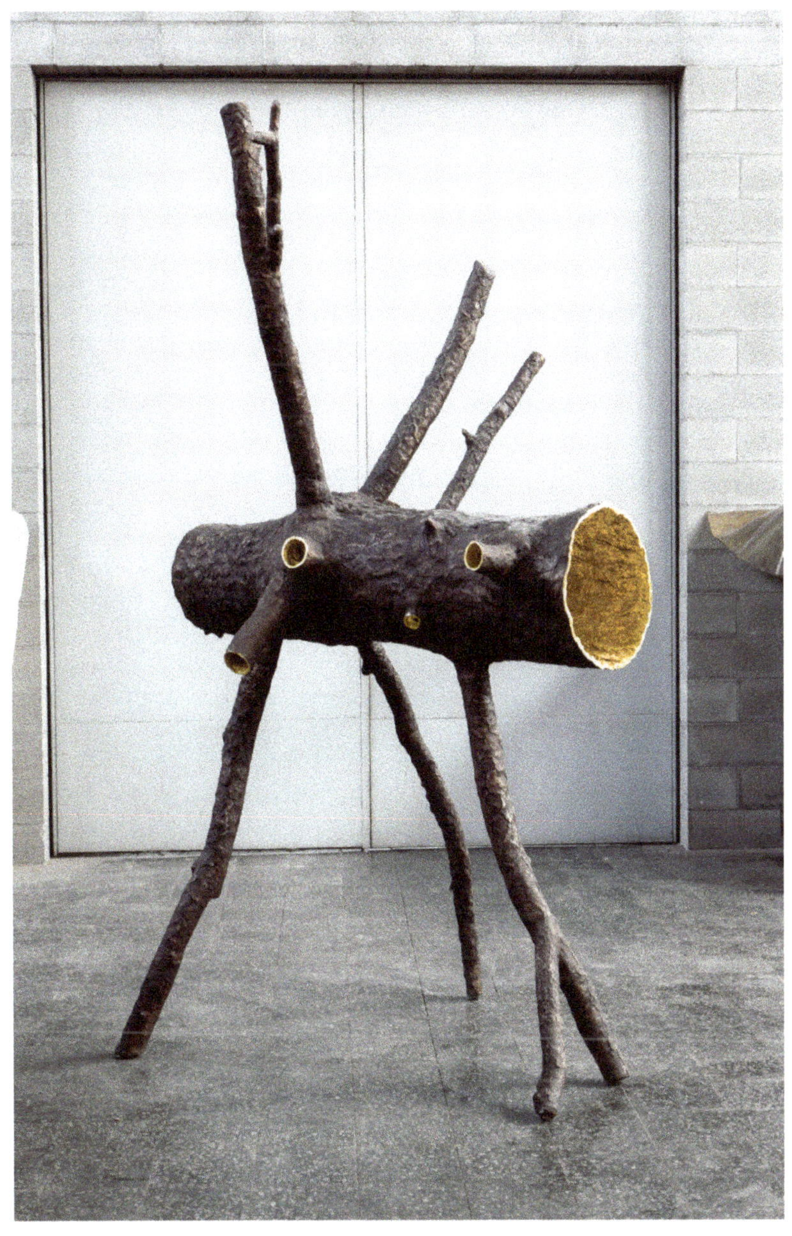

4.17 Giuseppe Penone, *Spazio di luce* (*Space of Light*), 2008 (detail). Bronze and gold, 240 x 200 x 200 cm.

Photograph: © Archivio Penone

forms and processes. That is, the hand of the artist recedes in favour of the organic relationship between the tree and the sun.

The sculptures exhibited at Versailles in 2013 did not constitute Penone's first encounter with these storied gardens.[50] Indeed more than a decade earlier the artist had purchased some of the property's trees, which had been felled by a series of violent storms in 1999. From the two massive trunks acquired at auction Penone created two distinct works. The first is *Cedro di Versailles* (*Versailles Cedar*, 2000–3), a recovered "wooden tree," which provides a profound example of the vast distances of time that can be demonstrated through the archaeological process begun by Penone in the late 1960s. Here a pale, slender sapling emerges through a carved fistula in the centre of a massive trunk (figure 4.18). Its smooth, youthful form denotes the age when Louis XIV and his courtiers promenaded through the gardens, in contrast to the dark, rough bark of the tree's most recent living form. However, it was not this Versailles cedar, but the second of the two trees sourced from the royal estate, that was returned to the gardens for Penone's 2013 exhibition.

When Penone found this second trunk too diseased to carve it in the same way that he had approached the first one, he instead cast the exterior of the colossal cedar. The resulting work, *Tra scorza e scorza* (*Between Bark and Bark,* 2003–7), consists of the two halves of the enormous bronze skin installed about three metres apart from each other, with a living tree planted between them. This work was on display at Versailles, but its placement in these gardens was temporary. Despite this symbolic return of the sick tree to the place where it had grown, the central living tree planted here had no chance to grow, no time to adapt to the conditioned way in which light entered its bronze container. This fact is significant because it highlights the circumstances in which Penone's large-scale works succeed best. When shown at Versailles from 11 June to 31 October 2013, this work was merely a representation of a sculpture that was "living" somewhere else. Seen from another perspective, the short life of these installations at Versailles mirrored the fleeting, constructed spectacle of Le Nôtre's fantastical designs.

Fluid, Integrated, and Autonomous

The material matrix of *Between Bark and Bark* may have had its origin at Versailles and returned there briefly in 2013, but the first version of the work itelf had been installed six years earlier as part of a long-term installation at La Reggia di Venaria Reale, just outside metropolitan Turin (figure 4.19).

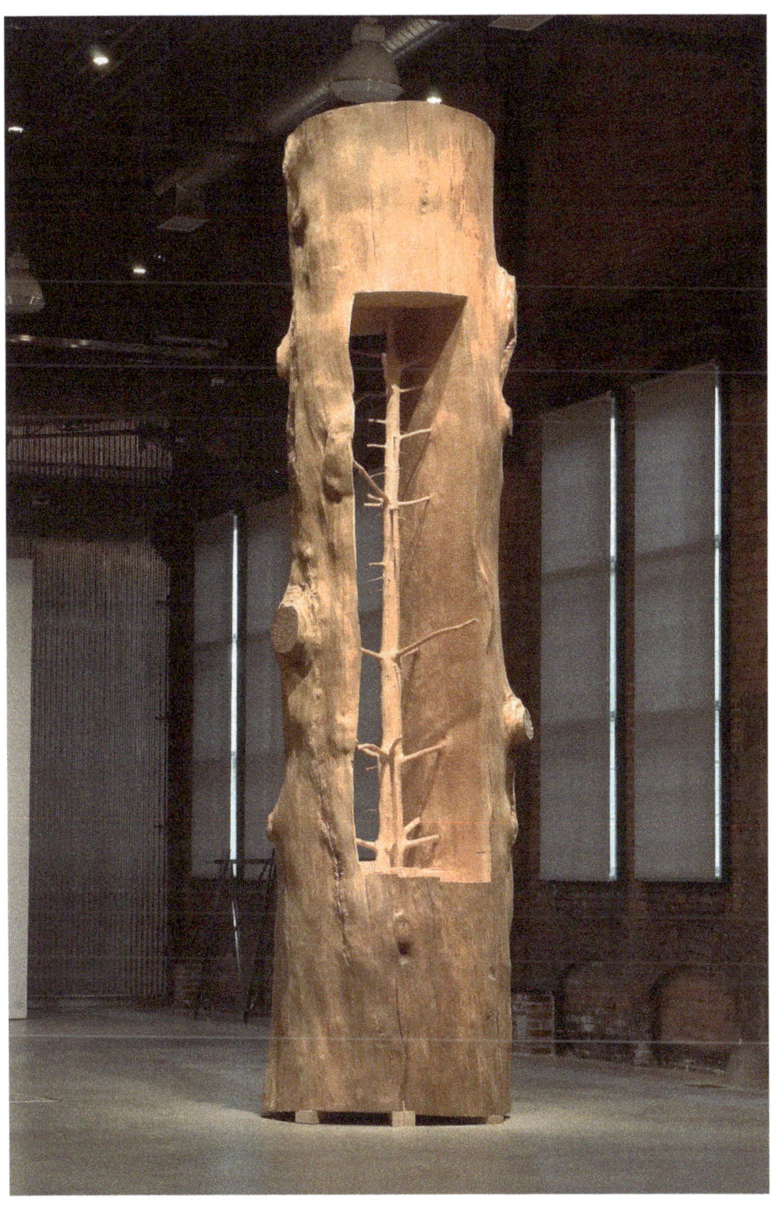

4.18 Giuseppe Penone, *Cedro di Versailles* (*Versailles Cedar*), 2000–3. Cedar wood, 630 x 160 cm diameter. Installation view of *Les éléments de la nature* at La Cité de l'Énergie, Shawinigan, 11 June–2 October 2005.

Photograph: © Archivio Penone

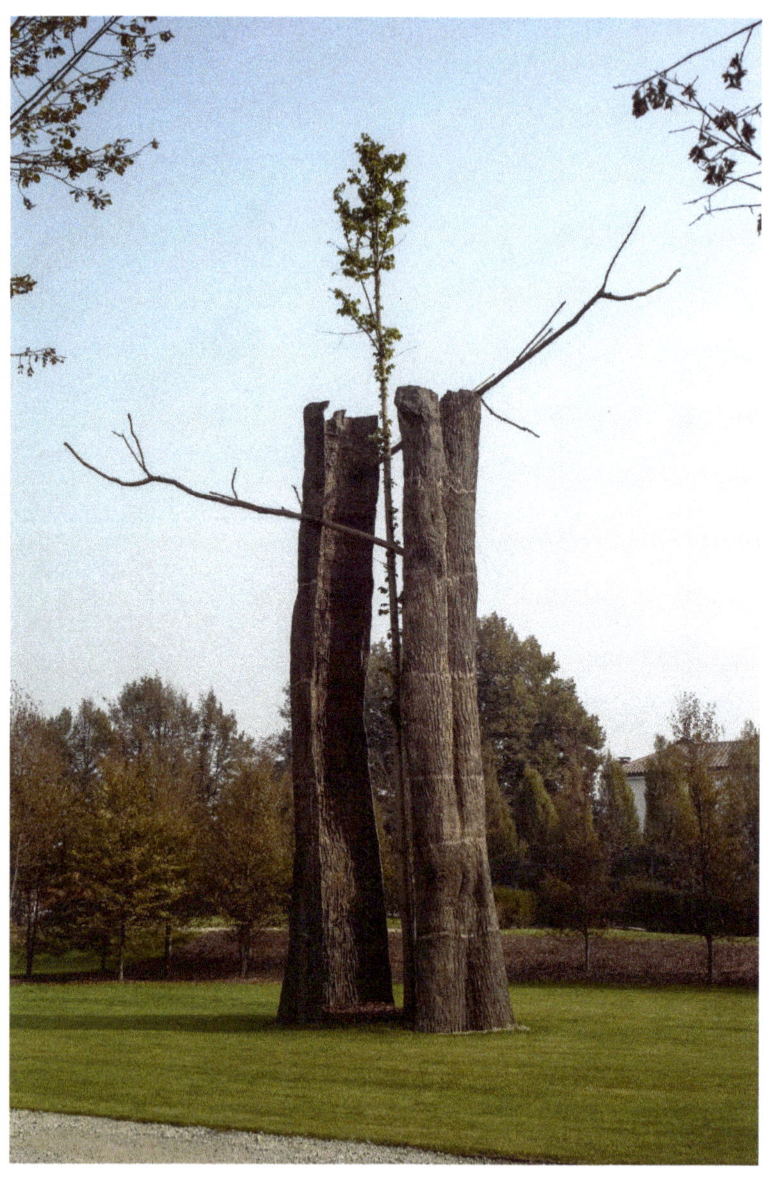

4.19 Giuseppe Penone, *Tra scorza e scorza* (*Between Bark and Bark*), 2003–7. Bronze, living linden (lime) tree, 1,030 x 430 x 280 cm. Permanent installation, *Il giardino delle sculture fluide* (*The Garden of Fluid Sculptures*), at Parco Basso della Reggia di Venaria Reale, Turin.

Photograph: © Archivio Penone

Penone's outdoor sculptures take on their fullest, most fluid potential here, at Carlo Emanuele II's emulation of Versailles. One of fourteen sculptures that the artist was commissioned to make for the re-establishment of these long-fallow gardens, which had been left in ruins after Napoleonic armies stormed over the Alps, *Between Bark and Bark* maintains an active relationship with the adolescent flora of the Italian palace's restored gardens.[51] As the live trees and plants of this garden grow and mature, having been replanted in the early 2000s, the bronze bark of Penone's sculpture takes on a new patina and continues to look more at home. Importantly, the relationship between the sculpture and the one tree that it encircles will change. Some day the central living tree may fill or even incorporate its bronze container. The temporal perspectivalism that powers this work emanates from the viewer's encounter, rather than from its representational form or a reflection on artistic intention.

Between Bark and Bark prompts consideration of past, present, and future in its very structure, directing the experience of the viewer through co-ordination of its multiple parts. Upon entering the towering enclosure to get closer to the living tree, one sees that the presently occupied space corresponds to the past of the felled tree from which the bronze bark was cast (figure 4.20). This is simultaneously the future space of the live tree at the centre, making the sculpture a kind of conceptual time machine. Penone argues that while this work has a representational element in its tree form, the meaning of the work as a proposition is precisely this consideration of time that it engenders through the physical experience of the work, through putting one's body in the space between the bronze bark of the sculptural element and the vegetal bark of the living tree.[52] Further, in the case of long-term installations like *Between Bark and Bark*, if one revisits them over time, the locations of past, present, and future are exposed as conditional and shifting. New perspectives on historical moments and future possibilities are produced through an embodied encounter with the sculpture's distinct parts, which are also held in a relationship to each other. The implied perspectives offered by a Baroque garden on its own might reinforce notions of the distance between the natural world and human culture, implying humans' right to dominate nature. Penone's long-term interventions in such historical constructions of the natural serve as a radical counterpoint to the master narratives made from within the philosophical foundations of European modernism.

Penone's installation at La Reggia di Venaria Reale is collectively titled *Il giardino delle sculture fluide* (*The Garden of the Fluid Sculptures*),

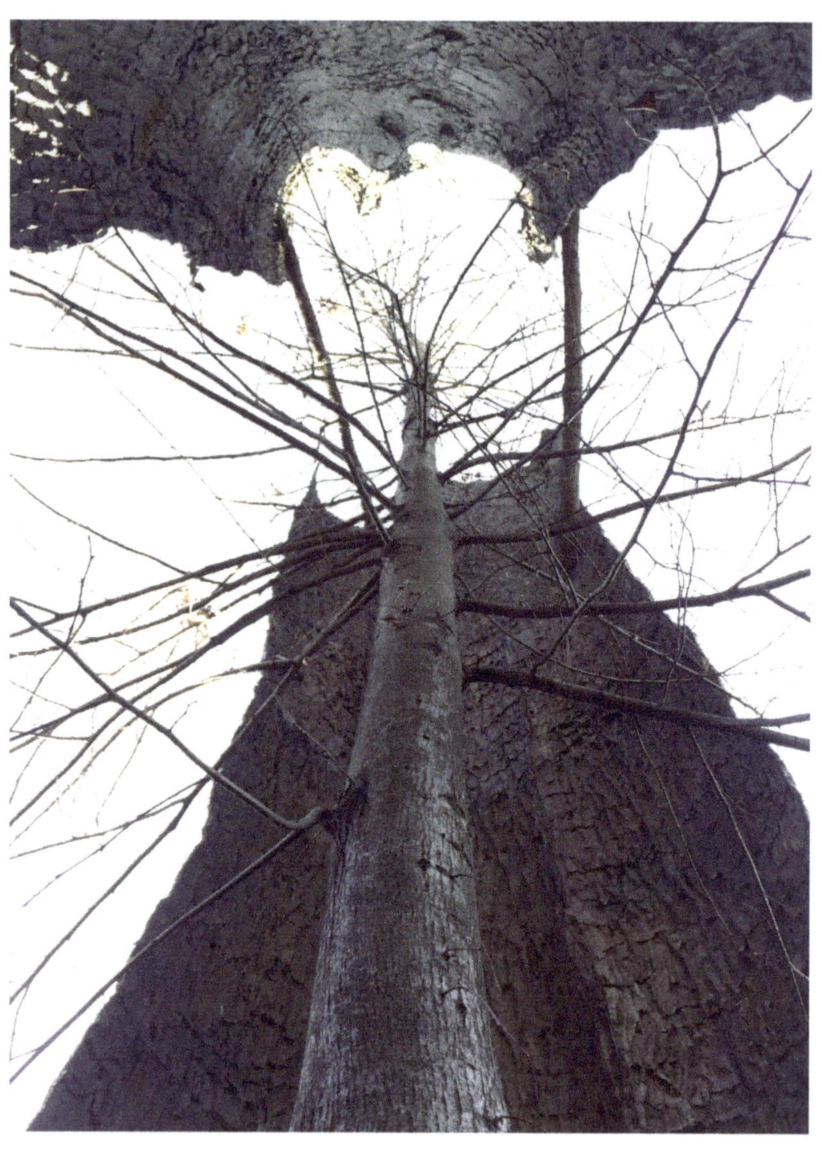

4.20 Giuseppe Penone, *Tra scorza e scorza* (*Between Bark and Bark*), 2003–7 (detail). Bronze, living linden (lime) tree, 1,030 x 430 x 280 cm. Permanent installation, *Il giardino delle sculture fluide* (*The Garden of the Fluid Sculptures*), at Parco Basso della Reggia di Venaria Reale (Turin).

Photograph: © Elizabeth Mangini

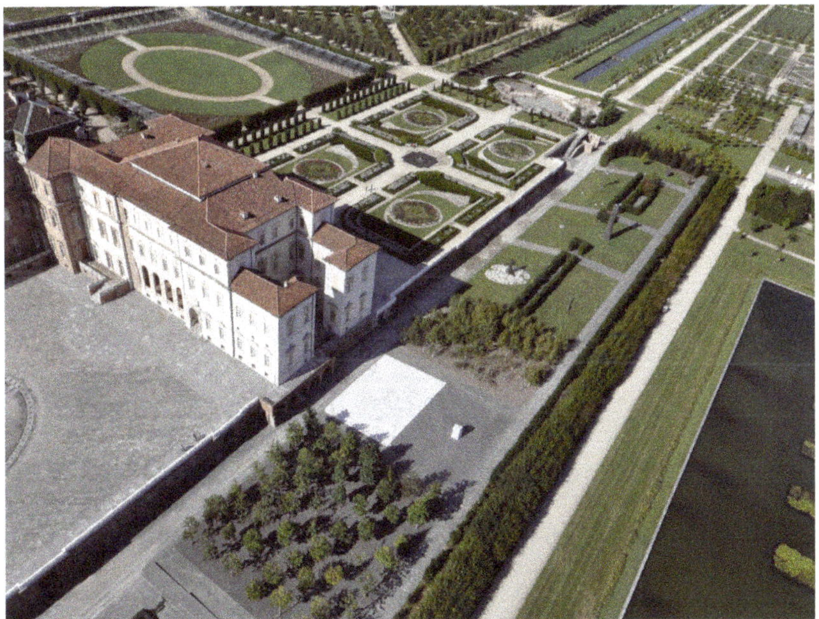

4.21 Giuseppe Penone, *Il giardino delle sculture fluide* (*The Garden of the Fluid Sculptures*), 2003–7 (aerial view, with Penone's works to the right of the palace). Parco Basso della Reggia di Venaria Reale (Turin).

Photograph: Courtesy Archivio Penone, © Reggia di Venaria Reale – Torino

and the various parts co-ordinate to posit the interconnected fluidity of matter when seen on a non-anthropocentric scale. Three of the fourteen works that make up the installation emphasize the concept by directly incorporating water: *Biforcazione* (*Bifurcation*, 2007), which is reminiscent of his earlier well in Münster; *Direzione: Verso la luce* (*Direction: Towards the Light*, 2007), which is a twelve-metre-tall bronze tree that emits "branches" of steam from its top; and *Disegno d'acqua* (*Water Drawing*, 2003–7), a large, black granite reflecting pool and fountain. These three works can be read as a symbolic nod to the historic use of water in such gardens, which often featured canals, fountains, and grottos to activate diverse views of the landscape and to provide a means of traversing the various divisions of the gardens. In fact, Penone's sculptural project occupies three hectares of land that boasted the palace's main water features in the time of Carlo Emanuele II, and the adjacent exterior walls of the palace still show remnants of having been encrusted with shells and coral arranged in decorative patterns. Penone's use of the term *Fluid Sculptures* for the program here hints at this connection to the site, and simultaneously it indicates the way his works are in perpetual flux, continually offering new perspectives on the relationship between nature and culture.

In some cases the bronze sculptures in the palace gardens will continue to shift in appearance as they are exposed to seasonal variations in weather and moisture. More obviously, works such as *Between Bark and Bark* and *Vegetal Gesture* are activated by the inclusion of living trees or plants in direct relation to the bronze objects. One of the fourteen sculptural incursions is hidden in a sparse copse of trees planted by the artist; only by walking through the thicket does one displace fallen leaves and mulch to reveal bronze "tree roots" underfoot. Titled *La luce dei passi* (*The Light of Steps*), the work consists of bronze elements that are effectively polished by being trodden upon, a physical engagement that increases the chances they will be visible to subsequent visitors. The work is typical of the symbiotic, fluid relationship among materials and bodies demonstrated in the installation as a whole.

The Light of Steps is one of five bosquets, or formal plantings of single species of trees, included among the fourteen works. Penone uses this historical garden device, characteristic of Le Nôtre's own garden designs, to give both pace and formal structure to the viewer's movement, demarcating one sculpture or outdoor "gallery" from the next. Two such bosquets, *Chiaroscuro* and *I colori dei temporale* (*The Color of Storms*), stand as sculptural installations in their own right. Each is a square area in which the artist has planted a single species: white-barked Himalayan birches and colourfully deciduous lindens, respectively. Since the living trees change with each season, they provide visible counterpoints to the relatively slower transformation of marble, bronze, granite, and river stones used by the artist in neighbouring plots. The remaining two bosquets are even more architectural, recalling classical exedra in their form: semicircular plantings of copper beech trees. In Ancient Rome, architectural exedra were designed for conversation, reflection, or veneration of sculptural deities. Penone's planted exedra fittingly act as parentheses, demarcating either end of the vast rectangle of his multi-part installation. Each also frames a sculptural piece that radically challenges one's temporal and spatial perspective: *Between Bark and Bark* at one end and *Direzione verso il centro della terra* (*Direction toward the Centre of the Earth*, 2007) at the other.

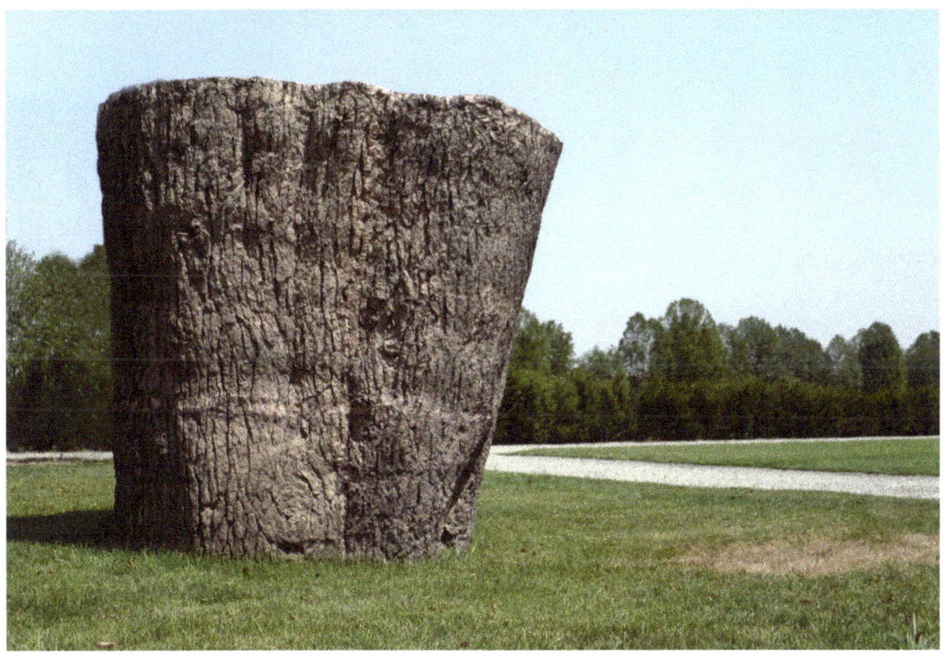

4.22 Giuseppe Penone, *Direzione verso il centro della terra* (*Direction toward the Centre of the Earth*), 2007. Bronze, 250 x 280 x 200 cm. Permanent installation, *Il giardino delle sculture fluide* (*The Garden of Fluid Sculptures*), at Parco Basso della Reggia di Venaria Reale (Turin).

Photograph: © Archvio Penone

Direction toward the Centre of the Earth may be the most succinct work in this fluid garden and a key to understanding Penone's ontology of sculpture. It is a massive bronze stump, narrower at the bottom and wider at the top, thus appearing to be growing downward into the ground (figure 4.22). In many ways this is the restaging, on a grand scale, of a fleeting gesture produced in 1969, one that goes unnoticed in many accounts of Penone's work. That year, Penone inserted a small lead-filled steel wedge into a crack that had naturally appeared on the concrete floor of Gian Enzo Sperone's Turin gallery.[53] Paolo Mussat Sartor, a collaborator of many Arte povera artists, snapped a photograph in which one sees the wedge as well as a partial view of the body of the artist who placed it. Titled *Verso il centro della terra* (*Toward the Centre of the Earth*, 1969), this ephemeral intervention was not part

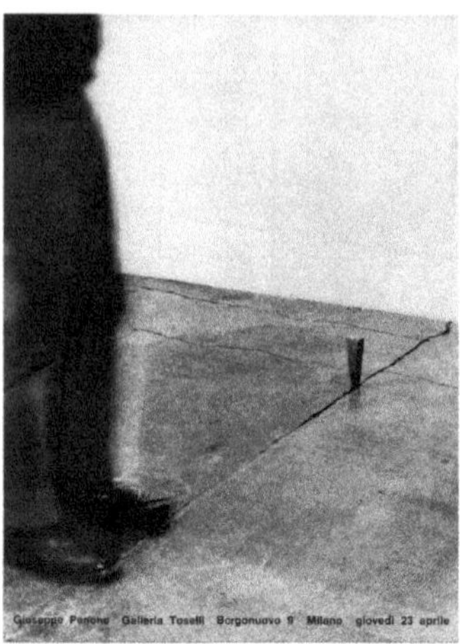

4.23 Exhibition announcement, Galleria Toselli, Milan, reproducing Giuseppe Penone's *Verso il centro della terra* (*Toward the Centre of the Earth*), 1969. Steel wedge, 15 x 4 x 4 cm. Intervention at Gian Enzo Sperone Gallery, 1969.

Original photograph: Paolo Mussat Sartor, © Paolo Mussat Sartor. Photograph of announcement: © Archivio Penone

of a specific show, and it lives on almost exclusively as a photograph, most notably on the invitation card for his April 1970 solo show at a different gallery in Milan (figure 4.23). Like the casual insertion of the wedge into the extant crack, the carefully cast and crafted bronze stump at La Venaria draws our attention to what was already present but unseen and underfoot. Like the roots of a tree, a whole world is hidden below the horizontal plane to which the sensory centres of our upright bodies are opposed. By positing the visibility of this invisible space, *Direction toward the Centre of the Earth* draws the viewer beyond the object itself, telescoping out to overturn perception of the phenomenal world itself.

Both of these works, *Toward the Centre of the Earth* and *Direction toward the Centre of the Earth*, might be read to nod to Piero Manzoni's *Socle du monde* (*Base of the World*, 1961), a stout iron-and-bronze box, with its title written "upside-down" (figure 4.24). Penone has remarked that this work of the Milanese artist, in particular, challenged him to think of sculpture in radically new ways. Having somewhat notoriously signed living bodies, sold his own excrement, and imprinted his thumb onto boiled chicken eggs, Manzoni here used a simple gesture of inverting

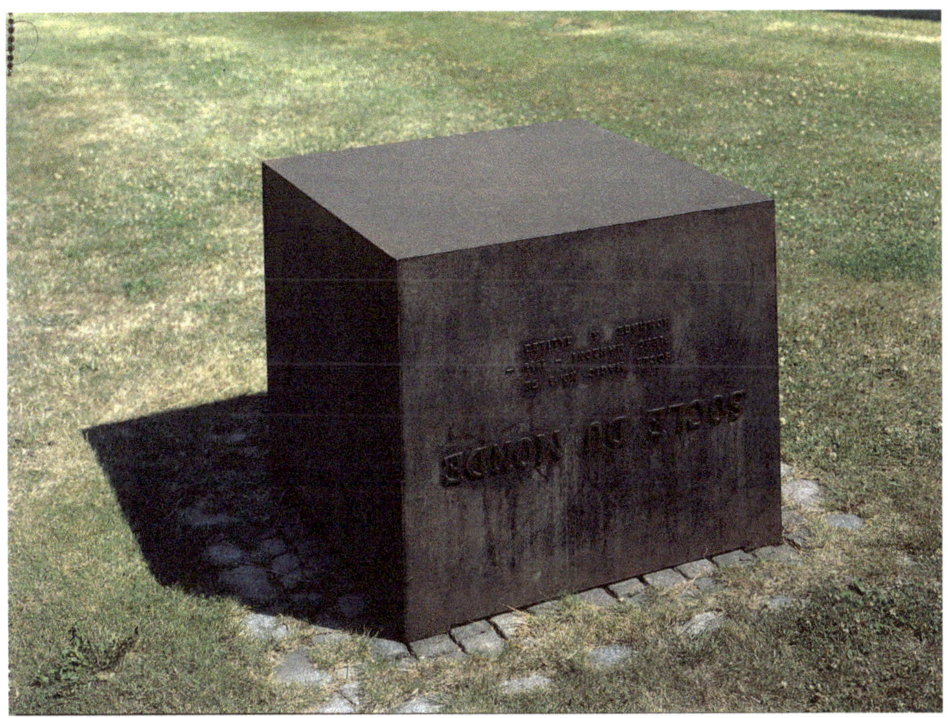

4.24 Piero Manzoni, *Socle du monde* (*Base of the World*), 1961. Iron and bronze, 82 x 100 x 100 cm. HEART, Herning Museum of Contemporary Art.

Photograph by Louis Schnakenberg, courtesy of Fondazione Piero Manzoni, Milan

a sign, taking the deictic aspect of artistic gesture to its logical extreme, and making the whole globe into his artwork. From the point of view of sculpture, however, Manzoni's *Base of the World* is evidence that a simple interruption of the flow of phenomenological perception can allow, if not provoke, revolutionary perspectives. Sculpture's ability to catalyse such conceptual perspectivalism emerges in ephemeral works like Penone's wedge and is monumentalized in projects like his inverted tree stump, an evolution traced here through the artist's foregrounding of time during his lifelong work with trees as a form and a subject matter.

The stated fluidity of the installation at the royal palace of Venaria demonstrates Penone's commitment to refining a theoretical position in which the ontology of sculpture, especially at a material level, is necessarily conditioned by time. Seen together, his tactics underscore what sculpture can do in the time and space of an encounter; further, they provide evidence that the palpable link between concept and embodied experience is central to the discipline. Sculpture is temporal in its very structure. Sculptures like Penone's, which are designed to amplify this aspect beyond the duration of a single encounter, expose the viewer to an unfolding entanglement of potential perspectives. The temporal aspect of Penone's ontology of sculpture is a theoretical position argued through the works themselves and emerging most distinctly in his works with trees. Each tautological wooden tree, each indexical bronze bark, and each long-term installation of sculptural elements with live flora prompts a radically autonomous perspective on time. Once such an expanded perspective is achieved, other binary categories – like nature and culture, plant and human – that would limit our reading of the work appear unworkably reductive. Sculpture, in Penone's hands, is a material means by which one can acquire a glimpse of the infinite perspectives that constitute the nature of being.

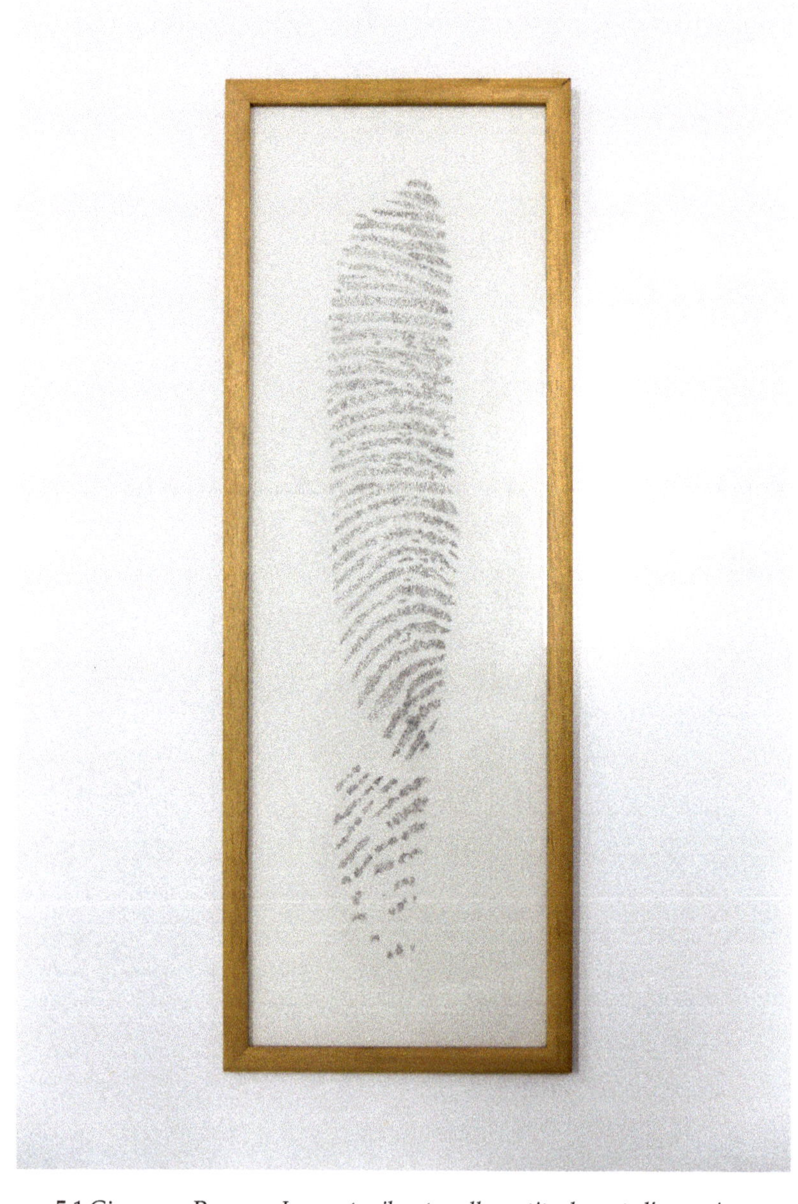

5.1 Giuseppe Penone, *Impronte rilevate sulla matita durante l'esecuzione* (*Fingerprints Revealed on the Pencil during Execution*), 1975 (detail). Graphite on paper. Four elements; this image, 61.5 x 28.5 cm (with frame).

Conclusion
An Ontology of Sculpture – Form, Process, and Palimpsest

In 1965 the Turin-based publisher Giulio Einaudi issued a series of short stories by the Italian fabulist author Italo Calvino that make a fantastic history of the cosmos. Together these *Cosmicomiche* (*Cosmicomics*) form a sweeping tale told from the fragmented perspective of Qfwfq, a fluid narrator, who, among other things, witnesses the big bang, discovers meiosis as a multicellular organism, is a dinosaur who recalls his own extinction, and captains a steamship sailing for Liverpool. Calvino weaves a counterpoint between microcosm and macrocosm through these stories, tasking his reader with beholding vast and moving swaths of time and space from the perspective of the chimerical narrator's present recollection. Among these pages, Qfwfq is also twice a mollusc, a seemingly insignificant identity that nevertheless allows the writer to examine form and, in particular, what any given form allows and what it limits.

In "The Spiral," Qfwfq the mollusc recalls that, as to form, he did not initially have any, "or rather I didn't know that you *could* have one."[1] It is only later, when the mollusc becomes aware of "others," that he wants to make something to mark his presence and to individuate himself from "all the rest." By secreting calcareous matter, Qfwfq eventually makes a spiral shell, which offers protection as well as formal subjectivity. In "Shells and Time," set 520 million years later, it is the now fossilized shell of Qfwfq the mollusc that gives rise to the concept of time. Here Qfwfq claims, "It if hadn't been for me, time would never have existed."[2] He explains that his making of a shell was an effort to fix the unwieldy continuum of presentness, with each turn of the spiral constructing a kind of clock of "shell-time." More importantly, although Qfwfq realizes that this effort was a personal failure because it could not continue beyond his individual lifespan, he maintains that his little "shell-clock," and others like it, contributed to the creation of what might be termed *an earth-clock*: a material strata through which contemporary humans read time. "Humanity," Qfwfq writes, "needed the cross-section of the Earth's crust to throw up our shells, which we had abandoned some hundred, three hundred, five hundred million years before, for the vertical dimension of time to open up to you and release you from the continual cycle of the stars' circuit in which you continue to pigeonhole the course of your fragmentary existence."[3] The mollusc laments that humans, with their blinding anthropocentrism, lack the perspective to see this complex evolutionary structure as anything but their own invention.

Like Calvino's mollusc shell, Penone's sculptures indicate more than their visible forms. Whether or not Penone read this particular book by Calvino is of little consequence for the comparison. It should be noted, however, that the artist traded one of his *Eight-Metre Tree* sculptures to Giulio Einaudi in exchange for over three thousand books published by the press. Beyond the evocative equivalence between objects with a shared vegetal substrate – ideas carved in wood traded for others written on paper – at least one of Calvino's books was among those received by the artist as part of the exchange.[4]

Penone's objects denote matrices as much as they do materials and, in so doing, they invite reflection on and measurement of sensory experiences. Within each artwork, remnants of the artist's touch model the complex negotiations brought to bear in the meeting of forces over time. Tool marks left on stone or wood offer visible signs of the artist's presence and labour. Yet the indicated labour often seems to be minimized, if not hidden, as in a beam returned to resembling the living tree from which it was milled, a stone carved to be identical to one found in a river, and a bronze sculpture destined to oxidize and blend into the surrounding woods. Penone's assertion of his presence is tempered by its effacement, demonstrating that artistic agency is only a fragment of the work's coming into form. Making sculpture, in this framework, is a declaration of subjectivity that merely intervenes in the life of a material without the hubristic recourse to domination. Such a notion of sculpture addresses itself to the future, while also testifying to moments of presence that have passed. In Penone's work, indexes of the body – in particular, fingerprints – shoulder the task of making legible this polyvocal entanglement of self and world, repositioning form and process as anti-anthropocentric, reciprocal, and contingent.

Penone uses fingerprints and other indexes to highlight the reciprocal formativity of touch. This has already been demonstrated in the previous chapters, including analyses of *Gli anni dell albero più uno*

(1969), *Vaso* (1972), *Palpebre* (1978), and *Gesti vegetali* (1981–4). The artist has also, over the decades, made many drawings that can be loosely described as drawings of fingerprints. Like wooden trees, the category "drawings of fingerprints" may at first seem like an inelegant description, if not a tautology. Nevertheless, such works come into meaning precisely in their probing of the gaps between a *fingerprint* as an instantaneous, often incidental trace of presence, pressure, or touch and a *drawing* as a slow, purposeful meeting of diverse materials in the service of rendering a concept. In each of these the artist contrasts the passive mark, which nonetheless differentiates his from other bodies, with the active response of materials to his touch. These interactions give rise to a purposeful, visual form of communication transmitted through that same epidermis.

Drawing is a particularly fecund form through which Penone can subvert his own subjectivity because works on paper are, stereotypically, framed as more direct, less inhibited, and generally closer to the germ of artistic intention and process than are other media. Penone's fingerprint drawings, however, are far from simple sketches or plans. Rather, they interrogate the meeting of artistic subjectivity and material agency through the making of the drawing. In *Impronte rilevate sulla matita durante l'esecuzione* (*Fingerprints Revealed on the Pencil during Execution*, 1975) the artist highlights the co-ordinated pressure exerted on the tool by the hand – its marshalling of nerve endings and muscles – in order to make a pencil mark appear on a piece of paper (figure 5.1). The artist coated his hands with charcoal and, after drawing with a pencil, used clear adhesive tape to lift the charcoal fingerprints off the implement. The resultant films, projected to enlarge the marks, became the basis for further drawings. They are drawings, in a sense, of the pencil's perspective or at least drawings of the pressure exerted on the pencil's shaft.[5] Here again, that thing which would seem to indicate the artist's presence and subjectivity – his fingerprint – transposes the artist's hand to a visual signifier of the places of its intersection with a tool (in this case, a pencil). Although the scale of these redrawn fingerprints reaches the point of near abstraction, they are still recognizable as human through the familiar organization of lines and whorls (figure 5.2). These works on paper thus make palpable the physicality of drawing through a subtle counterpoint between incidental fingerprint and purposeful lines. That is, while they are legible representations of the artist's skin, they only have meaning as *fingerprints* in connection with the act of drawing.

Twenty years later Penone introduced a new approach to the drawing of fingerprints. In *Propagazione* (*Propagation*, 1994–5) he made an

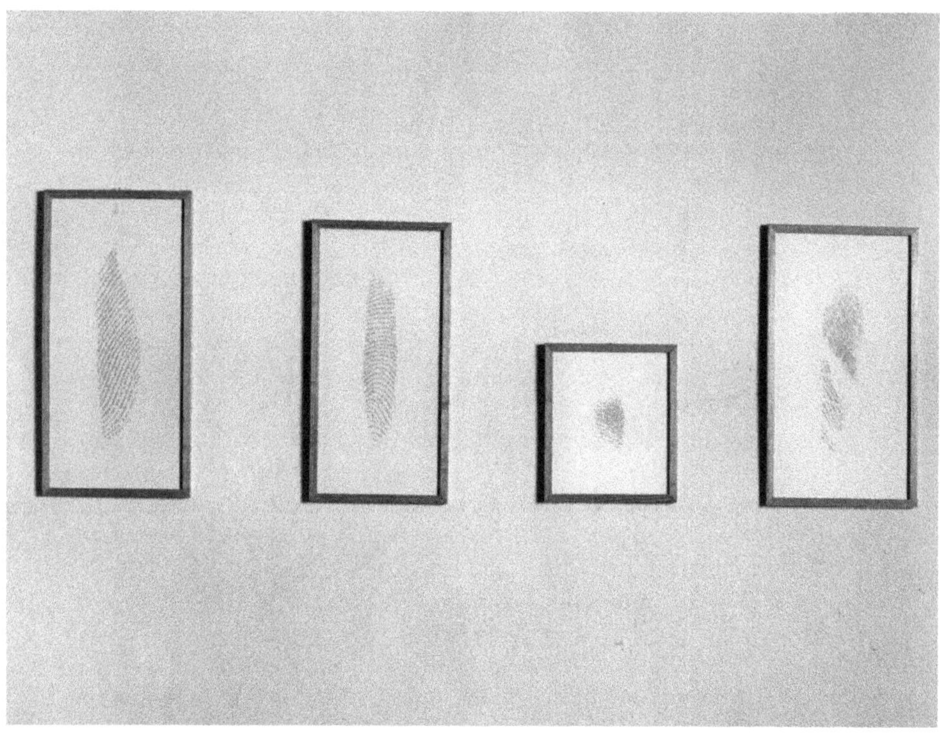

5.2 Giuseppe Penone, *Impronte rilevate sulla matita durante l'esecuzione* (*Fingerprints Revealed on the Pencil during Execution*), 1975. Installation view at Lucerne, 1977.

Photograph: Archivio Penone, © Archivio Penone

indexical mark – an inked fingerprint – at the centre of a piece of paper. This mark is doubly indexical in a semiotic sense because he specifically used the finger referred to as the *index*. (The duality is the same in English as in Italian, where *indice* also contains the possibility of both meanings.) In a profound paradox, the print from one's index finger merges the body with its politicized subject (as when one applies for a passport or a driver's licence), and the index finger is also used in a deictic gesture to "indicate" something apart from the body. Starting from this mark, simultaneously effortless and loaded with meaning, Penone drew expansive concentric lines, following the whorls of his skin and expanding the fingerprint to fill the page. These lines appear to

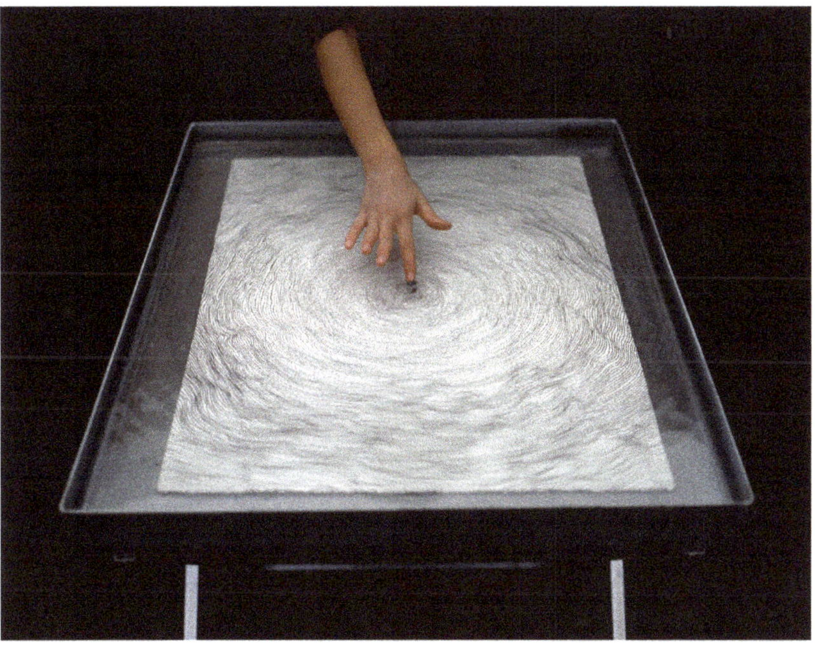

5.3 Giuseppe Penone, *Propagazione* (*Propagation*), 1994–5. Ink on paper, zinced iron, acrylic, water. Drawing, 69 x 49 cm; overall, 86 x 83 x 62.6 cm.

Photograph: Archivio Penone, © Archivio Penone

emanate from the single fingerprint, seemingly in response to the point of contact. The drawing was initially shown underneath a clear, shallow tray of water as if it were submerged in liquid (figure 5.3). The interactive installation tactic – rare in Penone's oeuvre – makes it plain that a touch like this is connected to its context. Even the gentle introduction of a single finger disturbs a still pool of water; the breaking of its surface tension is marked by the ripples and mirrored by drawn lines. Here the conditionality of touch becomes visible through the meeting of two substances, each of which is at least temporarily deformed by the encounter.[6]

By 1997 the expanding lines of Penone's fingerprint had exceeded the space of its support, running off the paper and onto the walls of Konrad Fischer's Düsseldorf gallery. Here the drawn lines flowed beyond the viewer's peripheral vision, extending his touch into phenomenological space. In 1999 Penone used all five fingers of each hand to create a truly immersive multi-part drawing (*Propagation 10*, 1997–9). Key to reading these works is consideration of the meaning of the term *propagation*. On the one hand, it refers to natural reproduction: the way a plant or animal is bred through a parent stock. In other usage, it describes a way of measuring the movement of energy through a material: a potential, lyrical means to gauge artistic labour in the making of sculpture.[7] Moreover, *propagation* provides an apt definition of sculpture itself: it has the dual character of something that has its own DNA and simultaneously is formed by physical interaction with its environment. Combining production and reproduction, propagation can also be understood as the way an idea is widely spread.

The poetic and tactical potential of the term *propagation* connects different areas of Penone's artistic research. Consider its meaning in relation to the way his works highlight fluidity, such as that between active and passive states or of a given material when viewed over time. *Wave propagation*, in particular, refers to electromagnetic, sonic, light, and seismic waves, as well to the movement of water. *Disegno d'acqua* (*Water Drawing*, 2003–7), mentioned in chapter 4 as part of Penone's fourteen-part outdoor sculpture program at La Reggia di Venaria Reale, could be said to propagate the traces of touch through a fluid fingerprint (figures 5.4 and 5.5). *Water Drawing* is in fact a subtle fountain in which intermittent jets emit bubbles that "draw" the artist's enlarged fingerprint once every couple of minutes. Recalling the first drawing in the *Propagation* series, the fountain provides a visual demonstration of the way that touch sculpts even the most elusive, fluid materials. The effervescent water here becomes a literal but ephemeral index of his touch, appearing for a few seconds before the water regains its smooth surface. In the context of the *bosquets* and bronzes of *The Garden of the Fluid Sculptures*, this fountain provides a means to read all the fingerprint works in his oeuvre as connected to the temporal issues raised in Penone's work with trees.

In *Water Drawing* and each of the *Propagation* works, Penone's expanded fingerprints also take on the appearance of the cross-sections of tree trunks (figures 5.6 and 5.7). Here the visual resonance between human body and tree comes full circle, achieving new meaning through the conflation of the formal and the temporal. Although each actual fingerprint was made in a matter of seconds, the drawings are the result of a long, repetitive, and painstaking process. Penone further increases the duration of this action by purposefully using a very "toothy" or rough paper, which requires intense concentration and a steady hand as he moves the pen or pencil across the page.[8]

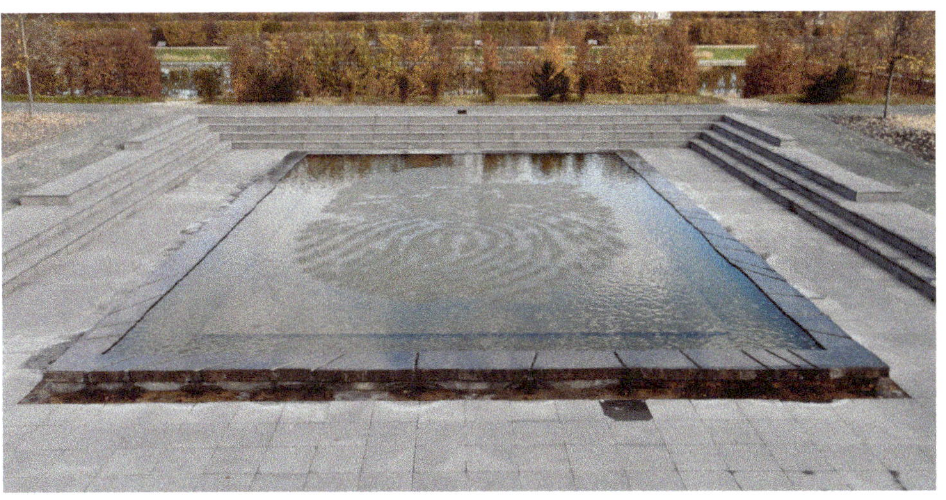

5.4 Giuseppe Penone, *Disegno d'acqua* (*Water Drawing*), 2003–7. Water, timed air flows, black granite, Verde Alpi marble, Volga Blu granite, 60 x 2,702 x 3,450 cm. Permanent installation, *Il giardino delle sculture fluide* (*The Garden of the Fluid Sculptures*), at Parco Basso della Reggia di Venaria Reale, Turin. Installation view.

Photograph: Archivio Penone, © Archivio Penone

In this way the fingerprint drawings challenge the fast, gestural bravado of mid-century modernism, offering instead a diachronic view of a work's making. The "rings" of the fingerprint become the rings of the tree and offer a slow, vertical perspective on time. Perhaps a tree does not know why it creates a new layer of bark season after season, any more than the average human considers why fingertips maintain a unique set of grooves over one's lifespan; yet the fact that each organism forms itself in this way provides the means to read human time and tree time together. In these fingerprint drawings Penone makes an iconic and purposeful image of something usually indexical and incidental, connecting the work of the artist to the natural processes of the material world.

The profound impact of reading the traces left by human hands on the material world as anti-anthropocentric again extends the impact of Penone's work beyond the presumed limits of aesthetics. Indeed, since the turn of the third millennium, some geologists have been arguing for a new conceptualization of time itself in strikingly similar ways. The term *Anthropocene*, which seeks to differentiate the moment human

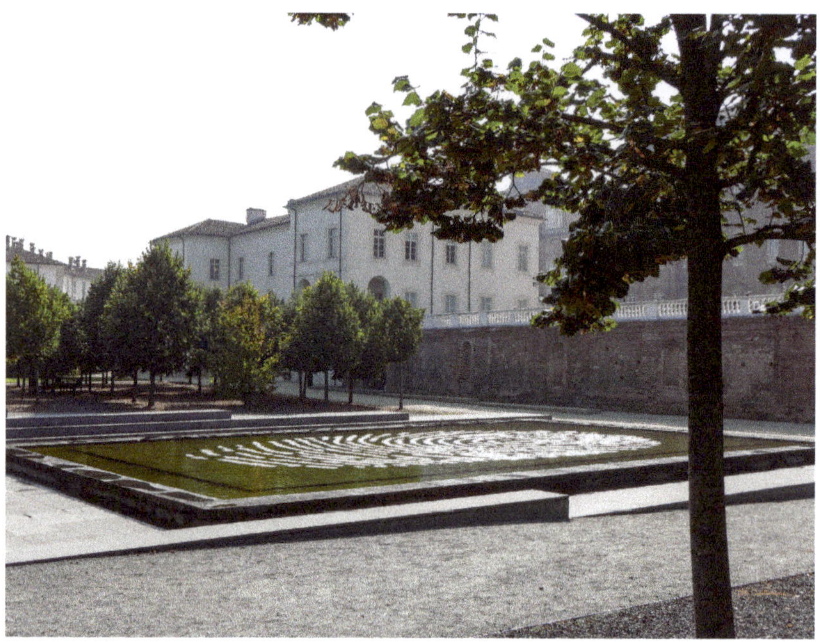

5.5 Giuseppe Penone, *Disegno d'acqua* (*Water Drawing*), 2003–7. Water, timed air flows, black granite, Verde Alpi marble, Volga Blu granite, 60 x 2,702 x 3,450 cm. Permanent installation, *Il giardino delle sculture fluide* (*The Garden of the Fluid Sculptures*), at Parco Basso della Reggia di Venaria Reale, Turin. Installation view.

Photograph: Archivio Penone, © Archivio Penone

activity began to shape the material strata of the earth in measurable ways, gives form to a line of thought that goes back for centuries but has gained new currency since the year 2000, owing to the rising environmental crises brought on by human-induced climate change.[9] Although the Greek root for "human" is privileged in the moniker, the supremacy of humans over other natural materials is compellingly problematized in the scientific and philosophical debates around introducing a new term to the geologic time scale.

Simon Lewis and Mark Maslin, professors of earth sciences at University College London, present a case for the ethical impetus of recognizing an Anthropocene. For them, the geological sediment from the year 1610 provides the earliest visual evidence of the effects of the

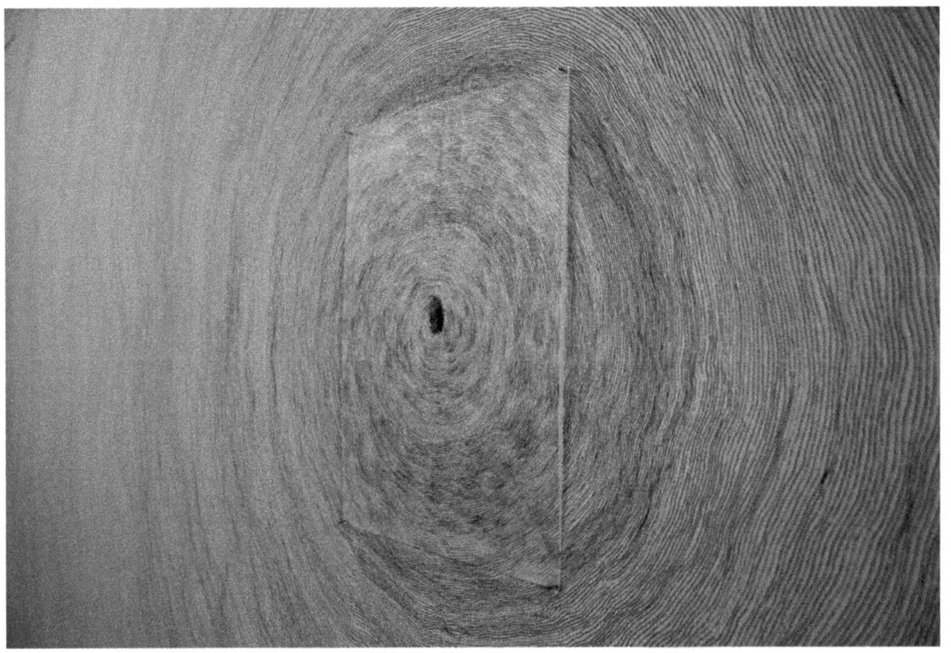

5.6 Giuseppe Penone, *Propagazione (Propagation)*, 1995–2009 (detail). China ink and typographic ink on paper, marker on wall; dimensions variable. Installation view at the exhibition *Cella. Strutture di emarginazione e disciplinamento* in Ex Carcere Minorile, Complesso Monumentale di San Michele a Ripa, Rome, 5–23 November 2009.

Photograph: Archivio Penone, ©Archivio Penone

Columbian exchange and indicates the beginning of a new relationship between humans and the planet, which is still pervasive in contemporary economic, political, and ecological systems.[10] European exploration of and colonialism in the Americas, which gave rise to the scientific revolution as well as mercantile capitalism, had a material impact that can be read in tree-rings, ice cores, lake sediments, fossil records, and even in human bones.[11] Lewis and Maslin argue that the geological foundation of the Anthropocene requires recognition of the interconnectedness of humans and the material strata of the earth, disrupting the idea that humans act upon a separate thing called Nature. Despite its name, the Anthropocene puts an end to an anthropocentric way of thinking that has dominated the West for centuries. This may, and

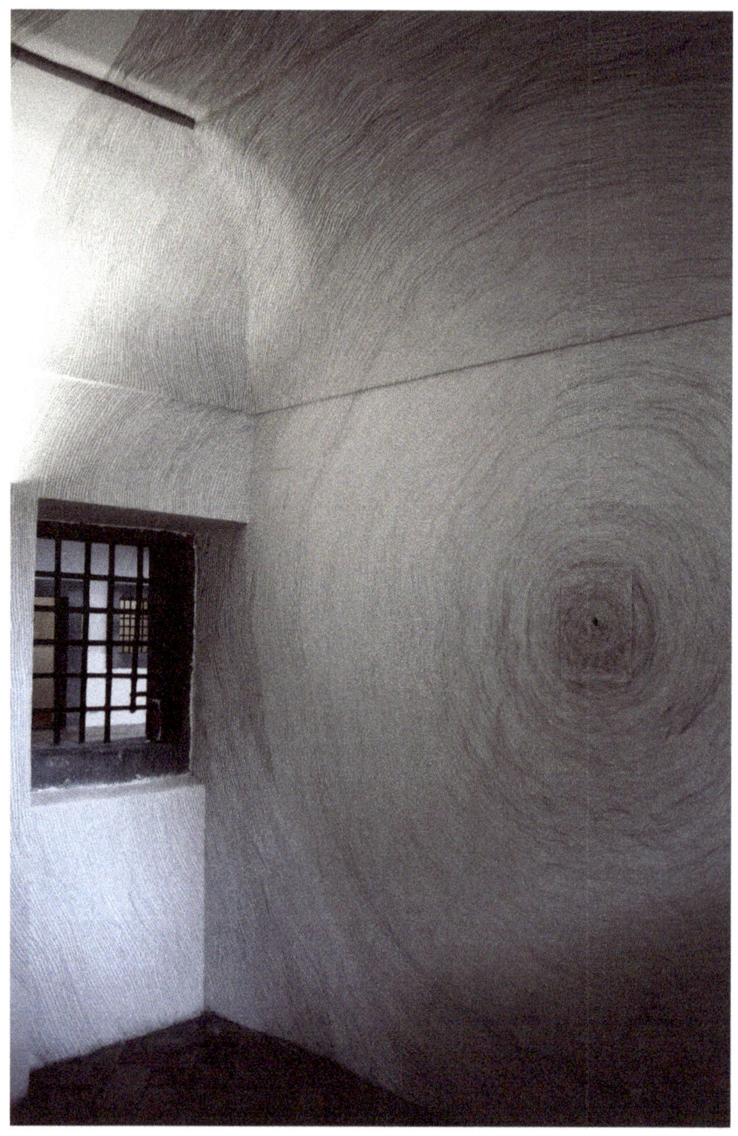

5.7 Giuseppe Penone, *Propagazione (Propagation)*, 1995–2009. China ink and typographic ink on paper, marker on wall; dimensions variable. Installation view at the exhibition *Cella. Strutture di emarginazione e disciplinamento* in Ex Carcere Minorile, Complesso Monumentale di San Michele a Ripa, Rome, 5–23 November 2009.

Photograph: Archivio Penone, ©Archivio Penone

perhaps *should*, affect our behaviour, making the academic naming of a geological period a pressing political issue.[12]

Similarly, Penone's diverse, evolving practice demonstrates that the nature of sculpture is not fixed within its disciplinary boundaries or limited to irreducible media; rather, it is realized through a constellation of corporeal, material, linguistic, and temporal perspectives. For more than five decades the artist's steady probing of the formal limits of the human body and organic matter, and their interaction over time, amounts to an ontology of sculpture that surpasses the confines of aesthetics. His sculpture provides a means to broaden one's perceptual horizons and, in so doing, critically challenges the stagnant dialectical structures of experience that have dominated human thinking since at least the time of Descartes.

Penone is adamant that, with regard to offering such perspectives, sculpture opens possibilities that other artistic media do not. In 1981 the artist identified that the importance of the discipline is rooted in the way that sculptures, although obviously human constructions, carry the possibility of being read or misread as natural forms.

> In sculpture there is a possibility of total coalescence with other elements, which does not exist in painting since this can be only a medium. My sculptures are supposed to be read also as being crafted by hand, but I want that they keep their strong load of reality. The traces of my fingers which apply the layers of clay make it possible to recognize the object as a cultural item made by man, but the way in which it was produced, the layering, could have been of a natural origin, could have been the work of a mollusc.[13]

Penone here expresses a desire to create works in a way that can be partially confused with the natural processes of other organisms. He imagines that a sculpture may appear to be at once a manifestation of human will *and* the product of an instinctive process. That is, when one approaches one of Penone's bronze tree sculptures in a public park, one might initially think it is a living tree and realize only upon reflection or closer inspection that it is an artwork. This notion is much more than an instance of the uncanny or a practical joke. It gets at the core of art's power to expand one's world view because it asks us to hold these two impressions together, simultaneously. Like the concept of the Anthropocene, this aspect of Penone's project shifts the balance of power away from single human actors towards a more entangled view of culture and nature. Such experiences, catalysed by his works, offer the potential to affect our ethics, politics, and ways of being in the world.

Art's means of address is always poetic, rather than prosaic, inviting us indirectly into such discourses. In their incorporation of the natural, the constructed, and the fantastic, Penone's works gently beckon viewers to inhabit a world view that resonates with the aspects of Italian culture that were most vital when the artist was forming the central questions of his artistic project. These aspects included a reckoning with the cosmic world views of Italy's ancient past (similarly reflected in Calvino's writings); a philosophical critique of Cartesianism (modelled in post-war painting discourses, and challenged by phenomenology's focus on the body); and the increasingly secular and industrialized future of a modern republic (in which autonomy over one's time and labour was a central concern). Encounters with Penone's artworks afford new ways of perceiving the material world – past, present, and future – in which humans play a limited role. In contrast to modernism's idealized anthropocentrism, his works marshal the body's multiple sensory organs in order to reveal the imbricated nature of being.

Giuseppe Penone's five-decade-long investigations – his objects, interventions, and provocations – have contributed to new ways of knowing the nature of human interaction with the material world. In his hands, sculpture is no longer mired in the battle between material and representational form that so troubled the Italian art critic Argan. Instead, Penone's practice is indexical, tautological, and deliberately palimpsest – a figurative page on which one reads multiple fragmentary texts simultaneously, sorting out meaning through constant rereading, reviewing, and taking up radically shifting perspectives in space and time. Engaging his sculptures requires the expansion of one's perspective to the point at which the phrase *seeing through closed eyelids* is perfectly sensible.

Notes

Introduction

1 Turin is the historic home of the Savoia (Savoy) family, who ruled the country following the "resurgence" of a unified "Italy" after centuries of foreign occupation, and who remained in power until the establishment of the First Republic in 1947 (though only nominally after Mussolini's ascendancy in 1922). Population figures come from Ginsborg, *A History of Contemporary Italy: Society and Politics, 1943–1988* (London: Penguin, 1990; reprint, New York: Palgrave Macmillan, 2003), 220. By some accounts, it was a city deeply divided between the remains of a genteel upper class and the many migrants who came to work in the factories.

2 The inaugural exhibition at the Galleria d'Arte Moderna (GAM) was *Capolavori di Arte Moderna nelle raccolte private* (*Masterworks of Modern Art in Private Collections*). See Giorgina Bertolino and Francesca Pola, eds., *Torino Sperimentale 1959–69: Una storia della cronaca: il sistema delle arti come avanguardia,*" exhibition catalogue (Turin, Italy: Giulio Baffi Editore, 2010), 20.

3 Germano Celant, "How to Escape from the Hallucinations of History," in *Arte Povera=Art Povera,* trans. Paul Blanchard (Milan: Electa, 1985), 22.

4 Other galleries included La Bussola, Galatea, and Il Punto. Additionally, exhibition spaces included the International Centre for Aesthetic Research and the Museo Sperimentale (Experimental Museum), which transferred its collection and varied activities from Genoa to Turin in 1964 when founder Eugenio Battisti departed for a teaching post in the United States. Il Deposito D'Arte Presente (DDP, the Warehouse of Contemporary Art) – a collaborative endeavour of the collector Marcello Levi and the young dealer Gian Enzo Sperone – was also an important venue for artistic exchange, and Penone would first show his works in public there. The DDP also played host to a somewhat notorious screening by Roman poet and filmmaker Pier Paolo Pasolini. The DDP was, in essence, a

constantly changing exhibition, storage, and event space, and there is little documentation of its short lifespan save a few crowded installation photographs. For more on Pasolini and his artistic contemporaries, see Ara J. Merjian, *Against the Avant-Garde: Pier Paolo Pasolini, Contemporary Art, and Neocapitalism* (Chicago: University of Chicago Press, 2020).

5 Claire Gilman notes that Francis Bacon, for example, had seventeen shows in Turin's galleries in the 1960s. Claire Gilman, "Arte Povera's Theater: Artifice and Anti-Modernism in Italian Art of the 1960s" (PhD diss., Columbia University, 2006), 45.

6 Anna Minola, et al, *Gian Enzo Sperone: Torino-Roma-New York; 35 anni di mostre tra Europa e America*, vol. 1, *Torino Milano 1963–1972* (Turin, Italy: Hopefulmonster, 2000), 106–7.

7 My translation. "Torino, nel giro dei due ultimi anni, è riuscita ad inserirsi tra i centri più vivi d'Europa." Lea Vergine, "Torino '68: Nevrosi e sublimazione," *Metro*, 1968, 22.

8 On 27 November 1967 the student occupation of the university's central location, the Palazzo Campana, and the Facoltà di Lettere e Filosofia (Department of Humanities and Philosophy) established a model for similar protests nationwide that have been likened by historians to the surprise attacks of guerilla warfare, with students regularly interrupting lectures and hijacking the discussions towards their own aims. They coalesced spontaneously in small-scale disruptions that succeeded in upsetting the institution's normal operations. These tactical impulses, which drew on Piedmont's anti-Fascist and partisan legacies, were perhaps most immediately inspired by Che Guevara, whose murder in Bolivia a month earlier had made him an instant martyr figure, and by Vietnamese responses to US and Soviet aggressions that made daily news in Italy. For more on the general climate around the university, see Pietro Derossi, "Anni Cinquanta/Settanta, alcuni ridcori," in *Un'avventura internazionale: Torino e le arti 1950–1970*, exhibition catalogue, ed. Ida Gianelli (Turin, Italy: Castello di Rivoli, 1993), 175–7.

9 Ginsborg, *History of Contemporary Italy*, 301.

10 Elizabeth Mangini, "1000 Words: Giuseppe Penone," *Artforum* 49, no. 2 (October 2010): 226–9.

11 Giuseppe Penone, interview by Elizabeth Mangini, 15 July 2013, at Café La Cicchetteria, Via Bologna 5, Turin, written notes.

12 Giuseppe Penone, interview by Elizabeth Mangini, 4 September 2014, in Los Angeles, written notes.

13 Penone initially felt somewhat apart from the Turin scene because he had arrived later than some of the others and he preferred focusing on his work to socializing. The loose structure of the art academy meant that he could go home to work on sculptures, using materials that were familiar,

but affinities with other artists in Turin grew nonetheless, and it has remained his centre of work for five decades. Giuseppe Penone, interview by Elizabeth Mangini, 15 July 2013, at Café La Cicchetteria, Via Bologna 5, Turin, written notes.

14 An excellent English-language account of the genesis, development, and afterlife of the term *Arte povera* can be found in Jacopo Galimberti's essay "A Third-Worldist Art? Germano Celant's Invention of *Arte Povera*," in *Art History*, April 2013, 418–41. In particular, Galimberti considers the divergence of the initial use of the term from its later reconfiguration in Celant's own historiography, in which he republished many of these original texts.

15 Gemano Celant, "Arte povera: Appunti per una guerriglia," *Flash Art* (November/December 1967). Printed in English as "Arte povera: Notes for a Guerilla War," in Celant, *Arte Povera = Art Povera*, trans. Paul Blanchard (Milan: Electa, 1985), 35–7.

16 Lea Vergine, *Dall'Informazione alla Body Art dieci voci dell'arte contemporanea: 1960/70* (Turin, Italy: Cooperativa Editoriale Studio Forma, 1976), 112.

17 Penone, email message to the author, 20 September 2009.

18 My translation; "È stato un incontro straordinario; fin dai primi giorni ha dimostrato un'eccezionale abilità a modellare (il nonno materno era scultore). Nel giro di un anno ha superato la prassi del modellare e ha cambiato completamente il tipo di lavoro." Gilberto Zorio, interview with Mirella Bandini, Turin, 1972, in Mirella Bandini, *1972: Arte Povera a Torino* (Turin, Italy: U. Allemandi, 2002), 109. Originally published in *NAC*, no. 3 (March 1973).

19 Giuseppe Penone, interview by Elizabeth Mangini, Café La Cicchetteria, Via Bologna 5, Turin, 15 July 2013, written notes.

20 Minola, *Gian Enzo Sperone*, 21.

21 My translation; "aveva visto delle cose che gli sono servite per la liberazione del linguaggio che cercava e vi è entrato con una scioltezza incredibile." Gilberto Zorio, interview with Mirella Bandini, Turin, 1972, in Mirella Bandini, *1972: Arte Povera a Torino*, 110–11. Originally published in *NAC*, no. 3 (March 1973).

22 Germano Celant, *Giuseppe Penone* (Milan: Electa, 1989).

23 Ida Gianelli and Giorgio Verzotti, eds., *Giuseppe Penone* (Turin, Italy: Castello di Rivoli, 1991).

24 Note that the interview with Buchloh was supposed to be material for an essay authored by Buchloh and ended up being published as an interview for lack of time. Laurent Busine and B.H.D. Buchloh, eds., *Giuseppe Penone* (Brussels: Mercatorfonds, 2012).

25 Giuseppe Penone, *Giuseppe Penone: Writings, 1968–2008*, ed. Gianfranco Maraniello and Jonathan Watkins, trans. Marguerite Shore (Bologna, Italy: Commune di Bologna [MAMbo], 2009).

26 Georges Didi-Huberman, *Being a Skull: Site, Contact, Thought, Sculpture*, trans. Drew Burk, English language edition (Minneapolis, MN: Univocal, 2016).
27 Martin Jay, *Downcast Eyes: The Denigration of Vision in Twentieth-Century French Thought* (Berkeley: University of California Press, 1993).

1 Presentness and Trace

1 Garessio is a semi-rural town near the Maritime Alps range that divides the regions of Piedmont and Liguria. Penone's maternal grandfather was an artist, and although Penone went to school for accounting, he followed his brother to the art academy in Turin. For more of his biographical background see Giuseppe Penone, interview with Mirella Bandini in Garessio, 1971, in *Data*, Summer 1973, 7–18, reprinted in Bandini, *Arte Povera a Torino*, 66.
2 See his artist's statement first included in Germano Celant and Galleria Civica d'Arte Moderna di Torino, eds. *Conceptual Art, Arte Povera, Land Art* (Turin, Italy: Galleria Civica d'Arte Moderna, 1970), reprinted in English in Penone, *Writings*, 90.
3 Bandini, *Arte Povera a Torino*, 65–6.
4 In a conversation with the author, Penone maintained that he had idealized what it would be like to work at the Accademia but was somewhat disillusioned when he got there. No one was doing their own thing – everyone was doing the same thing – and he thought that if he used what he knew, materials that he knew, he might be able to do his own thing. Working with the elements that he knew best could help him find what he really wanted. Giuseppe Penone, interview with the author, 29 January 2019, Archivio Penone, Turin.
5 The hand attached to this tree actually changed substantially over time, a testament to the experimental nature of the first interventions. First an iron hand was made, as evidenced in the writings published with these images in Celant's *Art Povera* (NY: Praeger, 1969). The artist notes that he considered using a bronze hand for durability, but, wanting to get away from the conventions of sculpture, Penone soon fashioned a stainless steel (*inox*) hand to replace the iron one. He wanted it to read as more a tool than a sculpture in itself. In later versions he replaced it with a bronze hand, for the colour, because it had a greater resonance with flesh and would oxidize in the weather. Interview with the author, Los Angeles, 4 September 2014, written notes.
6 Michael Fried, "Art and Objecthood," *Artforum* 5, no. 10 (Summer 1967): 12–23.
7 Interview with the author, Los Angeles, 4 September 2014.

8 Benjamin H.D. Buchloh, "Interview with Giuseppe Penone," in Busine and Buchloh, *Giuseppe Penone*, 16.
9 Giulio Carlo Argan, "Difficoltà della scultura," in *Studi e Note* (Rome: Bicca, 1955), 58.
10 Penone recounts that he took the photographs to Sperone to show them to him in 1968, which is how Celant saw them. Celant asked Penone to send them to him for inclusion in his 1969 book *Arte Povera*, simultaneously published in Italian, English, and German editions by various publishers.
11 Lucy Lippard, *Six Years: The Dematerialization of the Art Object from 1966 to 1972* (Berkeley: University of California Press, 1997), xviii.
12 Tommaso Trini, "Arte Povera a Genova," *Domus* 457 (December 1967), unpaginated.
13 Lippard, *Six Years*, 6.
14 Art historians Marcia Vetrocq and Adrian Duran have argued that the stories of American abstraction's post-war domination over European art have been largely overblown, ignoring the local traditions and schools of thought. In Italy it was, rather, that a particular desire to be internationally relevant, yet culturally specific, made post-war Italian painting ready to incorporate aspects of Abstract Expressionism into the mix of what was already going on. Each writer gives a strong account of the contemporary conversations, Vetrocq looking at the major figures in Italian criticism and examining their divergent prescriptions of post-war Italian painting, and Duran focusing on the specific critical response (or lack thereof) to abstract expressionism in the 1940s and 1950s. Duran specifically argues that in the immediate post-war period the majority of Italian painters agreed that they wanted their art to be "engaged," in the sense that all art is political, social, and potentially redemptive. Style, he argues, was not the key question until Togliatti wrote a scathing judgment on abstraction in 1948, and the conversation began to resemble that too-familiar split between abstraction and realism. This domestic context, Duran argues, largely overshadowed the reception of American painting in the Biennales of the early 1950s. See Marcia Vetrocq, "National Style and the Agenda for Abstract Painting in Postwar Italy," *Art History* 12, no. 4 (December 1989): 448–71; and Adrian Duran, "Abstract Expressionism's Italian Reception: Questions of Influence," in *Abstract Expressionism: The International Context*, ed. Joan M. Marter (New Brunswick, NJ: Rutgers, 2007), 138–51.
15 Greenberg's review first appeared in *The Nation* (24 January 1948), and Rosenberg "American Action Painters" first appeared in *Art News*, no 51 (1952). Both appeared excerpted and translated in the section "Breve antologia di poetica," edited by Enrico Crispolti, of *Il Verri*, no. 3. (1961): 135–6, 139.
16 For an English version of this essay see Clement Greenberg, *The Collected Essays and Criticism*, vol. 2, ed. John O'Brien (Chicago: University of Chicago Press, 1986), 200–1.

17 Enzo Paci, "Fenomenologia e Informale," *Il Verri*, no. 3 (1961): 159–61.

18 My translation; "In Italia l'intuizione nasce a livello individuale, l'arte è unmessaggio tra pochi; i migliori artisti oggi ... lavorano, se possibile, ancora più 'far out' degli americani, il loro terreno d'azione è ancora più esiguo e la loro forza di penetrazione più profonda e più sottile, perché costretta a concentrarsi per mancanza di ampia recezione." Marisa Volpi, "In margine a un dibattito: America o Europa?," *Bit* 2, no. 1 (March/April 1968): 12–14.

19 The Italian theorization of postmodernism would be made in precisely these terms. Turin-based philosopher Gianni Vattimo has theorized weak thought (*pensiero debole*) as the cornerstone of postmodernism. See Adelino Zanini, "Weak Thought between Being and Difference," trans. Michael Hardt, in *Radical Thought in Italy: A Potential Politics*, ed. Michael Hardt and Paolo Virno (Minneapolis: University of Minnesota Press, 1996), 53–9.

20 An artist like Pollock is but one example of the modernist associations of vision, verticality, and agency, but they are rooted in discourses that reach back to the origins of humanism. Indeed, the photographic documentation of Penone's action holds a visual correspondence with Leonardo da Vinci's drawing known as *The Vitruvian Man* (c. 1490). Whereas the well-known Renaissance drawing is a study in using the human body as an ideal unit of measurement for building, Penone's action exchanges the universalized anthropometry of Renaissance culture for a subjective occupation of an uncultivated terrain. Instead of standing erect in an ideal squared circle, Penone's rectangular form indicates a specific body, *his* body, which is lowered to the ground in a passive pose. That is, the position of Penone's body takes a critical stance on the anthropocentrism that corresponds to the humanist origins of modernism, as well as its more contemporaneous manifestations in such theories as Le Corbusier's Modulor system (1943).

21 Giuseppe Penone, interview by Elizabeth Mangini, 4 September 2014, in Los Angeles, written notes.

22 Rosalind Krauss, "Sculpture in the Expanded Field," *October* 8 (Spring 1979): 30–44. See page 33 in particular.

23 Krauss argues that Greenberg and Fried force the reading of Pollock's drip as one of pure opticality by insisting that the paintings are to be visually consumed on the wall, a ninety-degree turn that denies the physicality of works made on the ground. Of course, Pollock too showed them on the wall and, on at least one occasion, on the ceiling. Rosalind Krauss, *The Optical Unconscious* (Cambridge: MIT Press, 1996), 245–308.

24 Warhol, for instance, was the first of these three to show with Sperone in a one-person show in February 1965. On view were works from the 1963 *Death and Disasters* series, including several car crashes and a tuna-fish disaster. He was later included in group exhibitions in 1965, 1966, and

1967. In March 1969, Morris had a one-person show of his *Felts* of 1967–8, those works that echo the concepts elaborated in his "Anti-form" essay of 1968. (This was the only time Morris showed at Sperone.) Penone's *Maritime Alps* project, which had already been shown at the Deposito a year earlier, was again shown in a group show at Sperone (*Disegni progetti*) in May 1969. In February 1971, Twombly had a solo show at Sperone's relatively new space on Corso San Maurizio, and he continued to regularly show with the gallery through the 1980s.

25 Krauss, *Optical Unconscious*, 293.

26 Robert Morris, "Anti-form," *Artforum* 6, no. 8 (April 1968): 34–5.

27 Krauss is again one of the most prominent voices on the trace. She argues that Cy Twombly's graffito, begun in the period of his residence in Rome, and its inherent defacement of a surface signify the violence of a temporal rift between the action and the immediate, already-past status of the mark. Krauss, *Optical Unconscious,* 256. Twombly plays a central part of post–Abstract Expressionist discourses in the American context, but his 1960s residence in Rome and contemporaneous exhibitions in Turin make his project relevant to Penone's artistic context, too. Twombly frequented Rome's Caffe Rosati and showed at the Galleria la Tartaruga. The group of artists in this scene, active throughout the 1950s and early 1960s in Rome, is sometimes known by the location of these two venues as the Scuola Piazza del Popolo. Arte povera artists Jannis Kounellis, Mario Merz, and Pino Pascali all showed at La Tartaruga in the later 1960s.

28 Giuseppe Penone, interview with the author, 4 September 2014, in Los Angeles, written notes.

29 Rosalind Krauss, "Notes on the Index, Part 1" [1977] and "Notes on the Index, Part 2" [1977], in *The Originality of the Avant-Garde and Other Modernist Myths* (Cambridge: MIT Press, 1985), 196–219. In particular, Krauss argues that the photograph as index is a message without a code: "It is the order of the natural world that imprints itself on the photographic emulsion and subsequently on the photographic print. This quality of transfer or trace gives to the photograph its documentary status, its undeniable veracity … In the photograph's distance from what could be called syntax one finds the mute presence of an uncoded event. And it is this kind of presence that abstract artists now seek to employ" (211–12). Here Krauss is building upon the theories of French semiotician Roland Barthes. Note that the term *abstract artists* in Krauss's text does not merely mean painters; rather, it encompasses land artists, conceptual artists, body artists, video artists, etc.

30 Krauss argues that in the art of the 1970s the use of repetition or succession is another form of ordering that photography uses to create meaning external to the indexical image itself (*Originality of the Avant-Garde,* 218–19).

31 Decades later, for instance, American artist Richard Prince would use a similar tactic to question the desire for authenticity through his falsely "autographed" fan photographs of celebrities in his series *All the Best*.

32 Penone described *Write, Read, Remember* thus: "The books written in a matrix on metal wedges and set into the bark are assimilated, transcribed and remembered by the trees, acting as an intermediary between the author and the reader of the wood in the forests, avenues, woods, gardens, parks, orchards." Penone, *Writings*, 45.

33 Penone, 54.

34 Jacopo Galimberti cites the publication date of this book as late 1969. Jacopo Galimberti, "A Third-Worldist art? Germano Celant's Invention of Arte Povera," *Art History* 32, no. 2 (April 2013): 418–41. Looking at the American version of Celant's book, there are works in the book dated 1969, including an installation view of a Richard Serra exhibition from October 1969 at the Ricke Gallery in Cologne, making that the earliest the book could have been published. See Germano Celant, *Art Povera* (New York: Praeger, 1969), 224.

35 This work no longer exists, having been exhibited only in a temporary group show at Gian Enzo Sperone in 1969 and later destroyed.

2 An Artist Turned Inside Out

1 My translation; "Alla radice del divenire fenomenologico agisce questa decisione etica: è necessario incominciare da capo, rifiutare come deterministica la realtà direttamente rilevabile che non solo è fuori di noi, ma che ci educa e ci condiziona nell'intimo." Paolo Pompei, "Merleau-Ponty, politica e morale," *Il Verri 5*, (December 1961): 144–56.

2 While the earliest examples were made in Garessio, other photographs were taken in Ormea and Turin, as well as in international cities in which he was exhibiting. He even wore the mirrored contact lenses once at Cy Twombly's studio in Rome in 1971. Penone recounted to me how he had met Twombly in New York City in 1970 while in the United States to install work at the Museum of Modern Art's *Information* exhibition. He had been discussing a possible show with Ileana Sonnabend, and while in New York he visited her uptown gallery. She subsequently brought him to Robert Rauschenberg's studio (in a chapel) where he met also Twombly, who invited him to visit if he was ever in Rome. Giuseppe Penone, interview with the author, 28 January 2019, written notes, Archivio Penone, Turin.

3 I refer here to the French psychoanalyst Jacques Lacan's notion of the "mirror stage," the prelinguistic and pre-symbolic recognition of the self as "I." See Lacan, *Écrits: A Selection*, trans. Alan Sheridan (New York: Norton, 1977), 1–7. According to 2010 data from the World Health Organization, globally 39 million people are considered blind. See www.who.int/blindness/publications/globaldata/en/.

4 René Descartes, "Optics" [1637], in *The Visual Culture Reader*, ed. Nicholas Mirzoeff (New York: Routledge, 1998), 60–5.

5 The artist in fact had to wear two pairs of contact lenses for these images, a clear pair to protect his eyes and then the silvered or mirrored pair on top of that. Consequently, wearing them was painful, and they were not usually worn for very long at any one time. The action proposed to foreground sound, smell, and touch; however, Penone found that wearing the thick lenses made it hard to concentrate on anything other that the foreign objects touching his eyes. Giuseppe Penone, interview with the author, 28 January 2019, written notes, Archivio Penone, Turin.

6 Note here that the title of this work has changed and has had different translations over time. The initial translation of the longer title into English was *To Turn One's Eyes Inside Out*. See Achille Bonito Oliva, *Pèrsona: BITEF Festival Internazionale del Teatro, Belgrado, 10 Settembre 1971* (Florence: Centro Di, 1971), unpaginated. In the magazine *Studio International* one of the photographs is simply captioned *Contact Lenses*. See Tommaso Trini, "The Sixties in Italy," *Studio International* (November 1972): 169. Later books, including the catalogue by Mercatofonds, use the more placid *Reversing One's Eyes*.

7 That an essentially photographic work should be read as an anti-Cartesian sculptural manifesto seems contradictory, but in the case of *Rovesciare* the disembodying effect of the images on the viewer was an important part of the consideration. The work is fundamentally about the flaws inherent to visual perception, evidenced by the fact that the action grew out of a desire to make the finished images. Early sketches for these works, made in 1969, were followed by a series of photomontages in 1970, wherein Penone cut out photographs to place upon images of his face, just to see what the effect would be. He later exhibited these photomontages as a row of tightly cropped head shots, each nearly identical to the next. They read as a filmstrip, intimating a temporal relationship between images.

8 The artist has remarked that when he wore the mirrored lenses, people stopped looking at his eyes, since he seemed to be absent from there, and looked at his mouth, as if that were where the artist had "relocated." Giuseppe Penone, interview with the author, 4 September 2014, in Los Angeles, written notes.

9 Penone remarked about this in conversations we had in New York in 2012 and in Turin in 2013. Similar comments appear in one form or another in numerous published interviews held with Penone.

10 In the text that accompanied the 1977 publication of these photographs in an artist's book, Penone wrote: "Quando gli occhi, coperti dalle lenti a contatto specchianti, riflettono nello spazio le immagini che raccolgono con i movimenti abituali dell'osservare, si dilaziona nel tempo la facoltà

di vedere ... Il ritardo con cui mi approprio della immagine, rende le lenti a contatto specchianti divinatorie del vedere futuro." (When the eyes, covered with mirrored contact lenses, reflect back into space the image they gather with the usual movements one has when observing, the ability to see is deferred ... The delay with which I capture an image makes mirrored contact lenses into diviners of future sight; my translation.) Giuseppe Penone, *Rovesciare gli occhi* (Turin, Italy: Einaudi, 1977), 70–1.

11 In addition to the action that allowed the artist to experience the world corporeally, viewers' encounters with the artist via the photographs allowed them to see the reflected images at the same time as the artist could. Most of these works are only experienced as photographs or slide projections. Penone reportedly "performed" the work once in Rome in 1971. See Francesco Guzzetti, "Information 1970: Alcune novità sul lavoro di Giuseppe Penone," *L'Uomo Nero* 15, nos. 14–15 (March 2018): 215–31.

12 Busine and Buchloh, *Giuseppe Penone*, 95.

13 Celant, *Giuseppe Penone*, 12.

14 Giuseppe Penone, interview with the author, 15 July 2013, at Café La Cicchetteria, Turin, written notes.

15 Soutif writes: "This truly is one of the meanings of blinding, around which the works gravitate that deep down inside are Penone's most visual." Daniel Soutif, "Giuseppe Penone's Inverted Look," in Giuseppe Penone, *Giuseppe Penone: 1968–1998*, exhibition catalogue, Centro Galego de Arte Contemporánea ([Galicia]: Xunta de Galicia / Centro Galego de Arte Contemporánea, 1999), 34.

16 Penone, *Writings*, 57.

17 "Beginning with the Renaissance and the scientific revolution, modernity has been normally considered resolutely ocularcentric." Martin Jay, "Scopic Regimes of Modernity," in *The Visual Culture Reader*, ed. Nicholas Mirzoeff (New York: Routledge, 1998), 66–9.

18 Jay, *Downcast Eyes*.

19 However critical of ocularcentrism it may be, Merleau-Ponty's alternative philosophy of the sensible work refuses to give up entirely the nobility of vision. For instance, in his writings on artists like Cézanne, Merleau-Ponty explores the rejection of the visual through his two-dimensional medium. For the philosopher, Cézanne's paintings seem to visually implicate a viewing body. See Maurice Merleau-Ponty, "Eye and Mind," trans. Carlton Dallery, in *The Primacy of Perception* (Evanston, IL: Northwestern University Press, 1964), 164–5.

20 Jay notes that the later generation of French philosophers, such as J.-F. Lyotard, Michel Foucault, Luce Irigaray, and Christian Metz, therefore dismissed Merleau-Ponty's tepid critique, but that Merleau-Ponty was a pivotal figure precisely because his critique avoided the trap of giving up the visual altogether. Jay, *Downcast Eyes*, 286.

21 Whether or not Penone read Merleau-Ponty or other French philosophy is not the point. Phenomenology, in particular, was part of the intellectual milieu of 1960s Turin. The University of Turin was home to an important school of philosophy, in which scholars like Nicola Abbagnano, Luigi Pareyson, Norberto Bobbio, and their students Umberto Eco and Gianni Vattimo were among the main conduits of Continental philosophy. They notably resisted Benedetto Croce's then-dominant idealism by focusing instead on a blend of phenomenology, existentialism, and pragmatism, what Abbagnano called "il nuovo illuminismo." Nicola Abbagnano, "Verso il nuovo illuminismo," *Rivista di filosofia* 39 (October–December 1948): 313–25. The writings of Merleau-Ponty and those of American John Dewey were crucial to this Torinese philosophical school, especially with regard to ideas of anti-ocular perception and viewer participation in an aesthetic experience. For more on connections between Merleau-Ponty and Dewey see Victor Kestenbaum, *The Phenomenological Sense of John Dewey: Habit and Meaning* (Atlantic Highlands, NJ: Humanities Press, 1977), 5–7.

22 This parallels Jay's argument about Merleau-Ponty. Jay argues that Merleau-Ponty's emphasis on the imbrication of the senses highlights the way in which each "creates its own perceived world and at the same time contributes to an integrated world of experience." See Jay, *Downcast Eyes*, 298–9.

23 Marin Sullivan discusses *Narcissus Garden* at length in her book chapter "Reflective acts: Yayoi Kusama in Venice," including the legends surrounding the work's coming into being, its Italian patronage and sanctioning by the Biennale, and the critical response. Sullivan argues that the mirrored orbs were a means for a viewer to pick up and hold their reflection – resolving the dialectic of self and self-image that was the Narcissus's downfall. As art objects, Kusama's work critiques the self-congratulatory hubris of the international art world, especially those collectors who see themselves reflected in the objects they purchase. See Marin Sullivan, *Sculptural Materiality in the Age of Conceptualism* (New York: Routledge, 2017), 18–55. Note that the Tate Modern, which owns a version of Morris's mirrored cubes from 1971–6 (reconstructed), indicates in its records that, according to Leo Castelli, a version of the work was intended for Gian Enzo Sperone Gallery in Turin but was ultimately never fabricated. See http://www.tate.org.uk/art/artworks/morris-untitled-t01532.

24 It must be mentioned here that American artist Stephen Kaltenbach's series of *Personal Appearance Manipulations* (1968) includes a photograph of the artist's face with mirrored circles covering his pupils. Kaltenbach later remarked on the coincidence of his and Penone's works, neither of which was known to the other at the time, as evidence of similar thinking

among members of the same international artistic generation. See Roger White, *The Contemporaries: Travels in the 21st-Century Art World* (New York: Bloomsbury, 2015), 218. The two artists also exhibited together in 1970 in the Tokyo Biennale. See also mention in Francesco Guzzetti, "Information 1970: Alcune novità sul lavoro di Giuseppe Penone," *L'Uomo Nero* 15, nos. 14–15 (March 2018): 215–31.

25 Curator Daniel Soutif, on the contrary, says *Rovesciare* is "not surreal or even less surrealist." See Penone, *Giuseppe Penone: 1968–1998*, 25.

26 André Breton, "Surrealism and Painting" [1928], trans. David Gascoyne [1936], excerpted in *Art in Theory, 1900–1990*, ed. Charles Harrison and Paul Wood (Cambridge: Blackwell, 1993), 442; italics in the original.

27 Among the most notable examples of this are Eugène Atget's and other's reflective shop windows and opticians signs, Bunuel's infamous filmed slicing of an eye in *Un Chien Andalou*, and Andres Kertész's *Distortions* series.

28 In 1965, Magritte, who was still alive, had a big American retrospective, organized by James Thrall Soby of the Museum of Modern Art (MoMA) in New York, which travelled nationally during 1966. A recent gallery label from MoMA notes: "The Surrealist photographer Man Ray, who owned the work from 1933 to 1936, recognized this compelling duality when he memorably described *Le Faux Miroir* as a painting that 'sees as much as it itself is seen.'" *Magritte: The Mystery of the Ordinary, 1926–1938*, 28 September 2013–12 January 2014, https://www.moma.org.

29 Here the word *femme* or *woman* does not appear but is implied by the painted figure. Henri Béhar argues that this montage of text with automatic and painted images provides access to the surreal through the clash of form and imagery: "The dream is the expression of the inner world of man, the forest is enigmatic reality, woman being eroticism and mystery." Henri Béhar, "Réalisme surréalisme," *Mélusine*, 2001. This reference is made thanks to text authored by Pierre Ryngaert for the Centre Pompidou. https://www.centrepompidou.fr.

30 Photography, however, mirrors the unbiased, automatic nature of the subconscious. Rosalind Krauss argues in her essay "The Photographic Conditions of Surrealism" that photography, rather than painting and sculpture, should be made central to the legacy of surrealism, as it is shared by the Breton and Bataille camps. Krauss, "The Photographic Conditions of Surrealism," *October* 19 (1981): 3–34.

31 In *Documents 3 (June 1929*, Bataille defined *materialism* thus: "When 'materialism' is used, it should refer only to direct raw phenomena, 'excluding all idealism.'" Georges Bataille, *Visions of Excess: Selected Writings, 1927–1939*, ed. Allan Stoekl, trans. Allan Stoekl, Carl Lovitt, and Donald M. Leslie, Jr. (Minneapolis: University of Minnesota Press: 1991), 16.

32 Krauss, "Photographic Conditions," 28.

33 If the demonstration of vision's embodied limits in *Rovesciare* provokes an uncanny, even nauseating response, it may also be due to empathy for the artist, for whom the making of these works was distinctly physical. As previously noted, Penone had to wear two sets of lenses simultaneously. Thus the lens system created an uncomfortably thick barrier between his eyes and the outside world, making the artist painfully aware of the eyes as a boundary zone. When wearing these lenses, Penone could see just enough not to fall over, but it was essentially as if his eyes were closed. He became increasingly reliant on his other senses while wearing these lenses, especially his ability to touch and be touched. Giuseppe Penone, interview with the author, 4 September 2014 in Los Angeles.

34 See Penone, *Writings* [1970], 57.

35 Considering these actions and their documentation in 1971, Penone wrote: "Reflecting contact lenses are an actual reversal of the eye (eye intended as a recipient of images that are visualized in our mind). The mirror is an element that reflects images: contact lenses placed on the eye reflect images that the eye is able to perceive; in that way, the receptive element becomes an element of projection as well." Giuseppe Penone, "Note di lavoro," printed in Mirella Bandini, "Torino 1960/1973: Interviste – Note di lavoro – Dichiarazioni," *NAC*, no. 3 (November 1973). Reprinted in Bandini, *1972: Arte Povera a Torino*, I Testimoni dell'arte (Turin, Italy: U. Allemandi, 2002), 71–3.

36 Penone exhibited a similar piece, *Untitled* (1970), in the exhibition *Processi di pensiero visualizzati: 15 italienische Künstler*, in the Kunstmuseum Lucerne (31 May–5 July 1970). He also exhibited long rectangular mirrors placed on the wall and the floor, as well as a piece of magnetized calamite on the floor in the centre of the room, in a show at Toselli in Milan in April 1970, for which there are no photographs known to me or to the artist's archive. The archive has asked the gallery for photographs, to no avail. A similar project was proposed for the exhibition *Information* at the Museum of Modern Art in New York in July 1970, but it was unrealized due to lack of space. There are drawn plans for the MoMA installation, denoted as "mirrored room," but Penone ended up exhibiting photographs known under the title *Coincidence of Images*. For consideration of the artist's work in *Information* see "Information 1970: Alcune novità sul lavoro di Giuseppe Penone," *L'Uomo Nero* 15, nos. 14–15 (March 2018): 215–31.

37 The connections have recently been explored in curatorial form, from the 2013 installation at the Punta Dogana (Pinault collection) in Venice to the 2016 permanent collection installation at the Tate Modern. Here is not the place for me to go into this in detail, but it is a point of further research that I intend to undertake.

38 Fellow Arte povera artist Jannis Kounellis had particular difficulty, the museum rejecting his first three proposals before he settled on blocking the entrance to his gallery. Ningen Kokusai Bijutsu Ten et al., eds., *Ningen to Busshitsu: Between Man and Matter*, exhibition catalogue, vol. 2 (Tokyo: Mainichi Newspapers and the Japan International Art Promotion Association, 1970).
39 The critic, in what must be a rare combination, also happened to be an abstract painter and a Jesuit priest. Joseph P. Love, SJ, "Tokyo: 10. International Biennale of Art," *Art International* 14, no. 6 (Summer 1970): 70–5.
40 Love, 74.
41 Claire Gilman, "Introduction," *October* 124 (Summer 2008): 3–7. Gilman notes that Einaudi translated *Phenomenology of Perception* in 1961.
42 Maurice Merleau-Ponty, "Theory of the Body Is Already a Theory of Perception," in *Phenomenology of Perception*, trans. Colin Smith (New York: Routledge Classics, 2002), 235.
43 Merleau-Ponty, 237.
44 Merleau-Ponty, "Eye and Mind," in *Primacy of Perception*, 168.
45 Two hundred years later, Velásquez used painted mirrors, windows, and doors to communicate the complex visual field in his work *Las Meninas* (1656). The viewer of that painting is unceremoniously thrust into the position of the object of the artist's gaze and potentially that of the royal patrons who are reflected on the rear wall (whether it is a mirror or a painting is the subject of some debate).
46 Merleau-Ponty, "Eye and Mind," 168–9.
47 Perplexingly, Merleau-Ponty's discussion of this discourse ignores one of the most notable modern depictions of mirrors in art, Édouard Manet's *A Bar at the Folies-Bergère* (1882). Art historian T.J. Clark has authoritatively linked this enigmatic painting and its embodiment of "a kind of skepticism, or at least unsureness, as to the nature of representation in art" to the very foundations of the Modern era.[109] Clark notes that when Manet's depicted mirror fails to match with the viewer's conditioned expectations, the resulting discomfort aptly communicates the instability of modern life – producing what the historian terms "a texture of uncertainties." At the foundations of modernist reappraisals of representation, then, a painting of a mirror demonstrates how both paintings and mirrors are tools for communicating fleeting sensations and perceptions. See T.J. Clark, *The Painting of Modern Life: Paris in the Art of Manet and His Followers* (Princeton, NJ: Princeton University Press, 1984), 251.
48 Giuseppe Penone, "'Conversation: Giuseppe Penone / Catherine de Zegher' [March/May 2003]," in *Giuseppe Penone: The Imprint of*

Drawing, ed. Catherine de Zegher, trans. Jeff Fort (New York: The Drawing Center, 2004), 46.

49 These were first shown in the exhibition *Combattimento per gli immagini* at Galleria Civica d'Arte Moderna di Torino in 1973.

50 Michel Foucault, *Dits et Écrits, 1954–1988*, vol. 2 (Paris: Gallimard, 2001), 1575.

51 Penone, interview with Mirella Bandini, *Data*, 1973, 108.

52 Bonito Oliva, *Pèrsona*.

53 Giuseppe Penone, *Svolgere la propria pella* (Turin, Italy: Sperone, 1971).

54 Edmund Husserl, *Cartesian Meditations* [1984], (Dordrecht, Netherlands: Springer Kluwer Academic Publishers, 1999), 97.

55 In the study *Svolgere la propria pella: Finestrina*, the artist imagines being inside one's skin in the same way one is inside a car. The enlarged ridges of the artist's fingerprints, made through a tape-and-powder transfer similar to that used in forensic identification, read as an enclosure inhabited by the viewer.

56 Guy Tosatto has compellingly corresponded Penone's project and the *Santa Sidone* or Holy Shroud of Turin, a Catholic relic, claimed by believers to be the cloth in which Christ's body was wrapped for burial. See Guy Tosatto, cited in Penone, *Giuseppe Penone: 1968–1998*, 177–8.

57 Tommaso Trini, "Documenta 5," *Domus* 514 (September 1972): 47.

58 I am not suggesting that Penone necessarily knew of this work or was influenced by it, but Bochner did have exhibitions at Sperone in the late 1960s and early 1970s. If one is looking for other visual precedents, among them must surely be Man Ray's *Èrotique voile (Meret Oppenheim à la presse)*, or *Veiled Erotic (Meret Oppenheim at the Press)*, 1933, a photograph of the female artist with an inked arm near a printing press. In May 1971 Sperone hosted a two-person show in which Pisani projected this Man Ray photograph on the walls. Penone's works with body printing preceded this, but it shows that a broader interest in indexicality sometimes shared formal characteristics. I discuss Bochner here because of the connection to measurement, but of course there are other examples of more direct body prints from this era, most notably those made by Yves Klein, Jasper Johns, Ana Mendieta, and David Hammons.

59 Mel Bochner, interview with Hans Ulrich Obrist and Sandra Antelo-Suarez, n.d., http://projects.e-flux.com/do_it/notes/interview/i003.html.

60 In *Camera Lucida*, Roland Barthes writes: "Painting can feign reality without having seen it. Discourse combines signs, which have referents, of course, but these referents can be and are most often 'chimeras.' Contrary to these imitations, in Photography I can never deny that *the thing has been there*." Barthes, *Camera Lucida: Reflections on Photography*, trans. Richard Howard (New York: Farrar, Straus and Giroux, 1995), 76.

61 Giuseppe Penone, interview with Benjamin Buchloh, in Busine and Buchloh, *Giuseppe Penone*, 16.
62 Jean-Christophe Amman and Giuseppe Penone, *Giuseppe Penone: Bäume, Augen, Haare, Wände, Tongefäss* (Lucerne: Kunstmuseum Luzern, 1977).
63 I paraphrase here from Penone's own statement first published in the catalogue for *Projekt '74*, Cologne, p. 278, and reprinted in English in Amman and Penone, p 75. "1. The plaster thorax, which is the closest possible image of my reality; 2. Slide of my thorax, which is the realest [*sic*] possible image of my reality; 3. Body hairs, not any more image or fiction, but my reality, detatched from my body." In 1975 Penone repeated this operation of undermining the relationship between representation and experience, but with a different inflection. In *1216 peli (1216 Hairs)*, a series of eleven plasters records a state of the body that no longer corresponds to its real state. With each of these casts, hairs were ripped from the body as a result of the casting process. It is only in the coincidence of the two indexes that the body appears restored, albeit to a state that no longer exists for the living body.
64 Maurice Merleau-Ponty, "Eye and Mind," in *The Merleau-Ponty Aesthetics Reader: Philosophy and Painting*, ed. and trans. Michael Smith (Evanston, IL: Northwestern University Press, 1993), 125. Originally published as *L'Oeil et l'esprit* (Paris: Gallimard, 1961).
65 Maurice Merleau-Ponty, *The Visible and the Invisible* [1964], ed. Claude Lefort, trans. Alphonso Lingis (Evanston, IL: Northwestern University Press, 1968), 259. This posthumous text, *The Visible and the Invisible*, was published in Italian in 1969 and was mentioned in relation to Penone's art in an essay published by the Drawing Center, New York. See Michael Newman, "Sticking to the World-Drawing as Contact," in *Giuseppe Penone: The Imprint of Drawing*, ed. Catherine de Zegher, 103–10.
66 During the half century and more since their publication, Merleau-Ponty's challenges to Cartesian idealism have been central to studies of understanding how artists and viewers engage in communication through art objects. Amelia Jones chronicles the anglophone aspects of this trajectory in her essay "Meaning, Identity, Embodiment: The Uses of Merleau-Ponty's Phenomenology in Art History." Using the example of Courbet's *Birth of the World*, she also takes a feminist perspective on the gendered constructions available to artist, viewer, and viewed, and considers how Merleau-Ponty's late concepts like the chiasm point to a way out of dialectical thinking towards intersubjectivity. See Jones, "Meaning, Identity, Embodiment," in Dana Arnold and Margaret Iversen, *Art and Thought* (Malden, UK: Blackwell, 2003), 71–90.
67 For more on the infra-thin in Duchamp and its relevance for art of the late twentieth century see Thierry de Duve, *Pictorial Nominalism: On*

Marcel Duchamp's Passage from Painting to Readymade, trans. Dana Polan (Minneapolis: University of Minnesota Press, 1991), 159–61. More could also be said about Duchamp's notion of optical tactility in relation to Penone's work, and, although it is extraneous to this analysis, I flag it here as an area for future research.

68 Penone devised numerous projects aimed at making touch visible, including an installation that extended this experience to the viewer. In *Libro trappola* (*Book Trap*, 1972), a photograph album set on a music stand was filled with page after page of the same images – the recto and verso of Penone's open hand and forearm. Curious viewers could look through the album, trying perhaps to understand the meaning of the gesture. An open hand, however, indicates that it has nothing to hide. If anything, the exercise produces the amusing idea that, while flipping the pages, one touches the artist's hands through a photographic surrogate. The impact of engaging with this work is revealed later when the viewer realizes she has traces of pink dye on her hands. The pages have been coated with the same moisture-activated substance used by police to track stolen objects, thereby turning the viewer into an accomplice of an artwork about the visualization of touch. Touching the work is the key to unlocking its conceptual significance. To this end, one must also consider that Merleau-Ponty asserted the reversibility of touch: one can feel oneself being touched as well as actively touching. For him, touch is therefore simultaneously active and passive. See Merleau-Ponty, "Eye and Mind," in *The Primacy of Perception*.

69 Giuseppe Penone, "Conversation: Giuseppe Penone / Catherine de Zegher" [March/May 2003], in *Giuseppe Penone: The Imprint of Drawing*, ed. Catherine de Zegher, 49.

70 Giuseppe Penone, interview with Benjamin Buchloh, in Businc and Buchloh, *Giuseppe Penone*, 23.

71 Giuseppe Penone, in Amman and Penone, *Giuseppe Penone: Bäume, Augen, Haare, Wände, Tongefäss*, 80. The quotation appears in English, and no translator is listed.

72 John Dewey was central to the philosophy produced in Turin, and the subject of several of Nicola Abbagnano's writings. As evidence of the saturation of Dewey in Italian intellectual circles, Celant mentions Dewey in his opening essay in the 1969 monograph on Arte povera: "Among living things [the artist] discovers also himself, his body, his memory, his gestures – all that which directly lives and thus begins again to carry out the sense of life and of nature, a sense that implies, according to Dewey, numerous subjects: the sensory, sensational, sensitive, impressionable and sensuous." Celant, *Art Povera*, 225.

73 John Dewey, *Art as Experience* (New York: Perigee, 1980), 12.

74 Giuseppe Penone, interview with the author, 28 January 2019, written notes, Archivio Penone, Turin.

75 Penone's link between plaster casts and photography connects back to the surrealist's use of photography to provoke a rupture between the familiar and the strange. Rosalind Krauss argues that both surrealism and photography are orders of the indexical exploited by the surrealists. "On the family tree of images, [photography] is closer to palm prints, death masks, the Shroud of Turin, or the track of gulls on the beaches" Krauss, "The Photographic Conditions of Surrealism," 28.

76 Thierry de Duve, *Pictorial Nominalism: On Marcel Duchamp's Passage from Painting to Readymade*, trans. Dana Polan (Minneapolis: University of Minnesota Press, 1991), 161.

77 Penone, *Writings* [1988], 324–5.

78 The way in which sensory perception is constructive of experience in phenomenological theory also predicts subsequent readings of a body in which the senses are unified as a site from which power is exerted. The implications of the philosophical discipline known as "biopolitics," and in particular its elaboration by Italian theorists, will be explored in the third chapter.

3 Radical Reciprocity

1 "The solid, a condition of the inquiry into the void, is the sculptor / who with his tool and his hands exerts the pressure that produces volumes. / Vase as: substitution of the hands of the potter; / negative of the hands of the potter; sum of imprints; / the matrix to recreate, with his grip, the skin of the potter." Penone, *Writings* [1974], 204.

2 See, for example, the introduction to one of the first major edited issues on thing theory: Bill Brown, "Thing Theory," *Critical Inquiry* 28, no.1 (Autumn 2001): 1–22.

3 Such readings were already being rejected by Penone's Arte povera peers in the 1970s, with Zorio arguing, for example, that "today one writes (and I won't cite the authors) about *Arte povera* as using ugly materials, rough materials, and it is totally wrong. Of this use of materials a new materialism has emerged. The materials are what they are and are used for their own properties" (my translation; oggi si scrive (e non cito gli autori) sull'Arte Povera in quanto uso di materiali bruti, rozzi, e si sbagliato tutto. Di quest'uso dei materiali si è fatto un nuovo materialismo. I materiali sono quelli che sono e sono stati usati nella giusta dimensione). Zorio, "Interview by Mirella Bandini" [1972], in *Arte Povera a Torino*, ed. Bandini, 101.

4 In the epigraph for chapter 1, we have already seen some of Esposito's writings. In that passage Esposito refers to Elias Canetti's well-known

writings on the relationship between the masses and power. Canetti writes that whereas other animals might use an armoured mouth or a taloned claw to subdue prey, the fleshy human hand that grasps and never lets go is emblematic of human dominance. See Roberto Esposito, *Persons and Things: From the Body's Point of View*, trans. Zakiya Harafi (Cambridge, MA: Polity Press, 2016), 19. See also Elias Canetti, *Crowds and Power*, trans. Carol Stewart (New York: Continuum, 1978), 204.

5 I note here that these sculptures were made in a factory in Castellamonte, a Piedmont town famous for its manufacture of traditional clay stoves. That is, these sculptures were made in kilns used not for art or small wares but for hearths. Informal interview with the artist, summer 2016.

6 Giuseppe Penone, conversation with the author, 29 January 2019, written notes, Archivio Penone, Turin. I note here that a trove of examples of such use, in the form of Coptic jars, would have been accessible to Penone in Turin's Egyptian Museum, which continues to maintain one of the largest collections of ancient Egyptian funerary art outside of Cairo.

7 As with *Vase*, the interior surface of a pot is an index of the void waiting to be filled, of the air inside the pot, inasmuch as its exterior shell is a record of the hand that shaped it. Further, Penone has written that when an artist shapes clay on a wheel, the artist creates not only a form but also a force of air equivalent to an exhaled breath. Penone, *Writings*, 207.

8 Penone, 206.

9 Penone, 206.

10 As discussed in chapter 2, Merleau-Ponty argues that the externally sensible cannot be removed from the internally conceptual; they inform each other in such a way as to be distinct yet irrevocably intertwined (*The Visible and the Invisible*, 130–55).

11 Suspicious of the aura of his own artistic identity, Duchamp, under the name Richard Mutt, entered the infamous urinal-cum-fountain into a non-juried competition. He also wrote an "anonymous" defence for the work. See Anonymous, "The Richard Mutt Case," *Blind Man*, no. 2 (May 1917): 5.

12 Germano Celant, "Piero Manzoni: The Body Infinite," in *Piero Manzoni* (Milan: Charta, 1998), 22.

13 French psychoanalyst Julia Kristeva's concept of the abject is relevant to this reading. In *Powers of Horror*, Kristeva describes the abject as not merely a disagreeable or unclean object but that which "disturbs identity, system and order. What does not respect borders, positions, rules." Julia Kristeva, "Approaching Abjection," in *Powers of Horror*, ed. Kelly Oliver, trans. Leon S. Roudiez (New York: Columbia University Press, 1980), 232.

14 The larger series of *Breath* projects includes discrete, gilded casts of the interior of the artist's mouth – the negative space around his teeth and tongue where breath and language cross over and exit the body.

15 On the surface, the form of Penone's ephemeral body print made in a pile of leaves is not unlike the *Sileuta series* (1973–8) of the Cuban American artist Ana Mendieta, who photographically documented the outlines of her body made of and against a variety of natural materials. Both works are complex demonstrations of material interconnection, but Mendieta's evocative and effigial works remain in the realm of photography, visually experienced by the viewer at a remove.

16 Many early installations of *Breath of Leaves* used readily available box leaves, and later installations used myrtle, which is even more fragrant. Breath is addressed in a similar way in the later project *Respirare l'ombra* (*Breathing the Shadow*, 1999), a room-sized installation of fragrant laurel leaves that are held to the walls of a gallery at Turin's Castello di Rivoli by a cage-like structure. The experience of entering the room is a visual one, only on the most basic order. Instead it is chiefly an experience of scent, as the strong herbal fragrance of the dessicated leaves addresses the senses. Secondarily, the experience is auditory because the leaf-covered walls absorb the ambient sounds of the room. The visual experience is processed perhaps third as the leaves both colour and darken the space. A small sculpture of gilt-bronze lungs hanging on the caged walls becomes apparent to the viewer, reinforcing the tactility of air through this corporeal icon.

17 Penone, *Writings*, 208.

18 In fact, the essay is identical to the one Celant later published in Dutch in the 1980 Stedelijk catalogue and in English in the 1989 monograph on the artist. In the latter, the essay is preceded, without interruption, by a new introduction and followed by an interview between Celant and Penone. I cite the English translation here for ease of reference: Celant, *Giuseppe Penone*, 12.

19 Celant, *Giuseppe Penone*, 16.

20 Celant, 19.

21 Penone notes that only five of the sixty or so he made bore enough resemblance to his facial features to be used. This is evidence that he was simultaneously interested in the process of making a work that developed underground, and conscious of the way in which the resultant objects would communicate with the viewer. See Benjamin H.D. Buchloh, interview with Giuseppe Penone, in Busine and Buchloh, *Giuseppe Penone*, 22.

22 This work was first shown along with *Nero Assoluto d'Africa* (*Absolute Black of Africa*, 1978–9) at Zurich's InK, a short-lived alternative space that provided individual rooms and funding for artists to produce and exhibit new bodies of work. See Christel Sauer, "InK, die Halle für internationale neue Kunst," *Du: Die Zeitschrift der Kultur* 40 (1980): 6–11. *Absolute Black*

of Africa was made by laboriously carving the dense stone into a negative of the artist's three-quarter figure. The title of this work is meant to be plainly descriptive of the material. The granite type introduced in English contexts 1962 as Belfast Black was marketed in Italy as "Nero Assoluto" or "Absolute Black," and it is often quarried, as this piece was, in South Africa. Penone notes that he chose this specific stone because of its purity and density and also because it had been used by ancient Egyptians for external sarcophagi. The collection of the Museo Egizio in Turin has the largest collection of ancient Egyptian funerary art outside of Cairo. The artist imagined that this slab could be returned to the ground so that plants could grow within the carved cavity. The "impression" bears the softness of the body and its clothing as if it had been effortlessly cast of a fluid material. Together, with *Zucche*, this installation demonstrates the ongoing reciprocity of active and passive labours by probing a paradox that derives from the apparent differences of their forms and respective material malleability.

23 Note that this work has appeared in print with its title translated as *Pumpkins* and as *Squashes*. I will use the Italian *Zucche* to avoid confusion.

24 This story is often retold in the literature on this statue. See, for example, the epigraph and opening remarks of Daniel M. Zolli, "Donatello's Visions: The Sculptor at Florence Cathedral," in *Sculpture in the Age of Donatello: Renaissance Masterpieces from Florence Cathedral*, ed. Timothy Verdon and Daniel M. Zolli (New York: Museum of Biblical Art, 2015), 45–74. In another, sweeping overview of the collections of the Duomo Museum, Timothy Verdon writes: "More than any sculpture since classical antiquity, this prophet, probably carved in the mid-1420s, seems to be a living person." Timothy Verdon, "The New Museo dell'Opera del Duomo," *I Tatti Studies in the Italian Renaissance* 18, no. 2 (2015): 283.

25 Verdon et al., *Sculpture in the Age of Donatello*, 67.

26 This aspect of Donatello's work has been referred to as "ekphrasis" in Kenneth Gross, *Dream of the Moving Statue* (University Park: Penn State Press, 2010), 179–84. It has also been suggested that Habakkuk is used for a reflection on sculpture because the Old Testament iconoclast named sculptors as makers of false idols. For more on this line of analysis on Donatello see a contemporary review of an exhibition of Donatello's Florentine work: Peter Schjeldahl, "Entranced by Donatello," *New Yorker*, 2 March 2015, accessed online.

27 Penone has spoken of his admiration for Donatello, mentioning specifically the Renaissance artist's use of casts, unconventional materials, and novel techniques in a quest for verisimilitude in sculpture. He maintains that this interest is not strictly historical, because when one stands before a sculpture, however old it may be, it is present and

contemporary to the viewer. Giuseppe Penone, conversation with the author, 28 January 2019, written notes, Archivio Penone, Turin.

28 Tommaso Trini, "Nuovo alfabeto per corpo e material," *Domus* 470 (January 1969): 46–8. Reprinted in English as "A New Alphabet for Body and Material," in *Arte Povera = Art Povera*, ed. Germano Celant (Milan: Electa, 1985), 113. Page references are to the reprint.

29 Penone claims that his use of casting is separate from that of the contemporaneous works of artists like Jasper Johns; rather, his casts refer back to its use by Rodin, or to a bust by Donatello that was made after a rubbing of a death mask. See Benjamin H.D. Buchloh, interview with Giuseppe Penone, in Busine and Buchloh, *Giuseppe Penone*, 22.

30 Roberto Esposito, *Persons and Things: From the Body's Point of View*, trans. Zakiya Harafi (Cambridge, MA: Polity Press, 2016), 4–5.

31 Esposito, 144.

32 Esposito notes that even phenomenology has its limits, however, and he looks forward to the sociology of Bruno Latour and the potential of technological interpellation of the body to break the stronghold of the historic dialectic between persons and things (119).

33 Initially, when the works were shown at Konrad Fischer Galerie, the artist displayed one of the stones on a constructed base. This theatricality distracted from the message of the works and was removed from subsequent installations and later versions of the work. I illustrate the work known as *To Be a River I*, but for simplicity I will refer in the text to the work by its series title, without the distinguishing numerals.

34 Penone knows the work of Vija Celmins now; however, he did not know of the artist's work with stones at the time he made *To Be a River*. Giuseppe Penone, conversation with the author, 28 January 2019, written notes, Archivio Penone, Turin.

35 Penone writes: "It is not possible to think of stone or work it in a manner which differs from the river. The blows of the chisel, the scoop, the gradine, the drill, abrasive stones and sandpaper are the tools of the river." Penone, *Writings*, 151.

36 The viewer's experience is key to this work. When Penone first exhibited *To Be a River*, the stones were shown in two different rooms, and he notes that the effect was lost on viewers, who could not easily hold the details of a non-geometric form in mind at such a distance. He later brought them together and exhibited one on a metal pedestal to draw attention to their difference, but he later conceded that the demonstration worked best with the two stones set side by side, without a clear indication of which one was made by him and which one was made by the river. Giuseppe Penone, conversation with the author, 28 January 2019, written notes, Archivio Penone, Turin.

37 Penone, *Writings*, 151.
38 Indeed, around the time Penone was conceiving this work, his description of a river epitomized the idea that human touch modelled the simultaneity and reciprocity of encounters between things, active and passive. He wrote: "The nature of a flow of water such as a river is such that it cannot be thought of outside its course because it is conditioned and characterized by its flowing and draws from this many qualities. However, at the same time, it conditions, characterizes and shapes its container through the anger of its floods, the calm of its droughts and the continuousness of its flowing." Penone, *Writings*, 150.
39 Didier Semin, *Giuseppe Penone: The Politeness of Matter*, exhibition catalogue (Geneva: Galerie Guy Bärtschi, 2002), 9.
40 Penone, quoted in Busine and Buchloh, *Giuseppe Penone*, 353.
41 Bill Brown, "Thing Theory," in "Things," special issue, *Critical Inquiry* 28, no. 1 (Autumn 2001): 1–22.
42 Philippe Descola, *Beyond Nature and Culture*, trans. Janet Lloyd (Chicago: University of Chicago Press, 2013; first published 2005), xv.
43 Stanford anthropologist Ian Hodder provides a nearly exhaustive account of the different terms used to approach the relationship between humans and things, such as *actor network theory* (Latour), *engagements* (Renfrew), *equipmental totality* (Heidegger), *operational chains* (Lemonnier), *co-evolution* (Darwin), *enchainment* (Strathern), and *creolization* (Nuttall). See Ian Hodder, *Entangled: An Archaeology of the Relationships between Humans and Things* (Malden, MA: Wiley-Blackwell, 2012), 89–96, for a historiographic review of each term and its use.
44 Hodder, 59, 96, and 207.
45 Hodder, 213.

4 *Tempus Arborus* (Tree Time)

1 Penone, *Writings*, 78.
2 The artist does not have any archival images of the stamped number on the walls, which is likely the reason for this early intervention being rarely known. Subsequently, he has continued to use numbers to mark enigmatically the duration of his own existence. Sometimes this happens within an exhibition space, and at other times it is only written or reproduced in the catalogue.
3 Trini wrote, "As it already was for the futurists, the idea of energy or of force is not an equivalent of life." Tommaso Trini, "Anselmo, Penone, Zorio e le nuove fonte d'energia per il deserto dell'arte," *Data* 3, no. 9 (Autumn 1973): 62.

4 My translation; "Ecco allora che le sollecitazioni e gli stimoli su cui lavorano Penone, Zorio, e Anselmo, che li espandono nello spazio e nel tempo, non più solo metaforicamente, sottendo la ricerca di apportare *rinnovata energia alla critica* dell'esistente (arte esistente, realtà esistente, non più scisse, il conflitto elevandosi al livello della libertà contro la necessità). Non stanno neppure più dalla parte dell'arte, ma sui suoi confini materiali e mentali, dove attingono da nuove fonti d'energia quale la tensione sistematica, la contraddizione svelata, la esplicita deperibilità – materializzate in oggetti." Trini, 67.

5 Lee cites Michael Fried's rant against theatricality as one of the prime indicators of this anxiety because it is fundamentally about duration and time. She argues that the minimalist object in Fried's terms is both anticipatory (it waits for the beholder) and repetitive (it holds onto the beholder once engaged) and this is the essential fear that Fried has the 'endlessness' of the minimalist object. See Pamela M. Lee, *Chronophobia: On Time in the Art of the 1960s* (Cambridge: MIT Press, 2003), 43–5.

6 Lee, 307.

7 This is one of the central arguments of Merleau-Ponty's *Phenomenology of Perception*, especially its opening essay, "The Theory of the Body Is Already a Theory of Perception." See also Monika M. Langer, *Merleau-Ponty's "Phenomenology of Perception": A Guide and Commentary* (London: Palgrave Macmillan, 1989), 25–6.

8 Rosalind Krauss, *Passages in Modern Sculpture* (Cambridge: MIT Press, 1996), 4–5.

9 Krauss, 6.

10 Benjamin Buchloh has argued that the apparent "anti-technological stance" of Arte povera owed to the movement's misreading of American minimalism. See Buchloh's foreword to *Arte Povera: Selections from the Sonnabend Collection*, by Claire Gilman (New York: Wallach Art Gallery, Columbia University: 2001), 7.

11 Mangini, "1000 Words," 226–9.

12 The first tree was a four-metre tree that is now in a private collection and hangs in the Hotel du Parc in Turin. The second was *His/Its Being in the Twenty-Second Year of Life at a Fantastic Hour*, which after having been brought to Sperone's gallery to show the dealer and to be photographed, was loaned out to be displayed in the editorial offices of Einaudi. In 1970 the artist took it back to exhibit it in the Rome Quandriennale, but it was badly damaged in Rome and considered destroyed. Penone later arranged to make a new tree sculpture for Giulio Einaudi and was paid for the work with around 3,500 books from the Einaudi catalogue. Giuseppe Penone, interview with the author, 28 January 2019, Archivio Penone, Turin, written notes.

13 In a salient example, when Konrad Fischer included Penone in the 1969 exhibition *Konzeption/Conception: Dokumentation einer heutigen*

Kunstgerichtung / Documentation of a To-Day's Art Tendency, the artist submitted a plan to insert a text-laden object into a tree. This project was not fully realized – it was not inserted into a tree – but Penone did create the matrix. In the exhibition catalogue, charcoal rubbings of the object reveal the following text: "8161 pagine di un libro scritte a matita su cunei di ferro; conficcato in altrettante alberi, i questo cresceranno assimilando i cunei ed esprimendone il contenuto" (8161 pages of a book written in pencil on iron wedges; stuck in as many trees, that grow assimilating wedges and expressing the content; my translation). The number 8161 refers to the days the artist had been alive at the time the work was conceived, drawing viewers' attention to the distinctions between conception, execution, and reception. The artist thus positions sculpture as a physical and conceptual relationship between artist and material, which unfolds over time. Rolf Wedewer and Konrad Fischer, *Konzeption/ Conception* (Cologne: Westdeutscher Verlag, 1969), unpaginated.

14 Gerd-Rainer Horn, "Outcasts, Dropouts, and Provocateurs: Nonconformists Prepare the Terrain," in *The Spirit of '68: Rebellion in Western Europe and North America, 1956–1976* (New York: Oxford University Press, 2007), 5–15.

15 The German enterprise was short-lived but prolific: fifty artists showed their works at Aktionsraum over a period of one year. The bulk of the documentation was handed over to Egidio Marzona, who was one of the primary sponsors of the space. Several of the works made there were purchased out of the shows and now form part of the Marzona collection. https://www.mumok.at/en/events/aktionsraum-1.

16 My translation. "Ich werde eine Aktion ausfüren die als 15 bis 20 Tage dauert. Ich werde ein Holzbrett in die Zeit zuruckbringen, in der es ein Baum war und zwar in eine Zeit des Baumes, die ich an Ort und Stelle festsetze. / Jeden Tag werde 2 bis 4 Stunden daran arbeiten auf einem Raum von ungefähr 12 x 4 m. / An dem Tag an dem der Stamm wieder jung geworden ist, werde ich abreisen. Natürlich werde ich dem Baum nach Italien zurückbringen, aber wenn ihn irgandjemand kaufen will, kostet er 1000 Dollar. (Die Arbeit wurde von Hulten für des Moderna Museet, Stockholm angekauft.)" At the end of that passage Penone stated that he would take the work back to Italy with him, which would cost $1,000, but the magazine's editors note in a parathetical that Pontus Hulten bought the work directly out of that show for the Moderna Museet in Stockholm. The work is still in the collection of that museum. Giuseppe Penone, "Giuseppe Penone: Aktion," *Interfunktionen* 5 (1970): 144.

17 In an interview with Matthew Teitelbaum for the Art Gallery of Ontario, Penone said tautology was one of the most important themes of the 1960s. The notion of "wooden trees" and its relation to tautology is my own

contribution and is not mentioned in the Teitelbaum interview. Penone, *Giuseppe Penone: The Hidden Life Within*, ed. Matthew Teitelbaum (London: Black Dog Publishing, 2013).

18 Curator Giorgio Verzotti has argued that, with the *Trees*, Penone intends to show the ontology of cultural practices like sculpture as fundamentally engaged in presenting new ways of seeing the natural world. Questions of intentionality aside, Verzotti reads the way in which process is doubly visible in these sculptures as central to such expanded perception. In short, he argues that the visible "in-betweenness" of the physical states of the *Tree* sculptures is a de facto argument that the work of an artist is not of the same measure as a work of nature or the work of a factory. Giorgio Verzotti, "Alberi," in *Giuseppe Penone*, ed. Gianelli and Verzotti, 47.

19 Penone, *Writings* [1976], 92–3. When Celant published this text in the 1989 Halifax/Electa monograph, it was cited as being from the 1973 interview with Mirella Bandini in *Data* 7/8. However I have a looked at the original source, and it was not printed in *Data* 7/8. It is also not reproduced as part of this same interview in the 2002 book that reprints Bandini's interviews with Arte povera artists of this period. Further, I asked Archivio Penone if this text was ever exhibited along with the photographs and the tree itself, and the answer was no. Email exchange with the author, 27 July 2017.

20 See Diego Giachetti, *Il giorno più lungo: La rivolta di Corso Traiano (Torino, 3 luglio 1969)*, Biblioteca di cultura storica (Pisa: BFS Editore, 1977).

21 "Striking Workers Fight Turin Police," *New York Times*, 4 July 1969, 4.

22 This movement was supported by the local unions, which in Turin were relatively autonomous from the national organizations and parties compared to those in other areas of the country. Eddy Cherki and Michel Wieviorka, in *Autonomia: Post-Political Politics*, ed. Sylvère Lotringer and Christian Marazzi (Los Angeles: Semiotext(e), 1980), 72. These authors claim that Autoreduction "cannot be isolated from the climate of social and police violence which reigns in Italy." (73)

23 Sylvère Lotringer, "In the Shadow of the Red Brigades," in *Autonomia*, ed. Lotringer and Marazzi, v.

24 Paolo Virno, "Dreamers of a Successful Life," trans. Jared Becker, in *Autonomia*, ed. Lotringer and Marazzi, 116. This essay is illustrated by two pages from the artist Mario Merz's book *Fibonacci 1202: Mario Merz 1970* (Turin, Italy: Sperone, 1970). See my essay "Solitary/Solidary: Mario Merz's Autonomous Artist," *Art Journal*, Fall 2016.

25 Penone, interview by the author, 20 May 2006, Turin, written notes.

26 See notes in the collection catalogue of Kunstmuseum Luzern, attributed to Chonja Leem http://sammlungonline.kunstmuseumluzern.ch/.

27 The 1991 monographic exhibition catalogue produced for his show at Castello di Rivoli twice cites the Stedelijk show as the first time that

Ripetere il bosco was used as a title and that the *Tree* sculptures were shown together; however, the Stedelijk exhibition catalogue lists the works separately. See Gianelli and Verzotti, *Giuseppe Penone*, 192.

28 Penone, *Writings*, 121.

29 Curator Giorgio Verzotti argues that in the collective installation the *Trees* sketch the "phenomenal complexity" of the forest, in both its natural state and the state affected by human labour. Giorgio Verzotti, "Alberi," in *Giuseppe Penone* ed. Gianelli and Verzotti, 47.

30 Some authors claim that the verticality of these trees makes them more anthropomorphic because "man relates more easily to the vertical," but I am using it figuratively here to emphasize the natural state of the tree as organism. The former sublimating reading is indeed an American, if not a Greenbergian, perspective. Diane Waldman, ed., *Italian Art Now: An American Perspective; 1982 Exxon International Exhibition* (New York: Guggenheim Museum, 1982), 90.

31 It is only in the installation views taken from the top tiers of the galleries, looking down, that one sees that this work has been anchored to the interior of Frank Lloyd Wright's spiral rotunda to keep it steady. The hidden support system is reminiscent of the way ancient Roman sculptors often incorporated pillars into figurative statuary, the ankles of which had a tendency to break under the massive weight of the marble figures. At the Guggenheim Museum it is apparent from installation photographs that Penone also installed live trees along the sloping walkway of the rotunda in a manner that allow a vertical back-drop of live foliage to emerge in certain views of the *Twelve-Metre Tree*.

32 Nowhere in the exhibition catalogue, which likely was produced in anticipation of the show, do the curators acknowledge that this tree in inverted. See Waldman, *Italian Art Now*, 89–90.

33 Hodder, *Entangled*, 65.

34 Hodder, 221.

35 These felled trees are documented in the catalogue of the 1991 exhibitions at Castello di Rivoli and Strausbourg.

36 These forms were mostly female, and since the artist whose gestures created them is male, several male critics have focused on these forms as being highly sensual. On a more conceptual level, that the figures intertwined with living plants are female might also be read as relating to the personification of nature as female, to the ancient artistic association of the female body with fertility.

37 Early fragmentary examples like *Gesto vegetale (Vegetal Gesture*, 1981) were exhibited indoors at Centre Pompidou and the Museum of Modern Art, New York, in 1981–2, along with examples of the artist's *Pressure* drawings. These initial pairings suggest a visual relationship between

skin and bark and reinforce the notion that, on a processual level, the way a tree's trunk retains marks of its encounters over time is similar to the way clay holds onto the immediate touch of the artist. For the artist, clay's malleability makes it an ideal mediator between the immediacy of human gesture and the slowness of vegetal time. Penone writes, for example, that "[plant life's] slow and exasperated fossil fluidity make[s] it a paragon of plasticity. The clay that fixes or memorizes the action, retains the imprint, solidifies the trace of the fluid, and makes the sculptor's work a plant." Cited in Celant, *Arte povera = Art povera*, 239.

38 The effect achieved here was markedly different from that which occurred when they were shown in white cube spaces like Durand-Dessert (1986), Marian Goodman (1985), MoMA PS1 (1985), or Musée des Beaux-Arts Nantes (1986).

39 Giuseppe Penone, quoted in Patrick Frey, "Giuseppe Penone," in *InK Halle für internationale neue Kunst: Dokumentation 7*, ed. Sauer (Zürich: InK, 1981), 32. The text appears in English and German, and no translator is listed.

40 In the early 1980s Penone remarked on the importance of the opposition of liquid and solid in describing sculpture: "I am fascinated with making sculpture out of a liquid element, out of an element which actually is the opposite of any sculptural idea. The form which liquids assume is the horizontal, the horizontal is non-energy, sleep, or death, a re-absorption or retrieval of things by nature. That which stands up again this, that which attempts to escape gravitation is the basis on which sculpture springs up." Giuseppe Penone, quoted in Patrick Frey, "Giuseppe Penone," in Sauer, *InK Halle für internationale neue Kunst: Dokumentation 7*, 35. In the terms he lays out here, sculpture can most radically affect our thinking when, instead of merely standing against the forces of nature, it is designed to, at least in part, flow together with natural processes, to succumb to entropy, and to welcome transformation. *Münster Well* creates a collision of liquid and solid, or horizontal and vertical, which allows the pluralistic temporal frame of sculpture to come into view.

41 Penone writes: "The definition between fluid and solid is uncertain, and depends on temperature and time ... It is incredible to think that the same material may assume different states from the solid to the liquid and from the liquid to the gaseous." Giuseppe Penone, quoted in Matthew Teitelbaum, "Moments of Astonishment: An Interview with Giuseppe Penone," in *Giuseppe Penone: The Hidden Life Within*, 89.

42 In an unparalleled study of the German Romantic painter Caspar David Friedrich, art historian Joseph Leo Koerner counters the prevailing notion that the subject of early nineteen-century landscape painting is a longing or attempt to belong to the natural world. Instead of demonstrating synthesis, he argues, such paintings speak to human estrangement in the

natural world. Joseph Leo Koerner, *Caspar David Friedrich and the Subject of Landscape* (New Haven, CT: Yale University Press, 1990).

43 For more on the competing formation of the people and the public, see Paolo Virno, "Introduction" and "Forms of Dread and Refuge: Day One," in *A Grammar of the Multitude: For an Analysis of Contemporary Forms of Life* , trans. Isabella Bertoletti, James Cascaito, Andrea Casson (Cambridge, MA: MIT Press, 2004), 21–6, 29–45.

44 Although not horizontal, a clear forerunner of this work is Penone's *Faggio di Otterloo* (*Otterloo Beech*, 1988), a bronze tree installed in an empty spot amidst live beeches. Over time, as the surface of the sculpture has come into contact with the environment, it has lost its visual differentiation and nearly disappears within the thicket. The sculpture stands tall, defying gravity as the trees do when they reach towards the sunlight, yet it is submissive. On the ground a bronze pile of leaves lies at the base of the sculpture, bearing vaguely corporeal impressions. Through these traces, as well as those denoted by another mass suspended high in the branches, the viewer perceives that the body, too, loses its definition and returns to a closer integration with nature.

45 Scholars of landscape architecture argue that the philosophy of a culture or era can often take shape in its approach to gardens – from the Zen principle of Satori modelled by contemplation of a Japanese dry garden, to the powerful humanism implied by the overviews of sloping terrain in an Italian Renaissance garden, to the reactionary tautology of the "wildness" of gardens cultivated in eighteenth-century England. See, for example, Allen S. Weiss, *Mirrors of Infinity: The French Formal Garden and 17th- Century Metaphysics* (New York: Princeton Architectural Press, 1995), 11 and passim.

46 Giuseppe Penone, interview by Germano Celant, in *Il giardino delle sculture fluide di Giuseppe Penone*, ed. Ida Gianelli (Turin, Italy: Allemandi, 2007), 73.

47 Carlo Emanuele II was the son of Christine of France, sister of Louis XIII and therefore the aunt of Louis XIV. It is argued that the Italian prince was jealous of the enormous wealth and power of his French cousin, and the second stage of the campaign to transform Venaria from a rural hunting lodge to a grand palace was influenced by Versailles through the reports coming from his emissaries there. Le Nôtre was later hired to design the gardens of the urban palace in Turin, known as Il Palazzo Reale. See Elisabeth B. MacDougal, *Fountains, Statues, and Flowers: Studies in Italian Gardens of the Sixteenth and Seventeenth Centuries* (Washington DC: Dumbarton Oaks, 1994), 169.

48 In Versailles, for instance, the logical paradigm of Renaissance perspective seems to order the central axis of the gardens, yet its indication of an infinite horizon takes on the new symbolism of the divine right of Louis

XIV. From every vantage point the organization of the grounds according to the movement of the sun – rising behind the chateau and setting beyond the vanishing point of the furthest bosquet – results in a spectacle of reflections on water and windows that aptly captures the infinite power (and vanity) of the Sun King. Weiss, *Mirrors of Infinity*, 34 and passim.

49 Nicoletta Speltra, "Le Nôtre: I 400 anni dell'architetto di Versailles e Racconigi," *La Stampa*, 14 March 2013; accessed via online archive.

50 For more on the relationship between Penone's sculptures at Versailles and the sculptural programs of these gardens, see Hervé Brunon, "Le Jardin, La Sculpture, et L'Arbre," in *Penone Versailles*, ed. Alfred Pacquement (Paris: Éditions de la Réunion des musées nationaux, 2013), 122–31.

51 Penone's project at La Reggia di Venaria Reale is a multimillion-euro project that began with the restoration of the gardens in the 1960s and now includes the restoration of the palace as a museum, as well as an art conservation laboratory and school. The latest phase was begun in anticipation of the city's hosting of the 2006 Winter Olympics.

52 "This work also lends itself to a symbolic reading. My purpose is instead a consideration of time. If you place yourself between the tree and the bark of bronze, you enter the tree's growth space. Since the years of the tree are counted in its growth rings, it is as if you were within the growth time of the tree, you occupy the space of a future time" (my translation). (Anche quest'opera si presta a una lettura simbolica. Il mio proposito è invece una considerazione sul tempo. Se ti poni tra l'albero e la scorza di bronze, entri nello spazio di crescita dell'albero. Poiché gli anni dell'albero si contano nei suoi anelli di crescita, è come se tu fosse all'interno del tempo di crescita dell'albero, occupi lo spazio di un tempo futuro.) Giuseppe Penone, interview by Germano Celant, in *Il giardino delle sculture fluide di Giuseppe Penone*, ed. Gianelli, 89.

53 Anna Minola, one of the chroniclers of his gallery, mentions that Sperone's then-new space on Corso San Maurizio in Turin functioned as an annex of artists' studios, and works like this, which she mentions specifically, were often made and informally shown there. Sartor was the gallery's photographer, and he documented many of these ephemeral events. Minola et al., *Gian Enzo Sperone*, vol. 1, xix.

Conclusion

1 I say *he* when describing the narrator because Qfwfq is suggested to be male by various inferences throughout the text, including his sexual reproduction with female species (of protozoa, molluscs, etc.). Italo Calvino, "The Spiral," trans. William Weaver, in *The Complete Cosmicomics* (Boston: Mariner Books, 2002), 137.

2 Italo Calvino, "Shells and Time," trans. Martin McLaughlin, in *The Complete Cosmicomics*, 360.
3 Calvino, 362–3.
4 The interesting story of this exchange begins with Einaudi hanging one of Penone's very first tree sculptures in the editorial offices in 1969, an idea hatched by Sperone as good advertising for the young sculptor. This is discussed in detail in an earlier note in chapter 4. Subsequently, the work was irrecoverably damaged when it was loaned out for a 1970 exhibition in Rome, leading the artist to make a new tree sculpture for the publisher in exchange for a huge shipment of books (of the artist's choosing). When I mentioned to the artist that I found it interesting that he had traded a tree for a bunch of books (wood for paper), he modestly, and somewhat jokingly, countered that he thought it was interesting that he traded one idea for so many ideas. Penone still has the books, which arrived at his studio on a huge truck. Giuseppe Penone, conversation with the author, 28 January 2019, Archivio Penone, Turin. Written notes, and various emails with the Archivio Penone, 2018–19.
5 In *Da 100 grammi a 1 kilo* (*From 100 Grams to 1 Kilo*, 1975) Penone makes even more explicit the relationship between his own force and the force of the material. Here the artist measured the pressure exerted by his touch by pressing his charcoal-laden fingertip onto a piece of adhesive tape set upon a scale. First he pressed down until the scale read 100 grams, and then he repeated the process on new pieces of tape at intervals of 100 grams until he recorded one kilogram of force. Like his fingerprints on the pencil, these impressions were re-transcribed by hand. The ten resultant drawings were put into frames that weighed 100 grams, 200 grams, and so forth, according to the weight exerted in making the original print. They were hung on the wall using small spring-operated scales, each of which visibly indicated the pressure used to make the drawn image and the weight of the framed object, while at the same time it provided the means to attach the framed drawing to the wall.
6 In this way *Propagation* resonates with Manzoni's *Egg with Thumb Print*, which Penone argues escapes from the problem of the fetishism of the artist in the conflation of the egg, which symbolizes life, and the thumb print which also more or less takes the shape of an egg. See Giuseppe Penone, "'Conversation: Giuseppe Penone / Catherine de Zegher' [March/May 2003]," in *The Imprint of Drawing*, ed. Zegher, 49.
7 *The Oxford English Dictionary* defines *propagation* as "transmission of motion, light, sound, etc., in a particular direction or through a medium." Accessed 31 January 2018, https://en.oxforddictionaries.com/definition/propagation.

8 These works also resonate with Alighiero Boetti's stack of hand-drawn gridded papers, titled *Contest between Harmony and Invention* (1969), which at first glance looks printed but is similarly meticulously made. In an interview with Catherine de Zegher, Penone says that the slowness of his own drawings contrasts with the gestural work of the 1950s. See Giuseppe Penone, "'Conversation: Giuseppe Penone / Catherine de Zegher' [March/May 2003]," in *Giuseppe Penone: The Imprint of Drawing*, ed. Zegher, 55.

9 Simon Lewis and Mark Maslin, earth scientists based at University College London, describe the long history of the idea in the eighteenth and nineteenth centuries and give credit for the modern use of the term to scientists Paul Crutzen and Eugene Stoerman, who used it independently, and later together from the year 2000. Simon Lewis and Mark Maslin, *The Human Planet: How We Created the Anthropocene* (London: Pelican, 2018), 20–1.

10 Lewis and Maslin argue that the Columbian exchange led to the deaths of an estimated fifty million people over a few decades as diseases to which the inhabitants had no natural resistance were introduced across two continents. By 1610, enough farmland had reverted to forest, removing carbon dioxide from the atmosphere, to enable the planet to cool to a degree measurable in its material strata. Lewis and Maslin, *The Human Planet*, 179–83.

11 Lewis and Maslin, 169, 172, 182.

12 Lewis and Maslin, 278–9.

13 Giuseppe Penone, quoted in Frey, "Giuseppe Penone," in Sauer, *InK Halle für internationale neue Kunst: Dokumentation 7*, 31. The text appears in German and English, with no translator listed.

Bibliography

Abbagnano, Nicola. "Verso il nuovo illuminismo." *Rivista di filosofia* 39 (October–December 1948): 313–25.

Amman, Jean-Christophe, and Giuseppe Penone. *Giuseppe Penone: Bäume, Augen, Haare, Wände, Tongefäss*. Exhibition catalogue. Lucerne, Switzerland: Kunstmuseum Luzern, 1977.

Argan, Giulio Carlo. *Studi e Note*. Rome: Bicca, 1955.

Bandini, Mirella. *1972: Arte Povera a Torino*. I Testimoni dell'arte. Turin, Italy: U. Allemandi, 2002.

Barthes, Roland. *Camera Lucida: Reflections on Photography*. Translated by Richard Howard. New York: Farrar, Straus & Giroux, 1995.

Bataille, Georges. *Visions of Excess: Selected Writings, 1927–1939*. Edited by Allan Stoekl. Translated by Allan Stoekl, Carl Lovitt, and Donald M. Leslie, Jr. Vol. 14 of *Theory and History of Literature*. Minneapolis: University of Minnesota Press, 1991. This translation first published 1985.

Bertolino, Giorgina, and Francesca Pola, eds. *Torino Sperimentale 1959–69: Una storia della cronaca; Il sistema delle arti come avanguardia*. Exhibition catalogue. Turin, Italy: Giulio Baffi Editore, 2010.

Bologna (Italy), and Ente bolognese manifestazioni artistiche, eds. *3 Biennale Internazionale Della Giovane Pittura Gennaio 70: Comportamenti, Progetti, Mediazioni*. Exhibition catalogue. Bologna, Italy: Alfa, 1970.

Bonito Oliva, Achille. "Informazioni Sulla Presenza Italiana: 25 Novembre–18 Dicembre 1971." In "Incontri internazionali d'arte, 1972," special issue, *Quaderni Del Centro d'informazione Alternativa* 1. n.p.

– *Pèrsona: BITEF Festival Internazionale del Teatro, Belgrado, 10 Settembre 1971*. Exhibition catalogue. Florence: Centro Di, 1971.

Brades, Susan Ferleger, Christine Taylor, and Hayward Gallery, eds. *Gravity & Grace: The Changing Condition of Sculpture, 1965–1975; Hayward Gallery, London, 21 January–14 March 1993*. Exhibition catalogue. London: South Bank Centre, 1993.

Brown, Bill. "Thing Theory." *Critical Inquiry* 28, no.1 (Autumn 2001): 1–22.

Bürgi, Bernhard, Luca Cerizza, Ingvild Goetz, Christiane Meyer-Stoll, Simon Baier, Sammlung Goetz, and Öffentliche Kunstsammlung Basel, eds. *Arte Povera: The Great Awakening*. Exhibition catalogue. Ostfildern, Germany: Hatje Cantz, 2012.

Busine, Laurent, and B.H.D. Buchloh, eds. *Giuseppe Penone*. Brussels: Mercatorfonds, 2012.

Bussmann, Klaus, Kasper König, and Westfälisches Landesmuseum für Kunst und Kulturgeschichte Münster, eds. *Skulptur Projekte in Münster, 1987: Katalog zur Ausstellung des Westfälischen Landmuseums für Kunst und Kulturgeschichte in der Stadt Münster, 14. Juni bis 4. Oktober 1987*. Exhibition catalogue. Cologne, Germany: DuMont, 1987.

Calvino, Italo. *The Complete Cosmicomics*. Translated by William Weaver. Boston: Mariner Books, 2002.

Canetti, Elias. *Crowds and Power*. Translated by Carol Stewart. New York: Continuum, 1978. First published 1960.

Germano Celant. *Arte Povera = Art Povera*. Milan: Electa, 1985.

– *Art Povera*. New York: Praeger, 1969.

– *Giuseppe Penone*. Milan: Electa, 1989.

– *The Knot: Arte Povera at P.S. 1: Giovanni Anselmo, Alighiero Boetti, Pier Paolo Calzolari, Luciano Fabro, Jannis Kounellis, Mario Merz, Giulio Paolini, Pino Pascali, Giuseppe Penone, Michelangelo Pistoletto, and Gilberto Zorio*. Exhibition catalogue. Long Island City, NY: P.S.1, 1985.

– *Piero Manzoni*. Milan: Charta, 1998.

Celant, Germano, and Mole Antonelliana, Turin, Italy, eds. *Coerenza in Coerenza: Dall'arte Povera al 1984*. Exhibition catalogue. Milan: A. Mondadori, 1984.

Celant, Germano, Giuseppe Penone, Arnolfini Gallery, and Dean Clough Art Foundation, eds. *Giuseppe Penone: Arnolfini Gallery, Bristol, 21 Jan.–1 March 1989, Dean Clough Art Found. 17.3 –17.4.1989*. Exhibition catalogue. Milan: Electa, 1989.

Celant, Germano, and Galleria Civica d'Arte Moderna di Torino, eds. *Conceptual Art, Arte Povera, Land Art*. Exhibition catalogue. Turin, Italy: Galleria Civica d'Arte Moderna, 1970.

Clark, T.J. *The Painting of Modern Life: Paris in the Art of Manet and His Followers*. Princeton, NJ: Princeton University Press, 1984.

Crispolti, Enrico, ed. "Breve Antologia di Poetica." *Il Verri*, no 3 (June 1961): 128–40.

Crow, Thomas E. *The Rise of the Sixties: American and European Art in the Era of Dissent*. Reprinted edition. New Haven, CT: Yale University Press, 2004.

Descola, Philippe. *Beyond Nature and Culture*. Translated by Janet Lloyd. Chicago: University of Chicago Press, 2013. First published 2005.

Dewey, John. *Art as Experience*. New York: Perigee, 1980. First published 1934.
Didi-Huberman, Georges. *Being a Skull: Site, Contact, Thought, Sculpture*. Translated by Drew Burk. English language edition. Minneapolis, MN: Univocal, 2016.
Duran, Adrian. "Abstract Expressionism's Italian Reception: Questions of Influence." In *Abstract Expressionism: The International Context*, edited by Joan M. Marter, 138–51. New Brunswick, NJ: Rutgers, 2007.
Duve, Thierry de. *Pictorial Nominalism: On Marcel Duchamp's Passage from Painting to Readymade*. Translated by Dana Polan. Minneapolis: University of Minnesota Press, 1991.
Esposito, Roberto. *Living Thought: The Origins and Actuality of Italian Philosophy*. Translated by Zakiya Harafi. Stanford: Stanford Universiy Press, 2012. First published 2010.
– *Persons and Things: From the Body's Point of View*. Translated by Zakiya Harafi. Cambridge: Polity Press, 2016. First published 2015.
Flood, Richard, Frances Morris, Walker Art Center, and Tate Modern (Gallery), eds. *Zero to Infinity: Arte Povera, 1962–1972*. Exhibition catalogue. Minneapolis, MN: Walker Art Center, 2001.
Foucault, Michel. *Dits et Écrits, 1954–1988*, vol. 2. Edited by Daniel Defert. Paris: Gallimard, 2001.
Fried, Michael. "Art and Objecthood." *Artforum* 5, no. 10 (Summer 1967): 12–23.
Galimberti, Jacopo. "A Third-Worldist Art? Germano Celant's Invention of *Arte Povera*." *Art History*, April 2013, 418–41.
Giachetti, Diego. *Il giorno più lungo: La rivolta di Corso Traiano (Torino, 3 luglio 1969)*. Biblioteca di cultura storica. Pisa: BFS Editore, 1977
Gianelli, Ida, and Giorgio Verzotti, eds. *Giuseppe Penone*. Exhibition catalogue. Turin, Italy: Castello di Rivoli, 1991.
Gianelli, Ida, ed. *Un'avventura internazionale: Torino e le arti 1950–1970*. Exhibition catalogue. Turin, Italy: Castello di Rivoli, 1993.
– *Il giardino delle sculture fluide di Giuseppe Penone*. Turin, Italy: Allemandi, 2007.
Gilman, Claire. "Introduction." In "Postwar Italian Art," special issue, *October* 124 (Summer 2008): 3–7.
Ginsborg, Paul. *A History of Contemporary Italy: Society and Politics, 1943–1988*. London: Penguin, 1990; reprint, New York: Palgrave Macmillan, 2003.
Gross, Kenneth. *Dream of the Moving Statue*. University Park: Penn State Press, 2010.
Guzzetti, Francesco. "Information 1970: Alcune novità sul lavoro di Giuseppe Penone." *L'Uomo Nero* 15, nos. 14–15 (March 2018): 215–31.
Hardt, Michael, and Paolo Virno, eds. *Radical Thought in Italy: A Potential Politics*. Minneapolis: University of Minnesota Press, 1996.
Hodder, Ian. *Entangled: An Archaeology of the Relationships between Humans and Things*. Malden, MA: Wiley-Blackwell, 2012.

Horn, Gerd-Rainer. *The Spirit of '68: Rebellion in Western Europe and North America, 1956–1976*. New York: Oxford University Press, 2007.

Jay, Martin. *Downcast Eyes: The Denigration of Vision in Twentieth-Century French Thought*. Berkeley: University of California Press, 1993.

– "Scopic Regimes of Modernity." In *The Visual Culture Reader*, edited by Nicholas Mirzoeff, 66–9. New York: Routledge, 1998.

Jay, Martin, and Sumathi Ramaswamy, eds. *Empires of Vision: A Reader*. Objects/Histories. Durham, NC: Duke University Press, 2014.

Jones, Amelia. "Meaning, Identity, Embodiment." In *Art and Thought*, ed. Dana Arnold and Margaret Iversen, 71–90. Malden, UK: Blackwell, 2003.

Kestenbaum, Victor. *The Phenomenological Sense of John Dewey: Habit and Meaning*. Atlantic Highlands, NJ: Humanities Press, 1977.

Kitagawa, Tomoaki, Kiyoo Uemura, and Toyotashi Bijutsukan, eds. *7nin no sakka: Silent Friendship, 1960–90's; 7 artists*. Toyota, Japan: Toyotashi bijutsukan, 1999.

Koerner, Joseph Leo. *Caspar David Friedrich and the Subject of Landscape*. New Haven, CT: Yale University Press, 1990.

Krauss, Rosalind. *The Optical Unconscious*. Cambridge, MA: MIT Press, 1996. First published 1993.

– *The Originality of the Avant-Garde and Other Modernist Myths*. Cambridge, MA: MIT Press, 1985.

– *Passages in Modern Sculpture*. Cambridge, MA: MIT Press, 1996.

– "The Photographic Conditions of Surrealism." *October* 19 (Winter 1981): 3–34.

– "Sculpture in the Expanded Field." *October* 8 (Spring 1979): 30–44.

Kristeva, Julia. *Powers of Horror*. Edited by Kelly Oliver. Translated by Leon S. Roudiez. New York: Columbia University Press, 1980).

Kunsteverein München. *Arte Povera: 13 italienische Künstler*. Exhibition catalogue. Munich: Kunstverein München, 1971.

Kunstmuseum Luzern. *Processi di pensiero visualizzati: 15 italianische Künstler*. Exhibition catalogue. Lucerne, Switzerland: Kunstmuseum Luzern, 1970.

Lacan, Jacques. *Écrits: A Selection*. Translated by Alan Sheridan. New York: Norton, 1977.

Lee, Pamela M. *Chronophobia: On Time in the Art of the 1960s*. Cambridge, MA: MIT Press, 2003.

Lewis, Simon, and Mark Maslin. *The Human Planet: How We Created the Anthropocene*. London: Pelican, 2018.

Lippard, Lucy. *Six Years: The Dematerialization of the Art Object from 1966 to 1972*. Berkeley: University of California Press, 1997. First published 1973.

Lotringer, Sylvère, and Christian Marazzi, eds. *Autonomia: Post-Political Politics*. Los Angeles: Semiotext(e), 1980.

Love, Joseph P., SJ. "Tokyo: 10. International Biennale of Art." *Art International* 14, no. 6 (Summer 1970): 70–5.

MacDougal, Elisabeth B. *Fountains, Statues, and Flowers: Studies in Italian Gardens of the Sixteenth and Seventeenth Centuries*. Washington, DC: Dumbarton Oaks, 1994.

Malsch, Friedemann, Christiane Meyer-Stoll, Valentina Pero, Maddalena Disch, and Kunstmuseum Liechtenstein, eds. *Che Fare? Arte Povera: The Historic Years*. Exhibition catalogue. Heidelberg, Germany: Kehrer, 2010.

Mangini, Elizabeth. "1000 Words: Giuseppe Penone." *Artforum* 49, no. 2 (October 2010): 226–9.

Merleau-Ponty, Maurice. *Phenomenology of Perception*. Translated by Colin Smith. New York: Routledge Classics, 2002. First published 1945.

– *The Primacy of Perception*. Translated by Carlton Dallery. Evanston, IL: Northwestern University Press, 1964.

– *The Visible and the Invisible*. Edited by Claude Lefort. Translated by Alphonso Lingis. Evanston, IL: Northwestern University Press, 1968.

Merleau-Ponty, Maurice, Ted Toadvine, and Leonard Lawlor. *The Merleau-Ponty Reader*. Northwestern University Studies in Phenomenology and Existential Philosophy. Evanston, IL: Northwestern University Press, 2007.

Minola, Anna, Maria Christina Mundici, Francesco Poli, and Maria Teresa Roberto. *Gian Enzo Sperone: Torino-Roma-New York; 35 anni di mostre tra Europa e America*. Translated by Lucian Comoy, Paolo Delmastro, Jeanette Hall, Luisa Piussi, Alberto Serra, and Simon Turner. 2 vols. Turin, Italy: Hopefulmonster, 2000.

Morris, Robert. "Anti-form." *Artforum* 6, no. 8 (April 1968): 34–5.

Ningen Kokusai Bijutsu Ten, Yūsuke Nakahara, Toshiaki Minemura, Aichi-ken Bijutsukan, Nihon Kokusai Bijutsu Shinkeokai, Mainichi Shinbunsha, Tōkyō-to Bijutsukan, and Kyōto-shi Bijutsukan, eds. *Ningen to Busshitsu: Between Man and Matter*. Exhibition catalogue. Tokyo: Mainichi Newspapers and the Japan International Art Promotion Association, 1970.

Paci, Enzo. "Fenomenologia e Informale." *Il Verri*, no. 3 (June 1961): 159–61.

Pacquement, Alfred ed. *Penone Versailles*. Exhibition catalogue. Paris: Éditions de la Réunion des musées nationaux, 2013.

Penone, Giuseppe. *Giuseppe Penone: 1968–1998*. Exhibition catalogue. Galicia, Spain: Xunta de Galicia / Centro Galego de Arte Contemporánea, 1999.

– "Giuseppe Penone: Aktion." *Interfunktionen* 5 (1970): 144–7.

– *Giuseppe Penone: The Hidden Life Within*. Edited by Matthew Teitelbaum. Translated by Fabrizio Bianchini and Erin Moure. Exhibition catalogue. London: Black Dog Publishing, 2013.

– *Giuseppe Penone: Writings, 1968–2008*. Edited by Gianfranco Maraniello and Jonathan Watkins. Translated by Marguerite Shore. Bologna, Italy: Commune di Bologna (MAMbo), 2009.

– *Rovesciare gli occhi*. Turin, Italy: Einaudi, 1977.

– *Svolgere la propria pella*. Turin, Italy: Sperone, 1971.

Penone, Giuseppe, Achim Borchardt-Hume, and Poppy Bowers. *Giuseppe Penone: Spazio Di Luce*. Translated by Michela Parkin. Exhibition catalogue. London: Whitechapel Gallery, 2012.

Penone, Giuseppe, Constantino D'Orazio, Giorgio Verzotti, and Ludovico Pratesi. *Giuseppe Penone: Paesaggi del cervello*. Exhibition catalogue. Turin, Italy: Hopefulmonster, 2003.

Penone, Giuseppe, and Guy Tosatto. *Giuseppe Penone*. Exhibition catalogue. Arles and Grenoble: Actes sud and Musée de Grenoble, 2014.

Pompei, Paolo. "Merleau-Ponty, politica e morale." *Il Verri* 5 (December 1961): 144–56.

Sauer, Christel. "InK, die Halle für internationale neue Kunst." *Du: Die Zeitschrift der Kultur* 40 (1980): 6–11.

– ed. *InK Halle für internationale neue Kunst: Dokumentation 7*. Zürich: InK, 1981.

Semin, Didier. *Giuseppe Penone: The Politeness of Matter*. Exhibition catalogue. Geneva: Galerie Guy Bärtschi, 2002.

Sullivan, Marin. *Sculptural Materiality in the Age of Conceptualism*. New York: Routledge, 2017.

Trini, Tommaso. "Anselmo, Penone, Zorio e le nuove fonti d'energia per il deserto dell'arte." *Data* 3, no. 9 (Autumn 1973): 62–7.

– "Arte Povera a Genova." *Domus* 457 (December 1967), unpaginated insert.

– "Documenta 5." *Domus* 514 (September 1972): 47.

– "Duchamp dall'oltreporta." *Domus* 478 (September 1969): 43–5.

– "Imagination Takes Command." *Domus* 471 (February 1969): 49–50.

– *Mezzo secolo di arte intera: Scritti 1964–2014*. Edited by Luca Cerizza. Monza, Italy: Johan and Levi, 2016.

– "Nuovo alfabeto per corpo e materia." *Domus* 470 (January 1969): 46–8. Reprinted in English as "A New Alphabet for Body and Material," in *Arte Povera = Art Povera*, edited by Germano Celant, 109–13. Milan: Electa, 1985.

– "Per una nuova biennale" and "Dialogo sui massimi sistemi politici e artistici." *Domus*, no. 466 (September 1968): 46–54.

– "The Prodigal Maker's Trilogy: Three Exhibitions: Berne, Amsterdam, Rotterdam." *Domus* 478 (September 1969): 46.

– "Rapporto da Amalfi." *Domus* 468 (November 1968): 50.

– "The Sixties in Italy." *Studio International*, November 1972, 169.

– "Towards Theater." *Domus* 480 (November 1969): 51–2.

Verdon, Timothy. "The New Museo dell'Opera del Duomo." *I Tatti Studies in the Italian Renaissance* 18, no. 2 (2015): 283.

Verdon, Timothy, Daniel M. Zolli, Museum of Biblical Art, and Opera di S. Maria del Fiore (Florence, Italy), eds. *Sculpture in the Age of Donatello: Renaissance Masterpieces from Florence Cathedral*. New York : Museum of Biblical Art , 2015.

Vergine, Lea. *Body Art and Performance: The Body as Language*. Milan: Skira Editore, 2000.

– *Dall'Informazione alla Body Art dieci voci dell'arte contemporanea: 1960/70*. Turin, Italy: Cooperativa Editoriale Studio Forma, 1976.

–"Torino '68: Nevrosi e sublimazione." *Metro* (1968): 22.

Vetrocq, Marcia. "National Style and the Agenda for Abstract Painting in Postwar Italy." *Art History* 12, no. 4 (December 1989): 448–71.

Virno, Paolo. *A Grammar of the Multitude: For an Analysis of Contemporary Forms of Life*. Translated by Isabella Bertoletti, James Cascaito, and Andrea Casson. Cambridge, MA: MIT Press, 2004.

Volpi, Marisa. "In margine a un dibattito: America o Europa?" *Bit* 2, no. 1 (March/April 1968): 12–14.

Vowinckel, Andreas, Ilse Czigens, and Württembergischer Kunstverein, eds. *Natur-Skulptur: Nature-Sculpture: Württembergischer Kunstverein Stuttgart, Kunstgebäude Am Schlossplatz, 1. September bis 1. November 1981*. Stuttgart, Germany: Der Kunstverein, 1981.

Waldman, Diane, ed. *Italian Art Now: An American Perspective, 1982; Exxon International Exhibition*. Exhibition catalogue. New York: Guggenheim Museum, 1982.

Wedewer, Rolf, and Konrad Fischer. *Konzeption/Conception: Dokumentation einer heutigen Kunstrichtung / Documentation of a To-Day's Art Tendency*. Exhibition catalogue. Cologne, Germany: Westdeutscher Verlag, 1969.

Weiss, Allen S. *Mirrors of Infinity: The French Formal Garden and 17th-Century Metaphysics*. 1st ed. New York: Princeton Architectural Press, 1995.

White, Roger. *The Contemporaries: Travels in the 21st-Century Art World*. New York: Bloomsbury, 2015.

Zegher, Catherine de, ed. *Giuseppe Penone: The Imprint of Drawing*. Trans. Jeff Fort. Exhibition catalogue. New York: The Drawing Center, 2004.

Index

Page numbers in bold denote illustrations.

www.ingramcontent.com/pod-product-compliance
Lightning Source LLC
LaVergne TN
LVHW060137070826
844660LV00035BA/1429

9781487556969